BATH
HISTORY

BATH
HISTORY

VOLUME IX

edited by Brenda J. Buchanan

Bath Archaeological Trust
in association with
Millstream Books
2002

Bath History gratefully acknowledges the support of Bath & North East Somerset Heritage Services

The Editor wishes to thank the expert readers who have helped so greatly in the preparation of this volume.

First published in 2002 by Millstream Books, 18 The Tyning, Bath BA2 6AL

Set in Palatino and printed in Great Britain by The Jensen Press, Yeovil

© John Ede & Roland Symons; Stephen Powys Marks; Chris Noble; Robert Bennet; John Cattell; Steven Blake; Philippa Bishop; Angus Buchanan 2002

ISBN 0 948975 65 2

British Library Cataloguing-in-Publication Data:
a catalogue record for this book is available from The British Library

CONTENTS

Notes on Contributors   6

Heraldry in Bath Abbey   *John Ede & Roland Symons*   7

The Journals of Mrs Philip
Lybbe Powys (1738-1817):
A Half Century of Visits to Bath   *Stephen Powys Marks*   28

The New Gaol in Bathwick (1772-1842)   *Chris Noble*   64

The Last of the Georgian Architects of Bath:
The Work and Times of John Pinch   *Robert Bennet*   87

Edward Snell's Diary: A Journeyman
Engineer in Bath in the 1840s   *John Cattell*   104

William Beckford and Fonthill Abbey:
A Victorian Showman's Account   *Steven Blake*   126

Walter Richard Sickert (1860-1942):
Painter of the Bath Scene   *Philippa Bishop*   138

Bath: University City   *R. Angus Buchanan*   160

Index to *Bath History* Volumes I-IX   181

In the notes at the end of each article in this volume, the place of publication of books, so far as is known, is London unless otherwise stated.

NOTES ON CONTRIBUTORS

John Ede and Roland Symons are members of Bath Heraldic Society and acted together as advisers on heraldic matters when the Abbey interior was cleaned in the 1990s. John Ede formerly taught Physics and Roland Symons History. They have acted in close collaboration for the present article but the former takes responsibility for the text while the illustrations are the work of the latter.

Stephen Powys Marks, great-great-great-great-grandson of Caroline Powys, has carried out and published extensive genealogical and other research on the Powys family. He is a retired architect and a Fellow of the Society of Antiquaries. Other recent work includes an article on the Survey of the Manor of Kilmersdon 1571, published in *Five Arches*, the journal of Radstock Museum, of which he is a director.

Chris Noble's career in the Probation Service led to his visiting many, and working in two, Victorian and later prisons. Moving to Bath he found to his surprise that the city had had two purpose-built gaols. His interests in both architecture and social policy made them an ideal subject for his MA in local history at Bath Spa University College.

Robert Bennet trained originally as a craftsman printer and describes his early days as being just one step from Fox Talbot. Since early retirement he has been able to devote his time to his great love of architecture, graduating at the University of Bath in the Conservation of Historic Buildings.

John Cattell, a Senior Architectural Investigator with English Heritage, has been involved in the investigation, research and conservation of historic buildings for over 20 years. He is co-author of *Swindon: The Legacy of a Railway Town* (HMSO, 1995) and *The Birmingham Jewellery Quarter: An Architectural Survey of the Manufactories* (English Heritage, 2002).

Steven Blake is Keeper of Collections at Cheltenham Art Gallery & Museum and has published a number of books and articles on the history of Cheltenham. He is currently researching, for eventual publication, a full-length account of John Bellamy and his British Model Gallery.

Philippa Bishop was formerly Curator of the Holburne Museum of Art (1961-65 and 1977-85) and has written the recent *Guide* to the collections. She has acted as Chairman of the History of Bath Research Group and is a previous contributor to *Bath History*.

R. Angus Buchanan joined the University of Bath in 1960. He is now Emeritus Professor of the History of Technology at the University. He is a Fellow of the Society of Antiquaries and a Trustee of Bath Archaeological Trust. He has written extensively on industrial archaeology and engineering history. His latest publication is *Brunel: The Life and Times of I.K.Brunel* (Hambledon and London, 2002)

HERALDRY IN BATH ABBEY

John Ede and Roland Symons

The cleaning of the stonework of Bath Abbey in the 1990s has given an interior which not only delights visitors to the City but produced gasps of astonishment from Bathonians who knew the building well. The smoke of centuries of candles and the succeeding gas lighting that existed until well after World War II had so blackened the vaulting and upper walls that, in spite of the excellent daytime lighting through the huge clear-glass upper windows, details of some of the many heraldic shields could not be identified even with binoculars.[1] These painted shields, over one hundred in number, are an important source of information on individuals, families, the Abbey and the City of Bath. It is with their interpretation and relevance that this account is concerned.

Reading Heraldic Displays

For those not familiar with the interpretation of heraldic displays some basic explanations at the start may be helpful. In England an heraldic pattern is legitimate only if officially granted by the College of Arms.[2] Once granted it descends by all male lines automatically (there are some differences in Scottish practice). Having the same name does not entitle you to use arms unless you can prove descent from the grantee. The terms *shield, arms, coat of arms*, are all used to describe the pattern on a shield. The word *crest* refers to a form of badge or device which is placed above the shield or on top of the helmet – to use it for the shield pattern is a common error.

A married man can indicate his state by dividing his shield vertically down the middle, putting his own arms on the left and his wife's father's arms on the right. These arms are then described as *impaled*. Office holders, eg bishops, can use this method to link their official position with their family arms. If a father has no sons to succeed him, his daughters all become heraldic heiresses. Their husbands, instead of impaling, can put the wife's family arms on a small shield covering the centre of their own. This has the charming name of an *inescutcheon of pretence*. Only in such cases do sons of a marriage inherit the right to combine their mother's family arms with their father's. They do this by *quartering* the shield, showing the paternal arms in the first and fourth quarters and the maternal arms in second and third quarters. If the shields already combine families, or if there is further inheritance in a later generation, the duplication can be dispensed with for up to four coats of arms. Beyond this the shields may be divided into more compartments though these are still referred to as *quarterings*. Where desirable for a balanced arrangement the last quartering can be a repeat of the first and main family coat. For the sake of clarity there is no compulsion to show additional inherited arms but pride can be a powerful factor.

The shape of shield has varied with period or artistic preference but has no heraldic significance. A shield has been felt inappropriate for women and a lozenge is used but this has an awkward shape for coats of arms which are so often on a triangular pattern of two objects above and one below, that fit a shield so well. A spinster's lozenge shows her father's arms; a widow's shows the same impaled arms that her husband bore on his shield. A wife had no occasion for heraldic display separately from her husband. Modern heraldry has had to come to terms with granting arms to women in their own right and may soon need to lay down clear general rules if it is to survive.

Finally, the words *left* and *right* are used in this article to indicate the sides of an heraldic display as viewed by the onlooker. In heraldic textbooks or descriptions (*blazon*) the Latin equivalents sinister and dexter are used but they refer, confusingly, to the sides in relation to the man behind the shield.

The Building of the Present Abbey

The Norman church had become very ruinous before the end of the fifteenth century. It was 'so utterly neglected, that, to employ the strong expression of Bishop King, it became ruined to the foundations – *imo funditus dirutam* – in consequence of the monks expending their large income in pleasurable indulgences, instead of appropriating some part thereof to the necessary reparations of the fabric'.[3] Oliver King was translated from the bishopric of Exeter to Bath and Wells in 1495 and was enthroned in March 1496. He was politician as well as prelate and held, among other offices, that of French Secretary to Edward IV and Henry VII. He was sent by the latter to conclude a treaty of peace with Charles VIII of France. The legend of his dream is well known: a vision of the Holy Trinity and angels ascending and descending by ladders with a voice saying 'Let an olive establish the crown and a king restore the church'. The new bishop ordered a reduction in the expenses of the Prior and 16 monks, with all possible funds put towards a smaller building which was erected on the nave of the Norman structure, leaving the choir available for services.

In one of the Bath Abbey 2000 lectures the Very Rev. Patrick Mitchell, Dean of London, called attention to Oliver King's career from boy at Eton College, student at King's College Cambridge, to Canon of Windsor, where he saw three chapels in the course of construction which must have influenced the architectural style of the new abbey at Bath.[4] He liberally supported the building but responsibility for the execution of the work lay with the Prior and Convent. Prior Cantlow died in 1499 and the Convent appointed William Birde (or Bird) as his successor. The Bishop objected to the nomination but finally gave way. Birde proved to be a good partner, able also to continue the task when Oliver King died, early in the project, in 1503. When Birde died in 1525 the building was still not completed and the finishing was in the hands of Prior Holloway, alias Gibbs, though the nave did not get the intended stone roof until much later.

Oliver King's successor as Bishop was Adrian de Castello, another statesman. He came to Scotland as Papal Nuncio in 1488 and the following year to England as collector of Peter's Pence. He appears to have become Henry VII's ambassador at Rome and also clerk to the papal treasury. His services to Henry were perhaps funded by the appointment in his absence to the bishopric of Hereford in 1502 and Bath and Wells in 1504. He was clearly, first and foremost, an intriguer. He left Rome in 1503 after the death by poisoning of Pope Alexander III, returning on the accession of Leo X in 1511 and, though implicated in another Vatican conspiracy, was dealt with leniently. He was deprived of his collectorship and also of the bishopric of Bath and Wells in 1518 and died about 1523, possibly murdered.[5] He appears not to have visited England after 1502 but he may still have contributed to the restoration of the Abbey and he certainly has a central heraldic presence.

Early Heraldry in the Abbey

The heraldry relating to this first stage of the present building can now be considered. It is over pedantic to quibble with the universally used name of 'Abbey' on the ground that in the period with which we are concerned the bishop was titular head but that, under him, the monks were led by a prior so that 'Priory' is the accurate term. Since neither word strictly applies to the building in its present function we can use the two words to make a useful distinction between two heraldic shields.

The Priory shield (fig.1) shows the sword associated with St Paul and the two keys associated with St Peter set diagonally on a red background, the two keys lying from top left to bottom right. This shield is seen in a number of places but most prominently in the choir vault. The present Abbey shield

Fig.1 Bath Priory

Fig.2 Bath Abbey

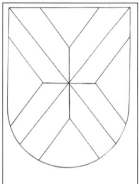

Fig.3 Bath & Wells

for the same building but different function reverses the diagonals of keys and sword and has a blue background (fig.2). This shield is also seen on items such as modern furnishings, headings for notices and the gowns of stewards. The arms of the diocese (fig.3) show a diagonal cross (*saltire*) on a blue field. This cross is divided along the diagonals into gold (or yellow) and silver (or white) in an attractive windmill pattern. In earlier centuries two keys, a sword and sometimes a crozier were often added, as may be seen in a number of shields in the Abbey. The origin of this practice may have been that the saltire stood for Wells where the bishop was based (except for a short period) and that the additional emblems served here to mark him as also bishop in Bath. We use the saltire alone today.

Bishop King's arms (fig.4) show three scallop shells on an heraldic chevron which points upwards, (unlike those on British service uniforms). These shells were common among pilgrims at the shrine of St James of Compostella and

Fig.4 Bishop King

acquired a wider heraldic connotation for religious people. Priests did not marry and their arms, therefore, were not inherited. King's shield is seen in the chancel north aisle vaulting and on the south side of the east window next to Prior Birde but also, less obviously, on the outside of the building, over the north entrance door in the west front. A small pilgrim-like figure is shown just above Oliver King's arms and below his rebus of a crowned olive tree. There is a much later statue of the Bishop's patron, Henry VII, over the central west door displaying his Royal Arms.[6]

Fig.5 Prior Birde   **Fig.6** Bishop Fox   **Fig.7** Bishop de Castello

Prior Birde has his shield (fig.5) carved on the inside of his chantry and it also appears in the choir north aisle and on the south side of the east window. Naturally the motif of birds is in allusion to his name. Such punning with names is common in heraldry though the connection is not always as obvious as here. King's predecessor as bishop was Richard Fox (or Foxe) who, after only two years at Bath and Wells, went to Durham and thence to Winchester in 1501 and did not die until 1528, so the appearance of his shield in the chancel south aisle may easily represent financial help or support during the period of the absent Castello. The heraldry of Fox's shield (fig.6) is another religious motif – a female bird on a nest of chicks pecking its breast and known as a *'pelican in her piety'*, though unlike the bird that the name now denotes. The legend was that the male bird killed the chicks and that three days later the female brought them back to life with blood pecked from her breast. The pelican was thus a strong Christian symbol. Some displays have the female bird pecking her breast but without nest and chicks and she is then blazoned as *'vulning herself'*. In either case drops of blood are often visible coming from the breast but no spots of red can be seen in this example.

Bishop Adrian de Castello, in spite of what has already been said about him, has pride of place as the central shield in the choir vault (fig.7). The castellated bands suggest his name. The making of the three shields into a special feature in the 1990s was the result of finding vestiges of earlier painting in the vaulting surrounding the shields, so they and their surrounds were newly repainted and not simply cleaned like the other shields. The shield to the east with its massive crown has the Royal Arms of James I (fig.8), king when the repairs after the Dissolution were finally completed

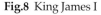

Fig.8 King James I

Fig.9 Glastonbury Abbey **Fig.10** King Edgar

around 1620. Two further shields of this time should be mentioned. In the lower row on the north side of the east window is a shield for the monastery at Glastonbury (fig.9) a large central cross and, in the top left corner, an image of the Virgin and Child. Next to it is a shield with a cross and four *martlets* representing King Edgar (fig.10) who, in 973, was crowned the first King of All England on this site.[7] Edgar lived well before the days of systematised heraldry but for such early heroes shields were devised from known or reputed emblems. The martlet is a legless swallow – a legend that will be more appropriately described below in connection with a nineteenth century shield. Edgar's shield can also be seen elsewhere, for example in the choir north aisle.

At the Dissolution the Abbey was surrendered to Henry VIII's commissioners.[8] The church was offered to the City for the sum of 500 marks but 'in the words of Fuller, the townspeople, fearing if they bought it so cheap to be thought to cozin the King, so that the purchase might come under the compasse of the concealed lands, refused the proffer'.[9] The glass, iron, bells and lead were sold to merchants, and nothing but the skeleton of the church was left standing. The shell of the church with the buildings in the precinct, lands at Bathwick, Holloway, Lyncombe and Widcombe and the advowson of the latter, were sold to Humphrey Colles. Colles immediately sold the site of the precinct with the partially roofless church to Matthew Colthurst, M.P. for Bath, whose son Edmund made, in 1572, a gift of the ruin to the Mayor and citizens of Bath for a parish church. In 1569 the main landed estates were sold by Colles and ultimately passed to the Duke of Kingston, and from him to his nephew Earl Manvers who has a later place in this account.[10]

The Post-Dissolution years

The sale of the roof lead had serious consequences, particularly for the nave where there had not been stone vaulting, and also created problems in the south transept which will be described later. The work of restoration was not completed until about 1620 but a manuscript once in the possession of the Abbey describes the stages with details of benefactors that have proved helpful in identifying the heraldic legacy of this period.[11]

This document reveals three distinct stages in the restoration and it is not surprising that details of benefactors are more numerous the nearer we come to its compilation. The first stage began when Letters Patent were obtained in 1574 from Queen Elizabeth, authorising collections for seven years in every part of the Kingdom to enable work to proceed. It makes no mention of Peter Chapman, son of a clothier, referred to by Leland as a member of the important Bath family of that name. Britton, however, states that after an army career Peter Chapman began the work by repairing the east end of the north aisle (still known as the Chapman aisle) in about 1572 and that the Queen's support came soon afterwards.[12] The Chapman shield (fig.11) can be seen at the top of a column on the north side of the choir and also over a window in the south transept, though there are differences in colour. The first stage of the work was limited to the east end, the north transept and part of the south transept. Named benefactors are only two: Thomas Ratcliffe, 3rd Earl of Sussex, K.G., Lord Chamberlain to Elizabeth I, 'at whose charge was glazed the uppermost of the high windows on the north side of the choir' and Walter Calcutt of Williamscot who gave £10 towards glazing windows. The shield of Thomas, Earl of Sussex, appears in the Benefactors' window in the north aisle of the nave. A shield on the south side of the west window must surely be for Edmund Colthurst (fig.12) – its main feature is three colts – though it does not agree exactly with other officially recorded arms for Colthurst, one of which adds three trefoils on the band across the shield and another has only two colts.[13]

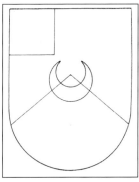

Fig.11 Chapman family

Fig.12 Edmund Colthurst

14

Fig.13 Thomas Bellot

In the second stage of repairs the south aisle was 'raised most from the ground, and covered as it is now, and the tower also now lofted with lead as it now is, with the clock set in it; and the bells to go; as they both now do.' The south end of the south transept was badly damaged by the collapse of the end wall when the support of the cloisters was removed. It was buttressed in 1576 and the date can still be seen on one of the buttresses. The plan of Bath in the corner of John Speed's map, dated 1610, shows the transept still gaping open, though buttressed, and the nave unroofed. The transept was repaired but not fully in stone vaulting until the nineteenth century. For this second stage the chief benefactor was Thomas Bellot, steward and executor to William Cecil, Lord Burghley, chief minister to Queen Elizabeth. Bellot seems to have given generously on his own account up to his death in 1611 and also for Cecil (the shield over the entrance to Bellot's Hospital shows the Cecil arms). Named contributions from Bellot at this stage are £60 to repair the east window and £30 towards the great bell. His arms are seen in glass at the top of the Benefactors' Window and, with more difficulty, above the end window of the south transept where there is a punning French motto *'Toujours Bellot'* – always handsome (fig.13). More than 30 other benefactors to this stage of restoration are named. Among them is Richard Hall, yeoman, of Wiltshire whose £5 is commemorated by his shield on the ceiling of the clergy vestry, not open to the public. John Still, Bishop of Bath and Wells 1593-1608, gave £20 and his shield is on the north side of the west window (fig.14).

Fig.14 Bishop Still

The third stage of restoration involved the church from the tower westward. The principal benefactor was Bishop Montagu who succeeded John Still in 1608. He gave £1000 and great energy to get repairs finished and persuaded others to contribute. Progress was rapid. Montagu became Bishop of Winchester in 1616 but his interest in Bath continued, though the restoration was not completed when he died only two years later. Perhaps the end of the repair programme may be marked by the west doors which were a memorial to the bishop and one of his four brothers. The

Montagu heraldry in the Abbey is impressive. Through inheritance the Montagu family had quartered their arms with those of Monthermer. The Montagu arms show a row of lozenges which might be seen as a row of mountain peaks and suggest *mont aguille, mons acutus* or *mont acute*! The west doors were given by Sir Henry Montagu, Lord Chief Justice and the fourth brother, in memory of the bishop and the brother who had already died. The lowest shield shows the family arms quartering Montagu with Monthermer. Above on the left the shield shows the diocese of Winchester impaling the Montagu quartered arms

Fig.15 Bishop Montagu

and shows James Montagu in his final office as Bishop of Winchester. The Winchester diocesan arms can easily be confused with those of Bath Abbey when uncoloured but the bishop had no connection with the former priory and no special office in the Bath church, although as bishop his arms are properly seen in the nave vault, impaled with those of the Bath and Wells Diocese (fig.15). On the west doors the small annulet at the centre of Bishop Montagu's arms is a cadency mark for a fifth son. The Montagu arms on the right have a different cadency mark – a crescent marking a second son, the brother who had died. Fig.15 shows the annulet near the top.

It was appropriate that Bishop Montagu should have been buried in Bath where he had done so much, especially as his remaining life at Winchester had been so short. His tomb inside the Abbey is a splendid heraldic display of 20 shields and badges. At the top he is shown as Bishop of Bath and Wells at one end and as Bishop of Winchester at the other, and his shield, quarterings and badges are everywhere. Binoculars will show that one of the shields in the nave vault bears the quartered Montagu/Monthermer arms and another shows the Bath and Wells saltire impaling Montagu. The detail is tiny but the difference mark here is not an annulet but a martlet, indicating a fourth son. This is an understandable error for it was the fourth son who gave the doors, but he was not bishop. Among the shields above the nave windows the Montagu lozenges may be seen on the north side and the Monthermer eagle on the south, together with another shield on the north side showing the family's griffin head crest.

What of the other donors whose gifts enabled Bishop Montagu to do so much? Bellot was prominent still, and there were many high-ranking peers. A number were recorded heraldically in stained glass that was damaged in World War II, but the restored remains were reassembled in a single window

Fig.16 William St Barbe   **Fig.17** Dr George Rives   **Fig.18** New College, Oxford

in the north aisle already referred to as the Benefactors' Window. Some uncertain quarterings have had to remain blank but the shields are named to assist identification. If you turn with your back to this window, high up on the south side may be seen the shield of John May of Charterhouse still, perhaps, in its original place. He paid for 'the glazing of four upper windows on the south side'. The gifts recorded are far more detailed for this third stage, presumably because the record was being compiled at that time. These gifts were mainly either money or undertakings to glaze a particular window. One donor of special interest is William St Barbe, 'Prebender of Hereford, at whose charge was glazed the fourth window westward, on the north side of the body of the church'. In the Kemble restoration in the nineteenth century, to which we come below, this window was chosen by Harriet St Barbe for a memorial to her husband and she replaced the plain glass with a fine heraldic display of her late husband and of some of his and her ancestors. The basic St Barbe shield (fig.16) is a simple check of black and white squares but the impalements and quarterings enable the particular individuals to be identified.

A few benefactors assisted construction by giving trees. Even for estates near Bath there must have been transport problems. One such gift with an heraldic connotation is detailed enough to be worth quoting in full.

> George Rives, Doctor of Divinity, and Warden (with the fellowes) of New College in Oxford, gave a goodlie oake that grewe upon their mannor of Cullerne, which yielded well neare 5 tunne of prime good timber, besides the topp and armes. The said Dr George Rives gave besides, of his own free gift, *5l.* [i.e. £5].

The shield of Rives (fig.17) can be seen on the north side of the west window (upper row, second from left). In the matching row on the south side are the arms of New College (fig.18).

The Arms of the City of Bath

The shield in use today (fig.19) has in its lower half a red battlemented wall and in the upper half two wavy bands on a blue ground representing water. This could be taken to represent either the River Avon outside the walls or the spa waters within. Over the whole is a sword, point upward. It seems more likely that the sword here stands for the Roman occupation than for St Paul but sometimes, in the past, the sword has been given a small key on the blade, perhaps to link saints Peter and Paul to whom the Abbey is jointly dedicated. But this is inappropriate in both size and number – St Peter has two keys. Modern displays have no key but you may find examples outside the Abbey – on the base of some street lamps, for example.

Heralds tried to control the use of arms through visitations round the country to record pedigrees and check the use of illegal displays. There was a visitation to Bath in 1623 when the heralds appended to one of their records, by way of a footnote, a drawing and description of the arms of the City. Contrary to the usual practice, this shows the wall at the top of the shield and the water below.(fig.20) This was not in any way a grant or confirmation but the shield received publicity in a Chapman genealogy now in the possession of the City. There are several clear examples from the sixteenth century to show the use of the accepted arms before and after 1623. This version does however have some support in a fifteenth century margin sketch which is in the shape of a shield but might be no more than a sketch of the spa bath.[14] The controversy as to which version was official surfaced again in the 1880s with Major Davis to the fore. There was no opposition from the heralds who were willing to make a new grant of the design with water at the top but the City objected to a 'new' grant for an ancient city. The supporters used were a lion and a bear which had even less authority than the shield. The matter was left in abeyance, but in preparation for cele-brating, in 1973, the 1000th anniversary of Edgar's coronation, a splendid compromise was reached. Appli-cation was made for an

Fig.19 City of Bath: traditional version

Fig.20 City of Bath: 1623 Visitation version

official grant of supporters, crest and motto and for a city badge. The grant gives details for a crest of two hands holding up Edgar's crown, and for lion and bear supporters decorated on their shoulders with the Abbey's sword and keys (with wards in the shape of B for Bath). The motto is *Aquae Sulis*, an old name of the City from the pre-Roman deity associated with the springs. The grant concluded with a mention of the arms with which these additions were to be associated and simply describes the ancient arms on which all parties were agreed![15] The 1623 shield is now simply an historical error but it can be seen in the nave vaulting. Among the Montagu shields are both the 1623 and the accepted arms. But do these stone carved shields date from the Montagu building or from the stone roof of the nineteenth century? When seen close up the style does look more seventeenth than nineteenth century. A more modern example of the City arms is in the vaulting of the crossing under the tower. Another curiosity is that the wall in the arms is occasionally white, as in one of the top corners of the east window. Could this error have been a reference to the colour of Bath stone? The arms are actually so blazoned in *Civic Heraldry* by a respected heraldic authority, C.W.Scott-Giles.[16] After this digression linked to two shields in the nave roof we now return to developments after the Montagu restoration.

Later Developments

It is not surprising that this great reconstruction was followed by two centuries without major alterations. The only addition of heraldic interest is the tomb, in the south transept, of the wife of Sir William Waller, the Civil War general. His own position, resting on an elbow and looking down on his wife's effigy, suggests that he intended to be buried here when the time came but he married a second

wife and is buried elsewhere. His first wife came from the Reynell family whose shield is basically black and white masonry – suggesting the wall that might have been an even better allusion to the name of Waller than the three walnut leaves that his shield bears. These two simple shields are seen on the monument, but its central shield shows many other quarterings inherited by Waller and Reynell families over the centuries. Waller and Reynell are impaled to show the marriage and all the Waller quarterings are on the left and the Reynell quarterings on the right. A simple impalement of the basic Waller and Reynell shields can be seen on one of the shields on the south side of the west window (fig.21).

Fig.21 Waller/Reynell family

The next major work was not until the 1830s, under G.P.Manners, when various pinnacles and parapets were added to the roof and the interior was filled with seats and galleries and there was a large new pulpit.[17] A far greater upheaval followed the appointment of Charles Kemble as Rector in 1860. A report by Sir George Gilbert Scott led to a major restoration which included replacing the roof of the nave and its aisles with stone vaulting to match the choir and transepts. Internal changes were made for liturgical reasons and the screen between nave and choir was removed. All the memorial tablets that had been placed on it, and also on the nave columns, were removed, and by careful jig-saw work and a little cutting were fitted on to the outer walls below the windows where they are now seen so densely packed. It is not surprising that there were a few errors – at least two heraldic shields have been separated from the tablets to which they belong. There were also new pews and some excellent heraldic carving on some of them. The work was well planned in three stages so that if funds were not sufficient some parts would be completed and others delayed rather than having to leave many aspects unfinished. Kemble was by far the greatest contributor to the funds, with his mother and uncle also giving very generously, but a wide range of mainly local people gave money in small amounts from a few pounds to the tens and hundreds from major landowners and gentry. The annual reports of the committee overseeing progress show long lists of names and many of these persons gave regularly year by year.[18]

Victorian heraldry was not strictly controlled and no longer provided an easily recognised division of society. Those aspiring to heraldic recognition of their rise in wealth and status did not always apply to the College of Arms and often assumed entitlement to arms granted to a family of the same surname. Two quotations from Thackeray's *Vanity Fair* illustrate this:-

'Captain Osborne, indeed! Any relation to the L ...... Osbornes?'
'We bear the same arms,' George said, as was indeed the fact; Osborne having consulted with a herald in Long Acre, and picked the L ...... arms out of the peerage, when he set up his carriage, fifteen years before.

The great red seal was emblazoned with the sham coat of arms which Osborne had assumed from the peerage, with '*Pax in Bello*' for a motto – that of the ducal house with which the vain old man tried to imagine himself connected.[19]

To identify some shields from the nineteenth century is therefore not easy. After the Kemble restoration, however, R.E.M.Peach, a contemporary writer, published a plan with names attached to most of the coats of arms[20] which has been helpful and time-saving to the present authors. The following cases

provide a few examples of identification problems with heraldry in the Abbey. The arms and crest for the family of Kemble (fig.22) are recorded in Papworth and Burke[21] and occur in several places in the Abbey, though some show variations from the recorded colours. Most examples show

Fig.22 Kemble family

Fig.23 Frederick Shum

the Kemble arms impaling arms for Charles Kemble's wife, Charlotte Cattley, which are not recorded by the authorities noted. Examples of Kemble's arms include a shield over the chancel arch and another in stained glass in a north aisle window. On the south side of the west window is a lozenge with Kemble impaling different arms that have also not been identified but the lozenge indicates a woman, and the display, authentic or not, can only be for the Rector's widowed mother who, second only to her son, was a large benefactor. Above the west window is a quartered shield for S.B.Brooke of Malmesbury, uncle of Charles Kemble, who was another generous donor. As an example of the links between families that heraldry can illustrate, the design in the second and third quarters of this shield can be seen again in the Benefactors' Window in the lozenge of the seventeenth century Baroness Hudson, who was a Carey. Charles Kemble's great-great-grandfather married a Carey heiress.

The second case concerns Frederick Shum. The Brothers Schumm had come to Bath from Germany in the eighteenth century and had anglicised their name. They were Methodists but Frederick had probably moved away from nonconformity. He was a prominent citizen and a trustee of St John's Hospital. It is most improbable that he was entitled to arms, German or English. The shield that Peach names as his shows the "lamb and flag" emblem of St John the Baptist, which is used by the Hospital, impaling a shield recorded for Cotterell, though as yet no record has been found that he married into this Bath family. The shield (fig.23) is in the nave south aisle. A third example is George Moger who was Mayor of Bath 1865-6. Correspondence with a descendant, Cdr George Moger of Exmouth, has made all clear. The Mogers were not entitled to arms but the Mayor's mother was a Slade whose mother was a Glover, both being heiresses in families having arms. The arms of Glover and Slade could have been added as quarterings to Moger arms but as he

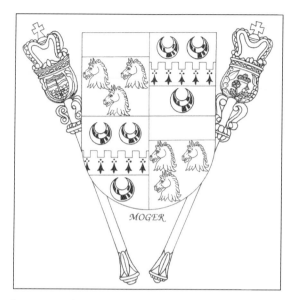

Fig.24 (*left*) Moger family

Fig.25 (*above*) Allen family

had none the Mayor simply, but incorrectly, quartered the Glover and Slade arms on their own. His display is near the east end of the nave north aisle and is a particularly fine one (fig.24) with the shield backed by two beautifully carved maces showing the City arms. The College of Arms confirmed that no arms were registered for the name of Moger. It was willing to make a grant but Cdr Moger declined the offer.

Lastly, Ralph Allen does not seem to have made any pretence to a coat of arms, though his biographer records that he used a Cornish chough unofficially as a crest.[22] However, his brother Philip's monument in Batheaston Church shows a coat of arms that Burke assigns to an Allen family of Pembrokeshire and to which the Bath family's humble background would have no likely entitlement. Philip's descendant, Major Ralph Shuttleworth Allen, was an MP (not for Bath) and a generous donor of £500 to the Abbey in 1868 and he is represented by the same shield in the nave north aisle (fig.25).

After these examples of Victorian heraldry problems we can now consider the heraldic legacy of the Kemble restoration in wider detail. The shields in the vaulting of the two nave aisles date from this time as do some of the shields at the sides of the east and west windows and a few elsewhere. The benefactors fall into several categories: those in official city positions during the 1864-73 period as mayors or members of parliament; important local families able to support the work generously; and local people working hard for the restoration project. Such persons account for most of the shields.

Fig.26 Long family   **Fig.27** Stoddart family

The Victorian period is regarded as a poor one for heraldic art, showing a lack of vigour in the representation of beasts and a lack of artistic balance in shields as a whole, but those in the Abbey, in spite of sometimes showing these faults, are in general well executed and a few, such as Moger and his maces, have good overall design. In the eastern part of the nave south aisle joint secretaries of the Restoration Committee, Long (fig.26) and Stoddart (fig.27), and the treasurer Gill (fig.28) have shields. Behind and below the Stoddart shield are two quill pens and the nibs have their tips coloured red and blue as if just inked. Below Gill's shield is a carved purse and chain. Fuller details of the names associated with the Kemble restoration are

Fig.28 Gill family

available elsewhere.[23] The following paragraphs will provide a few examples of the range of people commemorated.

Among the mayors, Jerom Murch (seven times mayor) is a similar case to Shum. He was an unlikely person to have family arms but he shows an unrecorded coat impaling arms for his wife (née Taylor), which match one recorded for a Taylor family. Murch has his shield in the nave south aisle and also at the north side of the east window where the impaled arms are uneasily distorted on a shield of mediaeval elongated shape (fig.29). Among Bath's MPs the names of Lord Grey de Wilton and Viscount Chelsea stand out with their courtesy titles as eldest sons of peers. Viscount Chelsea was elected in 1873. He succeeded his father as Earl Cadogan in the same year and at a further election Lord Grey became one of Bath's MPs until 1875 when he succeeded to the earldom of Wilton. These two have shields alongside Murch beside the east window.

Earl Manvers was an important local landowner, whose descent from the Duke of Kingston's sister had brought him the former Abbey estates. His shield (see the north side of the west window) was deliberately chosen to be similar to the Duke's, with the main charge of a lion, but the background of 5-petalled *cinquefoils* is replaced by 5-pointed stars (*molets*) (figs 30,31). The Gore-Langtons of Newton Park arose from a marriage of two Bristol merchant families. They reached a

Fig.29 Murch family

social peak with marriage to a daughter of the Duke of Buckingham in 1846 and subsequent inheritance of the title of Earl Temple, but they fell in fortune a century later. Their proud impalement with the Duke's many-quartered shield is on the south side of the west window.[24] The Dukes of Cleveland were inheritors of the Pulteney estates in Bathwick. Three brothers were duke in turn in 1864; the 5th Duke died in January without issue and his next brother succeeded as 6th Duke but died in September, also without a son to succeed. The youngest brother became 7th Duke and when he died in 1891 the title became extinct.[25] The Duchess of the 6th Duke was a benefactor and her arms, on a lozenge, in the nave north aisle illustrate well the unsuitable nature of that shape for arms, especially when quartered.

Fig.30 Duke of Kingston

Fig.31 Earl Manvers

Nearby the very simple shield of Boyle, two plain colours separated by an embattled diagonal, stands for the Earl of Cork and Orrery who was Lord Lieutenant of Somerset from 1864-1904. It may also provide a reminder of his ancestor who designed General Wade's house in Abbey Church Yard. Other local gentry of this period with shields in the Abbey are Miles of Leigh Court, west of Bristol, and Skrine of Warleigh, near Bathford.

The Kemble restoration saw a change of bishop for the Diocese of Bath and Wells. Robert John Eden (1799-1870) may have chosen the Church as a career suitable for a third son and thirteenth child of a baron but at the age of 50 he inherited the title as 3rd Baron Auckland. He was bishop from 1854 to 1869 and his shield is the most easterly of those in the nave south aisle. His successor was Arthur, Lord Hervey (1808-94), fourth son of the Marquis of Bristol and his shield is at the east end of the choir south aisle. The shield is held by two angels with clearly visible toed feet and supported from below by a more earthy Atlas figure – a most unusual display (fig.32).

Fig.32 Bishop Arthur Hervey

But notice the small bird on the shield. It is a martlet, the difference mark for a fourth son (as already mentioned in connection with the Montagu family). The martlet should be without feet, from the legend that swallows had no feet, for they were never seen to land on the ground. This martlet was given feet and although painted out with red the error was not rendered totally invisible. As John Aubrey wrote of another trivial matter, 'how these curiosities would be quite forgott, did not such idle fellowes as I am putt them downe!'[26]

The wood carvings on the end of the pews that completed the Kemble restoration provide a further heraldic display. These shields are beautifully carved in low relief and though uncoloured are hatched according to a convention developed for use with black and white printing and etching. Silver (white) is shown plain, gold (yellow) is stippled with dots, blue is marked by shading with horizontal lines, red with vertical lines and black with both. Diagonal lines from top left indicate green, those from the top right, purple. The original purpose of heraldry was instant recognition and it relied on a few colours easily distinguished. Except for small *charges* these carved shields can be 'read' in colour. In the choir stalls most of the ends are decorated with shields. Between the two groups of pews on the south side is a shield showing Noah's Ark – the arms of the Scottish family of Jolly who founded the Milsom Street shop. In the nave there are a few more such carvings, including Kemble and his wife, but lighting conditions are less favourable for spotting them. There are a number of other, but less notable, carved arms on screens.

The heraldry in stained glass relating to the early stages of restoration has already been mentioned and there are also shields in several nineteenth century memorial windows: two are worth describing. In the south transept, behind the Waller tomb, is a window given by a Mrs Elliott of Bath in memory of her father Robert Scott, and in gratitude for the recovery of the Prince of Wales from typhoid in 1872. The upper part is a Jesse window showing the descent of Jesus and the lower part indicates the sickness and recovery of King Hezekiah (Isaiah, Ch.38). Right at the top, but too small to be seen easily, are the badges of the 12 tribes of Israel. Such badges are part of heraldry's roots. Across the bottom of the window are five shields (not easy to see behind the tomb). They are, from left to right, Edward as Prince of Wales, showing the arms of Saxony for his father, Prince Albert, and a label for an eldest son; Diocese of Bath and Wells; Queen Victoria; City of Bath (1623 version); the Prince of Wales as husband impaling the arms of Denmark for his wife Alexandra.

At the west end of the north aisle the 'Guilds Window' was presented to the Abbey by the contractors for the Kemble restoration. The four figures are, appropriately, Moses (builder of the Tabernacle), David, Solomon and Zerubbabel (builders and restorers of the Temple). Across the bottom are shields of the Livery Companies of those who did the actual work of Abbey reconstruction – Masons, Joiners, Glaziers and Plumbers.

Conclusion

The rich heraldic legacy in Bath Abbey is worth study for several reasons. Each of the distinct stages in the development of the building has shields associated with people actively concerned in the work and of the donors who made it possible. In the nineteenth century especially, the wide range of social status and financial means become clear: the shields are not restricted to the upper classes. The heraldry, when understood, supplements the history as well as embellishing the building. To a smaller extent it also draws attention to the City's history: an abbey, walled off from the rest of the city, is dissolved and its church becomes a city church under the influence of its corporation. The growth of this city as a spa is further illustrated by the tablets on the walls. The individuals concerned are mainly visitors, not residents, but the heraldry on many of the tablets, though outside the present study, shows high social status, a number making full use of the prestige of quarterings. They also illustrate Heraldry itself with its changes in artistic style. A small amount of heraldic knowledge brings disproportionately large rewards and illustrates a dictum of T.L.Peacock who wrote of 'that commanding advantage, which, in all circumstances and conditions of life, a man who knows something, however little, always possesses over one who knows nothing.'[27]

Notes

1 Nimbus Conservation Ltd was responsible for the interior cleaning 1996-7.
2 The College of Arms is the authority in all matters of heraldry in England, Wales and Northern Ireland. The officers were incorporated in 1484 and assigned a building in London in 1555. This was destroyed by the Great Fire of 1666 (but records were saved) and it was rebuilt as the present College in Queen Victoria Street.
3 John Britton, *The History and Antiquities of Bath Abbey Church* (Longman, 1825), pp.45-6. For a general account of the early development of the Abbey see Peter Davenport, 'Bath Abbey' (*Bath History*, Vol. II, Alan Sutton, Gloucester, 1988), pp.1-26.
4 Patrick Mitchell, *Bishop Oliver King and the Present Abbey (Priory) Church* (Friends of Bath Abbey, Bath, 1996).
5 *Dictionary of National Biography*: Adrian de Castello (also known as di Castello).
6 Before the union with Scotland under James I and VI in 1603 the Tudors quartered France and England (in that order). Each sovereign chose favourite supporters: here a dragon and a greyhound. The use of a lion for England and a unicorn for Scotland was introduced in 1603 and has been unchanged since. Also from 1603 the Tudor arms were quartered with Scotland and Ireland. In Scotland the supporters are reversed with the unicorn on the left. For later changes and further details see, for example, J.H. & R.V. Pinches, *The Royal Heraldry of England* (Heraldry Today, 1974).
7 John Haddon, *Bath* (Batsford, 1973), pp.37-8.
8 *Ibid.*, Ch.5.
9 The quotation is attributed to Fuller in a guide to the Abbey by Sir Harold Brakspeare (n.d. but many editions). Thomas Fuller's *Church History of Britain* (1655) is a likely

source but its length and lack of indexing are daunting and a recent short search has not found the quotation. Haddon, *op.cit.* p.68, quotes without attribution.

10 Britton, *op.cit.* p.55, writes that these estates were sold to Fulk Morley in 1569 and descended to the Duke of Kingston and Earl Manvers. Haddon, *op.cit.* p.71, states that they were sold in 1611 to John Hall , a wealthy clothier of Bradford-on-Avon who was progenitor of a line which subsequently acquired the title of Duke of Kingston. There is heraldic support; the shield of Hall of Bradford on Avon is on the ceiling of the clergy vestry in the Abbey.

11 For copies of this manuscript see Richard Warner, *History of Bath* (Cruttwell, Bath, 1801), appendix 73, and Britton, *op.cit.* appendix V. Neither the archivist of Bath Abbey nor the librarian of Wells Cathedral has any knowledge of the possible present location of the manuscript.

12 Haddon, *op.cit.* p.68.

13 Sir Bernard Burke, *The General Armory of England, Scotland, Ireland and Wales* (1884; facsimile, Burke's Peerage, 1961), p.218.

14 Bath Record Office: Town Clerk's papers (unreferenced).

15 F.D. Wardle, *Arms of the City of Bath* (1953). Letter of 25 May 1972 from the Town Clerk to members of the City Council concerning the proposed new grant of arms. *The City Arms of Bath*: 4-page leaflet (April 1973) issued by the City Council to illustrate and explain the new grant.

16 C.W. Scott-Giles, *Civic Heraldry of England and Wales* (Dent, 1933).

17 G.P. Manners (*c.*1789 -1866), City Architect and responsible for many buildings in the 1820-60 period. See Charles Robertson, *Bath, An Architectural Guide* (Faber & Faber, 1975), pp.139-40.

18 Sir George Gilbert Scott (1811-71) was nearing the height of his career when he became involved with Bath Abbey in 1863. He worked on many cathedrals as well as being responsible for the Albert Memorial and St Pancras Station Hotel. Bath Reference Library has copies of the annual reports of the Restoration Committee bound with other material under the title 'Norman'.

19 W.M.Thackeray, *Vanity Fair* (Bradbury and Evans, 1848), Chapters 29 & 34.

20 R.E.M. Peach, *The History and Antiquities of Bath Abbey Church by John Britton continued to the present time by R.E.M.Peach* (Charles Hallett, Bath, 1887). Peach was author of many books about Bath in the last quarter of the nineteenth century. His work is not now held in high regard because of errors disclosed by later research.

21 Burke, *op.cit.*, presents an alphabetical list of names with recorded arms. J.W. Papworth, *Ordinary of British Armorials* (1874, facsimile, Tabard Publications, 1961) provides a means of attaching names to coats of arms. It depends on the correct order of describing the details on a shield according to the rules and language of blazon.

22 Benjamin Boyce, *The Benevolent Man* (Harvard University Press, Cambridge, Mass., 1967), p.198.

23 J. Ede & R.Symons, *The Heraldry in the vault of Bath Abbey: a tour* (1997), available in Bath Abbey shop.

24 Graham Davis, *The Langtons at Newton Park* (printed by Fyson & Co., Bath, n.d.); The Hon. Vicary Gibbs, ed., *The Complete Peerage of England, Scotland, Ireland, Great Britain and the United Kingdom* (new edn. St Catherine Press 1910), vol.12, part 1, pp.660-1.

25 Gibbs, *op.cit.*, vol.3, pp.285-6.

26 John Aubrey, *Brief Lives and other selected writings* (Cresset Press, 1949), p.49.

27 Henry Cole, ed., *The Works of Thomas Love Peacock* (Bentley, 1875), Vol.3, p.335.

THE JOURNALS OF MRS PHILIP LYBBE POWYS
(1738–1817)
A HALF CENTURY OF VISITS TO BATH

Stephen Powys Marks

I INTRODUCTION

Mrs Philip Lybbe Powys, née Caroline Girle, travelled extensively, as far afield as Devon, Staffordshire, Norfolk, Derbyshire, Yorkshire, Kent and the Isle of Wight, often staying with her family and relations, and she visited Bath with great frequency. She recorded these tours and visits in her Annual Journal and in several accounts of individual tours, as well as in letters to her father and to friends and relations.[1] Extracts from these were published in 1899.[2] The interest and extent of this output is all the more remarkable in view of the conventional attitude to the education of women in the eighteenth century. Caroline was well aware of the limitations which this imposed, observing that her ignorance of a scientific subject was 'more for want of instruction than capacity'. She asked:

> … is it any thing surprising the sex shou'd amuse themselves with trifles when these Lords of the Creation will not give themselves the trouble, (in my conscience I believe tis for fear of being out shone) to enlarge our minds by making them capable to retain those of more importance (BL vol. VI: Plymouth Journal, 1760, ff.28–9)

Despite these disadvantages, it is clear from two recent studies that her observations are highly regarded: praising her as a witness of prevailing tastes in country houses, one author concludes that 'None excel Mrs Lybbe Powys, not as an appraiser of architectural niceties but as a typical representative of the gentry class'; the other finds that the consistent interest in the interiors of a house shown by Caroline and the earlier traveller Celia Fiennes 'make particularly rewarding reading'.[3]

After an introduction to Caroline and her family, and to the journals themselves, there follow accounts of the visits to Bath from the original manuscripts. To give the full flavour of these visits, rather than to simply select 'interesting' passages, several accounts for the later years are transcribed in full.

Caroline Girle and her family

Caroline Girle was born on December 27th 1738,[4] the daughter of a prosperous surgeon, John Girle, and Barbara Slaney, an heiress. Her father's memorial tablet in Beenham Church, Berkshire, records that his death on July 5th 1761 occurred in his fifty-ninth year. He had retired, having made his fortune, and was planning to leave the house in Lincoln's Inn Fields in London into which the family had moved on September 14th 1754.[5]

According to Caroline, he died when he had 'just purchas'd' a house in the Circus at Bath (AJ, July 5th 1761), where building had begun in 1754.[6] His daughter would thus have become a resident in the newest and most fashionable part of Bath. Girle's purchase of a substantial house demonstrates that he must indeed have 'early in life acquired an ample fortune, the just reward of superior eminence , and unremitting diligence in his profession', as his memorial tablet informs us.[7] It is evident from Caroline's comments and her frequent visits that she was very attracted to the city, but Bath was not to be her future home. She and her mother moved instead to live in Caversham, Berkshire, near to a previous home. This was also close to where Philip Lybbe Powys (1734–1809) lived at Hardwick House, Oxfordshire;[8] his mother was Isabella Lybbe, sole heiress, whose family had owned Hardwick for many generations. The Girle and Hardwick families had been previously acquainted.

Caroline was married to Philip Lybbe Powys on August 5th 1762, and Hardwick became her much-loved home for twenty-two years. All her four children were born there; the first daughter died before she was a year old, the occasion of a consolatory visit to Bath, but the other three grew up at Hardwick. This house was, Caroline wrote in a letter to a close friend soon after her wedding, 'a large old House about twelve rooms on a Floor with 4 Staircases, The situation delightful on a declivity of a Hill ye most beautiful woods behind, and fine views of the Thames and rich meadows in Front' (BL vol. XIII: letter of October 24th 1762) (fig. 1 overleaf).

Philip Lybbe Powys's widowed father, Philip Powys, lived with the couple until he died in 1779. In 1782 Caroline's mother, Mrs Girle, moved to live at Hardwick House. She had planned to buy a house in Bath, but instead in 1783 and 1784 she took a house for the winter for herself and the young couple. In 1784, with most of the family gone, Hardwick House became too big, so Caroline and Philip, with their daughter Caroline, moved to live with his bachelor brother, Thomas Powys, Rector of Fawley, some 13 miles distant, leaving Hardwick with 'the utmost regret' (AJ, Summer 1784). Fawley Rectory was the home of Caroline and Philip for 25 years till the death of the latter in 1809; Caroline's last years till her death late in 1817 were spent in Henley. Their son Philip took over Hardwick in 1792 after a short period of letting. When they left Hardwick, Caroline's mother lived first in Reading and then in Henley.

HARDWICKE-HOUSE, THE SEAT OF PHILIP LYBBE POWYS, ESQ.

Fig.1 Hardwick House, Oxfordshire, engraved drawing by Skelton and Willis, 1827. The Philip Lybbe Powys in the title is the elder son of Caroline Powys. The drawing shows the rear of the house, looking entirely sixteenth- and seventeenth-century in character, and probably little changed from how Caroline would have seen it. (*reproduced by courtesy of Timothy Powys-Lybbe*)

The Journals

The journals are a valuable source of material on local customs, manners and celebrations, and on the the architectural development and interior decoration of the grand house in the late eighteenth century, when Caroline was both tourist and private visitor. They give a first-hand impression of the country life of the English upper classes at a time when rapidly increasing wealth gave rise to the building of new country houses everywhere, and the passion for entertainment was spreading from the town to the country. Caroline was clearly well read and extremely observant.

Caroline herself reduced her pocket diaries, which have not survived, into the three volumes of the Annual Journal, which runs to more than 500 pages; for example, in 1793 she wrote:

here ends my sort of journal for yᵉ year 1793, for though in my Annual pocket Book I always set down the visits of each day, yet that would take up too much room here, as in so excellent and agreeable Neighbourhood as this is it would be a constant repetition of dinners in each mansion within 7 or 8 miles round. (AJ, Dec. 28th 1793)

We know, therefore, that Caroline intended the surviving journals to be her record for posterity.

For whom was she taking the trouble to write up her journals from her letters and pocket diaries? The very first account, of a trip of several weeks to Norfolk in 1756, is in fact based on letters to her father. It was he who enjoined her to write about her journey and thus started her off in the diary habit. Caroline certainly took a long view, when she wrote of Holkham 25 years later, 'I shall say nothing of this place as in a journal in 1756 in a letter to my father, Ive given a description of it' (BL vol. X: Second Norfolk Journal, 1781).

Survey of Visits to Bath, 1759–1808

The first described visit occurred in 1759, when Caroline was 20 years old; it was part of a tour with her family which included Oxford and Bath. In Oxford they saw in one day Trinity College, the Ashmolean Museum, the Bodleian, New College, the Clarendon, Sheldonian, Schools, Radcliffe Camera, All Souls, the Physic Garden, Magdalen and the Walks, and then went off to lodgings in Woodstock. They arrived in Bath on August 21st:

… this is a place of great Antiquity, lying in a valley surround'd with an Amphytheatrical view of Hills from which Hills spring yᵉ waters so fam'd and which are of such advantage to this City, a City in my opinion more worth seeing than any I was ever at, the Grand Metropolis except'd. twice I have been there before, but tis infinitely improv'd by the building yᵉ Circus, and yᵉ noble street by which tis approach'd from yᵉ Square. they seem to fear yᵉ formers ever being finish'd its progress is so extremely slow 9 houses only are yet erect'd. there is intend'd to be 3 times that number, and yᵉ openings between give a fine view of yᵉ Country. those that are Compleat'd give one an idea of yᵉ elegance of yᵉ Whole they being in a magnificent taste in yᵉ Doric Ionic and Corinthian orders, and indeed tis so fine a design twou'd be great pity if it fail'd in yᵉ execution. there are many other fine Buildings in this City as the Parades &c, but yᵉ Bath Stone affords a fine opportunity to embellish and give an air of Grandure to yᵉ whole. we employ'd our morning as

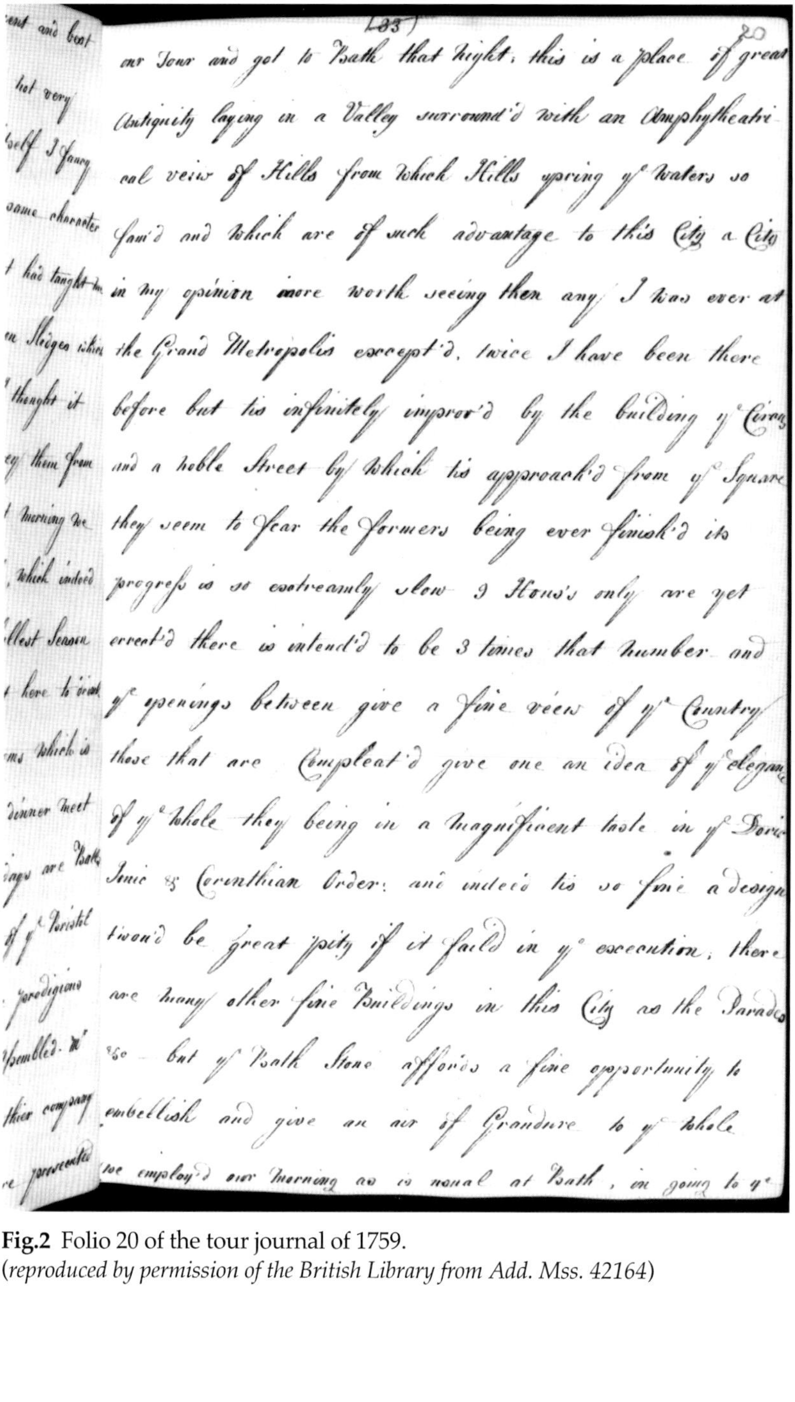

[20]

our Tour and got to Bath that night, this is a place if great Antiquity laying in a Valley surround'd with an Amphytheatri- cal veiw of Hills from which Hills spring y[e] waters so fam'd and which are of such advantage to this City a City in my opinion more worth seeing then any I was ever at the Grand Metropolis except'd. twice I have been there before but tis infinitely improv'd by the Building y[e] Circus and a noble Street by which tis approach'd from y[e] Square they seem to fear the formers being ever finish'd its progress is so extreamly slow 9 Hous's only are yet errect'd there is intend'd to be 3 times that number and y[e] openings between give a fine veiw of y[e] Country those that are Compleat'd give one an idea of y[e] elegance of y[e] whole they being in a magnificent taste in y[e] Doric Jonic & Corinthian Order: and indeed tis so fine a design twou'd be great pity if it fail'd in y[e] execution; there are many other fine Buildings in this City as the Parade &c — but y[e] Bath Stone affords a fine opportunity to embellish and give an air of Grandure to y[e] whole we employ'd our Morning as is usual at Bath, in going to y[e]

Fig.2 Folio 20 of the tour journal of 1759.
(*reproduced by permission of the British Library from Add. Mss. 42164*)

is usual at Bath in going to yᵉ Pump, yᵉ Abbey Church and yᵉ Rooms tho each were but little frequent'd there being but two or three families besides that of yᵉ Duchess of Marlboroughs. the heat of yᵉ waters is very extraordinary and People attribute it to different causes but most to its passing thro' certain Sulphurous veins of yᵉ earth, in taste tis not so agreeable as those at Bristol. Thursday afternoon [August 22nd] we went to Mʳ Busbys at Walcot; we had paid in the morning a visit to Mʳ & Mʳˢ Pierce, and early on Friday we quitt'd this agreeable Place. (BL vol. V: Oxford etc, 1759)

This was a brief visit perhaps, but particularly interesting for her comment that she had been there twice before, 'but tis infinitely improv'd by the building yᵉ Circus'. She and presumably her father must have visited Bath before the Circus, on which work began in 1754, was building (fig.3). When her father died on July 5th 1761, he had 'just purchas'd a house in the Circus

Fig.3 Portion of a deed of 1768 showing the south-west segment of the King's Circus, approximately what Caroline would have seen in 1759.
(*reproduced by courtesy of Bath Record Office*)

Bath, and our Goods were packing to remove there' (AJ, Jul. 5th 1761). It may be that the visits of 1759 and earlier mentioned by Caroline had shown how attractive Bath was. Forty years later it still had its enchantment: at the end of the visit in 1796–97, 'we walked about ye whole morning to take leave of our favorite place' (AJ, Jan. 12th 1797). It is perhaps not surprising that Bath was so congenial, since Caroline clearly disliked open landscapes: 'Suffolk … one of ye most horrid Countys I ever beheld' (BL vol. X: Second Norfolk Tour, 1781); Osterley Park's 'situation dreary and unpleasant' (AJ, May 22nd 1788); in the New Forest 'you … see your Straight Road for many Miles, which to me is ever a disagreeable View' (BL vol. XI: Isle of Wight, 1792). In Derbyshire, on the other hand, she found that 'what adds beauty to this county is the parks and forests, and inequality of hills and dales that so diversify the landscape' [9] – she was truly a devotee of the picturesque.

The next visit was in April 1764 after the death of her first daughter, born the previous June. Caroline, her husband, his brother and her father-in-law went to Bath because they thought 'a little Tour might be of service to my spirits at that time very indifferent' (AJ, Apr. 26th 1764). The next few years were occupied by the birth and childhood of her two sons, Philip Lybbe (1765) and Thomas (1768). The next visit to Bath occurred in 1773 when she and her husband went to Bath for five weeks 'for Mr Powys health, and the waters were of infinite service to him' (AJ, Jan. 6th 1773); she observed that 'The celebrated Miss Lindley [Mrs Sheridan] was now a capital singer at Bath, we heard her in "Acis and Galatea" and nothing but ye elegance of her figure can equal her voice.'

In 1775 another daughter was born, and the next Bath visit did not occur till in April 1780 they went again 'for Mr Powys health, but he soon received Benefit from the Waters, and having numbers of our Acquaintance there made us pass 6 most agreeable weeks.' We do not know if they planned other visits between these dates, but the weather could make the journey impossible: one year their six-week visit was delayed a fortnight by snow (AJ, Mar. 15th 1786). In another, the weather was so bad that they could not use their horses, and fuel ran short (AJ, Feb. 2nd 1795).

After 1780 the visits became much more frequent. Caroline's mother, who had moved to Hardwick House in the middle of September 1782,

> had long talked of … taking a house at Bath, but we could not reconcile ourselves to her being at so great a distance, or to her living there at all in Summer, so in the end we fixed on a scheme agreeable to us all, that of living with her at Bath in Winter if she would consent to be at Hardwick the other part of the year. (AJ, Sep. 1782)

There followed a pattern of nearly annual visits by the couple until the record ceases at the end of 1808. In 1783 and 1784 they went to Bath in February for three months accompanied by Caroline's mother who had taken a house, but she seems not to have come to Bath again. Thereafter, the couple took lodgings in many parts of the city, except in 1796–97 when they were invited by friends who had taken a house in Laura Place.[10]

On the penultimate visit in 1807 Caroline and her husband had their portraits done by Jacob Spornberg.[11] These were miniatures, that of Caroline being the only known representation of her (fig. 2). We do not know if Caroline ever visited Bath again, but as her husband died in April 1809, and as she was herself then 70, she may well have not felt the urge or had the energy to undertake a journey of two days, staying in Bath on her own, after more than fifty years' acquaintance with that city. In the 23 years from 1786 to 1808, there were 17 visits in all, usually in late winter running into spring; they lasted anything up to three months. From 1796 they truly became 'our annual Bath tour' or 'Excursion' (AJ, Feb.17th 1803, Jan. 12th 1807). In total, Caroline's visits to Bath accounted for three years of her life.

Fig.4 Mrs Philip Lybbe Powys, 'Etruscan profile' silhouette by Jacob Spornberg at Bath, 1807

The distance from Hardwick to Bath was less than 70 miles, a journey which it was possible to accomplish within a day. From Fawley, where most of the journeys started, the distance was some 12 or 14 miles longer, making an overnight stay unavoidable. The couple broke their journey most often at Marlborough, occasionally staying another night at Hardwick (where their son was in residence from 1792) or at Reading on the way.

The accounts of the visits to Bath reproduced below from the Annual Journal show the intensity of social life for those in a position to enjoy it, but evidently it could take its toll. In 1798, at the age of 60, Caroline wrote, 'we were so old Fashion a couple, as to enjoy ourselves (by ourselves), sometimes of evenings, rather than always in such immense crouded rooms.' (AJ, Mar. 10th 1798)

II THE LATER VISITS TO BATH IN THE JOURNALS OF CAROLINE POWYS [12]

1796 *February 25th* – Thursday yᵉ 25 Mʳ Powys and myself set off for Bath which we intended sooner as Mʳ P health had long wanted those waters, but I was too ill to go sooner and then very indifferent. We lay that night at Mʳˢ Micklems, Reading, and set off yᵉ next morning at ½ past seven.

26th – got to yᵉ White Lion Bath by six. we had sent about Lodgings, but it was so full none were to be had a week before, but luckily a family went out of N° 9 George St yᵉ next morn after we arrived, and we went into them in the Evening, liking that Situation, as we were tired of the high ones, having the last Time Lodged in Landsdown Place, and found the distance very Inconvenient.

28th – on Sunday the 28, I was much disappointed at not being well enough to go out, as Dʳ Randolph told me it was his last Time of Preaching, and I had never heard him, but I was so fortunate yᵉ next to find he had staid that week, and then had that pleasure. Text fifth Jeremiah 4 & 5.

March 9th – on The Fast day my Brother[-in-law], Dʳ Powys came from Bristol to preach at the Octagon, whose Sermon was so generally admired, he was much desired to print it and a most excellent one indeed it was, I seldom before went to the Octagon and those two Sundays thought it more than ever like being at an Assembly, for being a Friend of yᵉ one Dʳ & related to the Other, we were placed in the highest Seat in the Synagogue, and of course one of the most uncomfortable places to perform ones Devotions In.

I think tis unnecessary to write down a daily journal during our stay in Bath, only that I had the pleasure of seeing Mʳ Powys health mend daily, as to myself I was very indifferent the whole time I was there. as to yᵉ Amusements, we partook but a few of them, two very good Plays, and as usual amazingly well perform'd 'The Jew' (one of Cumberlands) and 'A Bell Stroke for a Wife', we were only at one dress Ball, but Parties tis impossible to escape, at Bath or London, though as diversion I believe so prejudicial to health from the intense heat of crouded rooms, one poor young Lady was a martyr to imprudence too common at Bath yᵉ walking if only a few doors from one Card Assembly to another, She was perfectly well, and I had met her at a Friend of mine in the morning, where she was talking of the many places she was to be at that evening, the next day but one She died of a most violent Cold caught by not taking a chair because it was only a few Doors She had to go, the wind was amazingly high and the Physician said that this was literally the cause of her Death, though quite unknown to her till two days before. I think I was hardly ever more shock'd.

15th – I forgot to mention being much entertain'd one Evening by Breslaus, who we had not seen for some years, indeed it appears very surprising, at one time he made Five or six of us not take up ye same Card that Ive often seen done but each of us think of the same Card, then he desired from different Gentlemen each to take a peice of money from their own pockets, mark them as they liked, then lay each down on ye Table themselves under a Card, he never came near the Table, but in a few minutes desir'd them to look for their own peices under some lids of boxes on another table, and see if their marks were what they made, two of the Gentlemen were our own party, which proved the Trial fair, as wonderful how he could deceive one.

April 4th – we left Bath at ten in the morn […] forgot to mention the Elegant new pump room being finish'd since we were last at Bath, which renders the croud in meeting there much more Comodious than it used to be.

1796 *November 22nd* – went to The White Lion Bath ye next day where we dined and then luckily got the same Lodgings in George Street for one week as we were in the last year. The Shrimptons had sent us word from London, they had taken a large house in Laura Place and we must come to them ye 28, though they knew it was not ye Time of year we generally went to Bath. This being all fixed, and Mr Powys being far from well, we thought of setting out, and taking Lodgings till they were ready to receive us, without telling them of our intentions and luckily we were quite settled before they knew we were around.

26th – The Duke and Duchess of York came to their House in the Crescent the Center one, which they have just purchased, and ye next day the Prince of Wales came to them. We were that Sunday at Queen Square Chaple,[13] the Duchess had taken a seat there and was handed in by one of the Gentlemen, her attendants, and the beautiful Mrs Bunbury was with her Royal Highness

28th – On Monday the 28 we left our Lodgings and went to the Shrimptons who had taken a large house N° 7 Laura place, Mrs Norman with them.

30th – at the Concert new rooms to hear Signora Storacé

December 3rd – at the play 'The Dramatist' and 'Agreeable Surprise', ye Duchess there, who was at all ye public Amusements.

4th – Sunday at Dr Randolfs new Chapel, Laura place, where we had taken a recess, being acquainted with him, it was not near so full as the Octagon used to be, and is at present a very cold one indeed, but the weather was remarkably severe at that time.

6th – at a party Mrs Hankles.

8th – to dinner Mrs Eyre Miss Purvis Sr George Colnebroke Mr Eyre and Mr Purvis, a party in the evening as usual.

10th – a large company to dinner

13th – a party at Mr Badderleys

15th – Mr Shrimpton & Mr Powys dined at the Marquis of Lansdownes. among many other Gentlemen The Archbishop of Bordeaux was there a very agreeable man, he could not talk english, he now lives on a pension from our Government, though formerly of such state and magnificence at Beaudeaux, as to have treated two Regiments in his Court Yard.

18th – Dr Randolf preach'd his Charity Sermon for ye Bath Hospital and got a larger Collection than any other Church.

19th – Company to dinner

20th – party at Mrs Eyres

22nd – at the play to see Miss Wallace in 'Beatrice' with 'ye Lock & Key', Miss Wallace perform'd it amazingly well indeed, and as I had often seen Mrs Pritchard in the same Character, I think I must say more in praise of this Favorite Bath Actress, who was come from London, to act for a week as usual

25th – being Sunday and Xmas day, the places of Worship were (as I must say they generally are at Bath) as full as possible but the service being very long and the weather colder than has almost ever been known, it was hardly possible to bear the severity, at Bath having been generally there only in Spring I never felt any thing like it, but it seems in London and Country it was at that time very remarkable.

28th – at the play to see Miss Wallace act 'ye Jealous Wife', which She performed Incomparably.

29th, 30th – each a large party at home. [visit continues into 1797]

1797 *January 2nd* – Monday, January 2nd, was Mr Tysons Ball at the Upper Rooms, and I fancy never any Master of the Ceremonies had a fuller or one more magnificent from the number of persons of Quality then at Bath, of whom I will set down a list of those I can recollect seeing there, we were obliged to go an hour before it began to get a tolerable place, but by that means were fortunate to get very good ones, near the Throne, Sopha, so call'd, plac'd there for the Royal family, when they entered, the whole company rose up, and continued standing while 'God Save ye King' and 'The Duke of Yorks march' was play'd. The Duchess of York, and Princess of Orange was first led up the room and seated on the Throne, next all the Ladies of quality and placed on benches on each side. the Gentlemen none of them set down, but the Prince of Wales, Duke of York, the Stadtholder, Prince of Orange, and many noblemen stood and talked to ye Ladies till the Ball began, when they mixed with the croud, which was immense, above fourteen hundred, indeed it was allow'd by all to be a most pleasing sight in so fine a room as that is. I will now put down the names of the nobility I remember to have been there, tho Ive no doubt I shall omit many.

Prince Wales, Duke & Duchess York, The Stadtholder & Princess of Orange, The Prince of Orange, Lord & Lady Harcourt, The Chancellor & Lady Loughborough, Lady Mary Howe and her sister, Lord and Lady Clifden, Earl of Sussex, Earl of Galloway, Earl Miltown, Earl of Strafford, Lord Molesworth, Viscountess Down, Earl of Peterborough, Lord Ashbroke, Lady de Clifford, Marquis & Marchioness Blandford, Duke and Duchess Beaufort, Duchess Rutland, Marquis Bute, Earl & Countess of Inchiquin, R^t Hon Lord Caledon, Lady Mary Knox, Earl & Countess Altamont, Countess Ormond, Lady E. Butler, Lady G. Sutton, Earl Milton, Lord J. Thynne, Marquis Worcester, Lord Malden, Lady Eliz Chaplin, Lady C. Johnstone, Count Travinville, Earl & Countess of Cork, Duchess Newcastle & two Daughters, Duke Newcastle, Earl of Peterborough, Earl of Plymouth, Lord & Lady Hood, Lord Coleraine, Marquis Landsdown, Countess of Ely, Countess of [blank], Lady Malmesbury, Lord George & J. Beresford, besides Baronets & their Ladies innumerable.

3rd – at the play 'The Duce is in Him' The Royal Family there, and when Signora Storacé sang 'God Save the King' I do believe half the Audience shed tears, as her manner voice and Action, was beyond anything one could imagine.

5th – a party at home

6th – Kings Ball the master of the ceremonies lower rooms a very full one, but nothing like Tysons, indeed, many of the nobility were gone and the Prince Duke and the Stadtholders family, and those Rooms being so much smaller, made the croud very disagreeable indeed so that people being sever'd from their own parties most left ye Ball very early, as did the Duchess of York.

While we were at Bath Mrs Norman had her post Chaise weigh'd, and it was Thirteen hundred[weight] & a half and 5 pounds, without ye Coach Box Trunk chaise Seat, or Imperial, we none of us imagined it would have been so much.

The pump woman gives a Thousand a year for the place and to mend the road two mile ye London way costs Twenty two pounds a week.

11th – we walked about yᵉ whole morning to take leave of our favorite place, the pump room very full of Company many Emigrants there, and one among them with large Gold Earrings, to us in England this appear'd extraordinary, but I believe common in France.

12th – we were to have set off on our journey this morning but it snow'd the whole day,

13th – but we went the next morning […]

1798 *March 2nd* – got to Bath about 3 to Mʳ Shrimptons Lodgings Nº 15 Gay St, they wish'd us again to be with them, as the house was a large one but we sent them word we would not only till we got Lodgings.

5th – Company to dinner, and large party evening.

7th – The Fast day Dʳ Chapman preach'd, Dʳ Sedley yᵉ Sunday before at Queen Square Chaple.

8th – a party at home evening

9th – dined at Mʳˢ Cassalets, large party in the evening.

10th – we went into our Lodgings Nº 34 Gay St, at which our kind Friends were very angry with us, but we really told them the truth, that we really wish to live a rather quieter life than theirs when we were at Bath, but would certainly see them every day as long as they stay'd but beg'd to be excused so many dinners and parties, as Mʳ Powys riding and I constantly walking all yᵉ mornings, we were so old Fashion a couple, as to enjoy ourselves (by ourselves), somtimes of evenings, rather than always in such immense crouded rooms.

12th – we called on Mʳˢ Munster yᵉ sister of old Lord Camden, who we had not seen some years.

14th – The Shrimptons to dinner a small party evening

16th – Lady & Mʳˢ Williams to dinner

17th – at a party Shrimptons evening

18th – Mʳ Smith (late of Prior Park) preach'd at Queen Square.

19th – we dined at Shrimptons party evening

20th – at The Play Biggs Benefit 'Inkle & Yanias', a Farewell address and 'yᵉ Blanders of Bingley'.

21st – The Shrimptons left Bath, at the pump room that morning we met Lady Eliz. Pratt and Lord Londonderry, who were on their journey to Bristol, with his Lordships Daughter who was very ill.

24th – at a party at Miss Cresswells in the evening, Miss Sally More Sister to Miss Hannah More, was there.

25th – Mʳ Ogle preach'd at Queen Square.

26th – we dined at Mʳ Lutwycheˢ 17 of us, Sʳ James Fitzgerald Collⁿ Burgoyne

& Lady, Coll^n & Mrs Northy a young Lady with them two Mrs Strouds Miss Cholmondley Miss Waller Mrs Ann Northey the two Miss Mayos Neices to Mr Lutwyches, went up to Coffee ye Gentlemen very soon after, and we then were most highly entertain'd by the Miss Mayos Singing and playing on ye Harpsichord. I think no one can hardly equal Miss Clementina in both, ye eldest only Sings. after ye Ladies had entertain'd us some time, almost ye whole Company adjourned to the Dress Ball upper rooms.

30th – In the morning we went to see the exhibition of Ivory Work, most exceedingly curious indeed, Windsor Castle, Greenwich Hospital, Eddystone Lighthouse, &c &c &c, most ingeniously carved from solid pieces of Ivory. Likenesses of their Majesties &c most astonishing well done, any device carved for Lockets, Bracelets, Rings, or toothpick cases, in as small peices as I did ye Cherry-stone Baskets, and done with somthing like ye same Knives, and must be equally trying to ye eyes. tis done by Stephany and Dresch, ye only Artists in this Line, and by whom is taken ye most striking Likenesses in Ivory.

April 3rd – Mrs Fanshawe to Tea, and at about 9 we all went to Mrs Lutwyches party (who is always at home on Tuesdays). we thought there was numbers of people, but that discovered our ignorance in these affairs, as Mrs Lutwyche express'd herself quite hurt, two or 3 times, that Mr Powys and myself should be there ye first time, when she had literally hardly any company, 'only seven tables, and that is so very few, you know, Ma'am', I really was ignorant, for I did not know it, and rather thought it a squeeze; but how unfashionable I am in disliking these immense parties I kept secret to myself.

7th – [?]—Mr Powys and myself went to Bristol […]

8th – Sunday we went to ye Octagon Chapel with ye Badderleys to hear ye famous Dr Gardiner, successor to ye no less famous Dr Randolph, indeed he is a very good preacher, and not quite so pompous as his predecessor which is certainly what makes him more pleasing to most of his congregation.

9th – at Tysons Ball, which appeared to be so thin of Company, though not reckon'd so, but we could not help comparing it with his last years in Jan: which was so crouded, and such numbers of high rank then present

10th – at a party at Mrs Vanbrughs

11th – we went in the evening to the Fantochini, the whole is in French and entertaining for once. […]

12th – paid our visits of taking leave

13th – we set off from Bath by 7 […]

1799 *March 29th* – […] to Bath, where we got by half past six, to Woodleys at ye White [Lion] where we lay, had enquired after Lodgings long before but none to be had for some time even for single Gentlemen, and ye next morning

30th – Mr Powys and myself walk'd about for 4 hours before we could meet with any, and at last were forced to be in Bond S^t where I never before could have an Idea of taking any, but fortunately it was very Cold weather, or certainly, tis as much too low in the Town as we have often before been too high, but we were obliged to be content and indeed can except ye above objection there was no other, as most excellent dining rooms and very civil people at Viners N° 13, we went into them on Satt evening.

31st – arrived the first news of the Austrians having beat ye French.

April 2nd – amazing cold weather even at Bath, I consulted Dr Mapleton who had formerly been a near neighbour to us, and was now ye second Physician at this place.

4th – at a party in the evening at Mr Vanbrughs.

7th – Mr Falkner, son of Dr Falkner preach'd at Queen Square Chapel, where we as usual had taken a pew.

9th – at Mrs Lutchwedgs party in the evening (always at home on Tuesday) 10 tables six to each, and numbers who like us did not play.

11th – at the play 'Laugh while you can' and 'Blue Beard'

12th – terrible cold weather and constant rain every day

14th – Sunday Mr Clark preach'd, I went to Church at $^1/_2$ past ten. Mr Powys was just then taken with a bleeding at the nose, but as much used to it he desired Id go and he would follow me, but having staid out y^e Service in great anxiety, I return'd home and found it still bleeding, and had never seaced. I sent to the apothecary, who gave him something without effect, I then sent for Mr Gaunt, ye Surgeon, who advised me to send for Dr Mappleton as acquainted with his constitution, ye D^r being out, it was between 4 and 5 in the afternoon before he came, poor Mr Powys was near fainting, and I from my fears could hardly support it, but the D^r beg'd me not to be so alarm'd, as he was almost certain he could stop it by Ruspinis Styptic, which was directly sent for, and almost as soon as applied stopt ye bleeding, and most thankful was I, as he was really nearly exhausted, and ye loss of blood must have been immense. The D^r told us he knew not what it is, but though a quack medicine, it was wonderful ye cures he had known by it, in wounds, inward bruises, or bleeding at the nose, and he advises every one to keep some in their house, which I certainly always shall, for if we had been at Fawley or any place where this remedy was unknown, the consequences might have been fatal.

15th – Tysons, yᵉ Master of yᵉ Ceremonies Ball at yᵉ Upper Rooms, we were to have been there, but of course after yᵉ fatigue & anxiety of the day before, we did not think of it. Mʳ P was better than could be expected, though extreemly weak for a long while.

18th – at a party at Mʳ Vanbrughs.

19th – having been very indifferent ever since Mʳ Powys illness, and too low & nervous to be blooded I was by Dʳ Mapletons advice cupt by Mʳ Grant (Charles Street, Bath)

20th – Mʳ Cookes family and Miss Warnford to Tea.

22nd – Miss E Powney dined with us, at Mʳˢ Vanbrughs night in yᵉ Evening 8 Tables, from thence I went to the Dress Ball upper Rooms

24th – drank Tea at Dʳ Mapletons

26th – at a party at Mʳ Purvis 6 tables, went from thence to a party at Mʳ Leigh Perrots,[14] 8 tables, 90 people.

27th – The few days we staid after this was spent in taking leave of our Friends there, as we now wished to return home as we had receiv'd a Letter lately from our Son Thomas to inform us he was going to add another Daughter to our Family, and indeed our excursion this Spring had not afforded us our usual pleasure, from Mʳ Powys illness, my apprehension on his account having made him unwell, and terrible cold wet weather yᵉ whole time, so that neither of us were so sorry as we often had been to quit that agreeable place, which we are both partial to.

May 4th – On Saturday we left Bath at half past 7 after having breakfast'd […]

July 11th – Bath anecdotes omitted

I forgot to mention the Prince of Wales being at Bath when we were. he was not very popular, from the company he brought with him Mʳ Sheridans Son, and another Gentleman whose name Ive forgot whose great merit seem'd to be that he could drink at a setting two bottles more than any one else. A Miss Fox, a very beautiful Girl whose Sister lives at Major Marsacks, was of yᵉ party but kept quite invisible. indeed His Royal Highness was almost constantly at Mʳˢ Carrs, attracted by the beauty of her two Daughters, yᵉ Miss Gubbins, though it was said yᵉ most beautiful Miss Honor was not yᵉ Princes favorite, but both play'd & sang to him every evening, and he generally supt there, poor girls are really to be pitied, as tis not their, but the mothers fault, to be in such a constant round of dissapation, and playing very deep at Cards, from yᵉ same bad example. I think yᵉ Prince look'd in better health than yᵉ year before, but they said he was not, and though he came to drink yᵉ waters, from his manner of living they certainly could not be of much service. Bath always abounds in drole anecdotes, & on its being thought yᵉ Prince look'd very dull, it was given as a reason, that a few days before he left London he had had his Fortune told. The manner of it is the person puts in his hand to a person that is invisible, who having observ'd it a little while said 'Youll not live long' the Prince not liking I suppose this observation, came again the next day in quite a different dress. When on again putting in his hand, ye voice said 'Youll not die a natural death', this still it was said discomposed him more, indeed it was no wonder, and we all could not help wishing it might be a warning to him to behave more proper to his high station. The Duke of York was fearful he might not be graciously received, & sent to ye Mayor before he came, that he might. however, ye lower class cannot always be led, and as he got out of his Carriage, call'd out very vehemently 'Where's your wife? Why did you not bring your wife, as your Brother does?' he did not stay long, and carried Mrs Carr and her Daughters to London, where it was said ye former was to set up a faro Table, how true these Bath reports time may discover.

The famous Mrs Maccartney left Bath this Spring, and is gone to a house her Nephew, Mr Greville, lent her in London. says she 'must come to Bath for her health sometimes, but had rather live in Hell than on ye Queens Parade, where ye families were so shockingly impolite as not one to visit her.' She offer'd her hand lately to Colonel Mckenzey, who refused it & kindly gave notice to her Nephew Greville, to look after his curious Aunt.

Mrs Dunn died at Bath this year on the 16 of April at 80 years of Age, she was a Miss Holman, and married when very ancient Mr Dunn a Young Militia officer.

The once celebrated Beauty Miss Wroughton, still keeps up her consequence by her large parties, and fine Concerts every Sunday evening, where Rauzzini and many amatures sing & play. the Prince always attended to hear Miss Mayo Mrs Lutwyche's neice, sing & play, and indeed I never heard any one so charming. Not that I ever attended Miss Wroughton's Sunday Concerts, as I quite agreed with the two amiable Duchess^s of Newcastle and Hambleton [Hamilton] who never would appear there on those evenings. The amiable Lady Nelson, who as usual was then at Bath with her Father in law, had some music sent her from Russia endeavouring to be expressive of her Lords Victories. She sent it to Rauzini, and some of the opera musicians came from London to perform it. the Great Ball room was ye place fixt on and there were above 1300 people, but the amateurs were disappointed as the 'Battle of the Nile' as one might suppose, was only a monstrous continued Noise, but however every one was grateful to her Ladyship. I think I never saw any one more altered in ye course of one year than Lord Nelson's Father, a most worthy old man with long grey hair, but seems now so broke which he says is litterally being overcome with joy, so much so that he can hardly bear it.

Dr Randolf, ye celebrated preacher, had ye Living of Bradford given him, but does not reside there, which The King when he heard that he was constantly at Bath, said ye Chaple there was no cure of Souls.

Mr Day [*in margin*] Ive now recollected ye Name of the Gentleman who came with ye Prince, for being so famous a man at the bottle. The Prince once said to him, 'you are a jolly Fellow Day. When I am king, Ill make you a peer by the title of my Lord Cinque Port.' Not a bad pun of his Royal Highness.

Coals in April 1799 were only 10^d a Bushell in Bath, when 5^s in London, viz., £9 a chaldron.

1800   *March 7th* – We […] got to Bath at $^1/_2$ past 7, to Mr Shrimptons Lodgings, N° 36 Melsom Street, as they were so kind as to insist on our going to them, for a few days, till we got Lodgings to our mind, but we walk'd about y^e next morning for many hours and none were to be had, Bath was so full.   *8th* – […]

9th – went to The Octagon heard Dr Gardiner

10th – morning return'd visits (Snow)

11th – at The Play Diamonds Benefit 'The Stranger' & 'Shipwreck'

12th – The Fast Day at The Octagon Dr Gardiner preach'd an excellent Sermon (Rain)

15th – we left our kind Host & Hostess as we had at last got Lodgings, N° 32 Gay St rather too small but very airy & comfortable.

18th – at two Parties that evening Mrs Cazalet and Mrs Lutwytchs ye latter she told me a very small party only Seven Tables

19th – a party at Mrs Shrimptons

21st – at Mrs Vanbrughs party

22nd – at Mrs Shrimptons party

23rd – we had taken a pew at Queen Square Chapel chusing that as ye most private place of Worship. Mr Bowen preach'd

25th – at Mrs Shrimptons party

26th – Mr Powys at Mrs Vanbrughs party, I was not well enough to go

27th – I went with Mrs Shrimpton to Charltons benefit 'The School for Scandal' and 'ye Chimney Corner'

28th – at Mrs Henkles party.

30th – Mr Stafford Smyth preach'd

April 2nd – a party at home, the Shrimptons & Miss S Nicols had dined with us. As usual when ye weather permitted walk'd all morn

3rd – M^r & Mrs Shrimpton left Bath.   *4th* – […]

6th – Mr Ricards preach'd

8th – Mr Powys at Mrs Henkles party, I was not well.

9th – Miss S Nicolls to Tea. (Constant wet weather) *11th* – […]

13th – Mr Falkner preach'd, incessant rain and high Winds

15th – at Mrs Vanbrughs party.

19th – at Mrs Lutwydges party staid Supper, the two Miss Mayos & Mr Maddox (who married Lord Craven Sister) and Mr Walsh Porter sang after Supper, we did not return home till near one.

20th – Dr Davis preach'd a Charity Sermon for The Bath Hospital

21st – began my visits of taking leave

23rd – drank Tea at Bloombergs. The Marquis & Marchioness De La Peire and all my young Cousins met us there & M^r & Mrs Fane.

24th – call'd on Coll & Mrs Schutz. […]

25th – we set off from Bath at half past 8, […]

1801 *March 13th* – we […] got to Bath by half past two to N° 34 Gay St

14th – […] it rain'd all day, Mrs Freeman who had been at Bath some time on account of poor Mrs Winford her Sisters illness call'd on us, and Mrs Fanshawe drank tea with us

15th – at Queen Square Chapel Mr Spry preach'd a very good Sermon, we walked after Church to Mrs Freeman and Mrs Winford.

16th – call'd at ye Fanshawes Eyre Masons, Vanbrugh Mapleton.

18th – ditto on Badderleys, Perrot Lillingston Page Freeman.

22nd – we had taken a pew at Queen Square Chapel, a Mr Wood preach'd a most pompous discourse but not pleasing, call'd on M^{rs} A Northy, who had been to see us as well as ye above mention'd Families

23rd – call'd on Mrs Freeman, it rain'd almost every day some could not get out, and wind amazingly high, I began y^e waters but left them off as had some fever.

24th – at Mrs Lutchwydges party Tuesday evening being her Night, Sixteen Card Tables 156 people.

25th – walk'd up to Mrs Winfords, Sommerset Place, I was $^3/_4$ of an hour getting there and found her very poorly indeed. in y^e Evening at Mrs Vanbrughs party, 4 Card Tables

27th – return'd visits of Miss Nicolls Ricks and Mrs Freemans we drank tea.

28th – morn Mrs Tubb Henkle and Piggot.

28th – Mr Ogle Preach'd, we drank tea at Mrs Badderleys.

30th – call'd on Mrs Stead and ye Masons and Weggs.

31st – at Mrs Northys party evening, had walk'd up to Mrs Winfords morn

April 1st – we had to dinner ye two Mrs Sherwoods M^{r}S: jun Mr Pettman and M^r

Manisty sen: in yᵉ Evening at Mʳˢ Lutwydges stay'd Supper Mʳˢ Freeman there, and Lady Fermanagh & Mʳ and Mʳˢ Wright who we had met at Mʳ Wheatleys at Lesney. 24 staid supper, we had singing after and as usual highly entertain'd by Miss Clementinas fine voice, her Sister Miss Mayo too sings vastly well, we did not get home till one.

3rd – Good Friday Mʳ Sibley and two other Clergymen gave yᵉ sacrament.

4th – a Mʳ Townshend read prayers most exceedingly well.

5th – Sunday a Mʳ Pinnock preach'd, walk'd up to Mʳˢ Winfords & Mʳˢ Freeman.

6th – went to see The Model of Rome, at Tysons Ball in yᵉ evening, The Duke and Duchess of York at it, 'God save The King' play'd as they walk'd up The Ball Room […]

7th – we dined with Mʳˢ Freeman at Mʳˢ Winfords.

8th – at Mʳˢ Tubbs Ricks Freemans Nicolls Fanshawes Weggs T.T.L. [?To Take Leave]

10th – at Mʳˢ Eyres party   *11th* – […]

15th – a party at Mʳ Weggs.

17th – at the Play, Mʳˢ Siddons Benefit 'Lady Macbeth', She perform'd certainly very well, but I think her gone off in manner as well as person. Mʳˢ Freeman left Bath.

18th – morn at Mʳˢ Henkles Badderleys Perrots Vanbrughs T.T.L.

19th – Mʳ Wood Preach'd, we walked afterwards to take leave of Mʳˢ Winford, yᵉ last time we ever saw our kind and beloved Friend.

20th – we set out from Bath about 12, […]

1802 *February 4th* – […] we went to […] Bath. we went to Woodhouse's The White Hart where we dined and lay.

5th – we went to get Lodgings, and got very Elegant ones at Halances Nᵒ 11 Henrietta St, to which we went that evening. […]

6th – I was not well or able to walk out, that day or yᵉ next,

7th – Mʳ P went to The Abbey Church. Mʳˢ Fanshawe and Mʳ & Mʳˢ Austin.

8th – call'd on the Austins Fanshawe Eyre and Masons, yᵉ latter and Dʳ Mapleton on us.

9th – call'd on Capt & Mʳˢ Hardy, Pages, Mapleton, Perrot, Lillingston.

12th – Lord Pembroke Mʳˢ Eyre Pages.

13th – call'd on Badderleys Pages Bennet

14th – went to Dʳ Randolfs Chaple where we had taken a Seat as in our Sᵗ, his Sermon ³/₄ of an hour.

15th – call on yᵉ Hardys, Miss Emily Hardy, Pages, Austins, Fanshawes, Mʳˢ Pigot & Pages call'd on me when out.

16th – Mʳˢ Powys of Shropshire morn, we drank Tea at Mʳˢ Pages Catherine Place, The Miss Pages there.

17th – call'd on Mrs Powys and her Daughter Lady Feilding.

18th – we were both very ill with violent colds M^r P did not drink ye waters […]

20th – call'd on Mrs Cazalet.

22nd –at a party at Mrs Northys

23rd – at the upper Rooms which were opend this Season on Tuesdays, as they used to be formerly, but never had been since Mrs Lutwidge parties on that day, but that Family had left Bath, 25 Tables.

26th – at Mrs Steads and Eyres morn, in the evening at Mr Austins

March 2nd – Tuesday at the Upper Rooms, 27 Tables.

3rd – The Pages to Tea and Cards

6th – The Austins to Tea and Cards   8th – […]   13th – […]

15th – at Mrs Vanbrughs party.

19th – went to Bristol in the morn, call'd on Miss Nicolls's Boices Buildings N° 3, and dine with my Cousin Wheatley who was with one of their Sons very ill, at Duncan House, at home by 8

20th, 21st – this day and the following one paid morning visits and took leave of our Bath acquaintance.

22nd –Set out from Bath a little before 12, […]

1803 *February 17th* – Mr Powys and myself set off for our annual Bath Tour, […]

18th – […] we got to Bath to a late dinner at the White Hart Woodhouse's where we were obliged to stay three nights as no Lodgings were to be got though we had tried to procure them by our Friends who were there for more than three weeks who all advised us to come as if any empty one day they were taken the next, and they knew we liked to see them ourselves but not one board could we see out, when most fortunately I went to buy some things at Cowards Bond Street and beg'd her to enquire every where for us, 'La Ma'am if our Lodgers are not going to night and if the appartments would but suit you how happy I should be.' I know it was not a time to be difficult and we got into them ye next evening.

23rd, 24th – return'd visits to Mrs Eyres Hodges Fanshawe Bennet Austin Badderley Lillingston Tubb M^{rs} A Northy Lady Cotton & Dormer

27th – at Queen Square Chapel where we took Seats in the Gallery, as we always do ye other Churches being so like going to public Assemblys. The weather was so alterd ye last week that we set with one of our Windows open 2 or 3 evenings.

March 1st – returnd visits to Mrs Jenkinson Stead Perrot Page Manley Masons Townshend Pigot & Powys Paynes.

5th – Snow'd a little and very Cold, such alterations is there in our English Climate.

7th – I Baythed in the Warm Bath

8th – we went to the Tuesday Card Assembly which are very pleasant indeed, 23 Tables […]

9th – I was at Miss Candelis Concert with yᵉ two Miss Paynes.

10th – many visitors most mornings

12th – we were at The Cotillon or Fancy Ball […]

13th – Mʳ Sibley preached we staid the Sacrament   *14th* – […]

15th – at the Tuesdays Card Assembly.

16th – returnd visits to Mʳˢ Bullock &c &c

17th – saw the Wax Work, & returnd visits to Mʳˢ Beedon &c

19th – at the Fancy Ball.

22nd – at the Card Assembly, 26 Tables

24th – Saw the Panarama of London.

25th – went to see 'The Invisible Lady made Visible', a foolish thing

26th – at the Fancy Ball.

27th – Mʳ Jackson preach'd.

29th – I was at Miss Daniels Benefit 'The Cabinet', Mʳˢ Eyres got me 2 Tickets in Miss Broughtons Box, I gave one to Miss Payne who went with me.

April 1st – at the Dress Ball Lower Rooms.   *3rd* […]

4th – we dined at Mʳˢ Powys (of Shropshire) in the Crescent, 13 to dinner and a large party in the evening

10th – Mʳ Bowen preach'd.

11th – at Tysons Ball. […]

12th – at the Card Assembly

14th – we dined at Mʳˢ Paynes Nᵒ 70 Pultney St […]

15th / 16th – paid our visits of T.T.L.

18th – ditto [*reference to later entry*]

19th – we set out from Bath at Ten, […]

[*Additions in journal for December 1803*] In March 1803 Mʳ Dutton Brother to Lord Sherbourne, married at Bath the Celebrated Beauty Miss Honoria Gubbins, settled on her in case of no Children Five Thousand pounds & 3 hundred a year in pin money and 15 Thousand on younger Children if any. We were then at Bath. […]

Coll Coterel drove four Cream Color'd Horses this year at Bath, which he bought of the King, who met him one day, when his Majesty told him he was quite happy they were in such good hands.

When The Influenza was so violent this Spring at Bath Dʳ Parry visited a hundred & 20 patients in two days; and Mʳ Crook, yᵉ apothecary only wish'd he could have a Lease of this same Influenza for 8 years, he should not desire a better fortune.

Oberne, The Bishop of Meath, preach'd an Excellent [sermon] this season at Bath, against Card parties and Concerts on Sunday Evenings. His wife, Mrs Oberne, went the day after to pay a morning visit to an Old Lady, who told her She was very angry with her husband, as She had just received 28 Cards of refusals to her next Sundays party. 'Oh, how glad I am' says Mrs Oberne, 'to hear this'. The Lady Bridled up and replied, 'however, it shall not hinder my parties', and Miss Wroughton declared She would always have her Sunday Concerts, for all The Bishop. This Latter Lady formerly one of the first of The Bath Beauties, was lately Stiled by Wit at that Place 'A proof print of Former Times'.

Mr Whaley, a fine Travelled young Clergyman, a Widdower who has spent already two good Fortunes a great Taste for Virtu, was married this year, after a 3 weeks Courtship, to a Miss Heathcote, aged Sixty with a fortune of Fourscore Thousand pounds in her own power. She had the finest dresses made for the Occasion I ever heard of, her Gowns Laced to the highest expense of fashion, and all jewels that was possible. She has an elegant House in the Cressant, and he has one in St James Square Bath, which, though most Elegantly furnish'd, after he returned from Paris, finding paper hangings were there call'd vulgar immediately took all down and hung all with Sattins.

1804 *January 12th* – Mr Powys and myself set out on our Annual Bath Excursion […]

13th – […] we got to our Lodgings at Bath to dinner, at Balleys No 11 Milsom Street, very good ones indeed at 5 Guineas a week and no other Family but their own in the House which makes it much more comfortable, but we were obliged to pay one week before we went, as they never keep them even a day or 2, nor indeed would one expect it.

15th – Mr Guise, Son of St John Guise read prayers Mr Drought preach'd, rain ye whole day ye 14 and this. […]

16th – morn, at Scotts Northys Fanshawe Eyre Masons, Mrs Fanshawe had left our Neighbourhood of Shiplake Hill and now lives at Bath.

17th – at a small party at Mrs Northeys

18th – called on us M^r & Mrs Powys of Shropshire M^r & Mrs Badderley, M^r & M^rs and Miss Austin, M^r & Mrs Mason M^r and Mrs Scott Mrs Stead Bennet Eyre

19th – return'd the above visits

20th – call'd on Mrs Arden, Scot, Lady Cotterel, Mrs Beedon, Cazalet Lillingston. […]

22nd – Mr Guise read Prayers, Mr Stafford Smyth preach'd a Charity Sermon for the Boys and Girls Schools, rain'd most part of every day the last week, but so warm we set with the windows open (I began y^e Waters)

23rd – call'd on Sr Tho & Lady Williams and Mrs Pigot

24th – at the Card Room only 7 Tables went $^1/_4$ after 7

25th – at Mrs Fanshawes and Mrs Tubbs morn, evening a party at Mrs Northeys, morn Lady Williams M^{rs} and Miss Cazalet M^r & Miss Badderley

27th – I was at The Ladies Catch Club, Mr Badderley was so obliging to get me a Ticket, a difficult thing to get one. About 372 mostly Ladies, no Supper, but Cakes Ices Jellies &c carried round between ye Acts.

29th – Mr Ogle preach'd at Queens Square Chaple where we always take seats for ourselves and Servants.

February 1st – we had M^r & Miss Powney and Mr Bennet to dinner.

2nd – I call'd on Mrs Arden &c &c &c

3rd – ditto ditto & this morning visitors when out ye 3d ditto & 4

5th – a Mr Ogle preach'd not the same as last Sunday, drank Tea at Mr Badderleys, Snow & hard Frost ye 4th and the first day we had no Rain since we came to Bath. […]

6th – at the Dress Ball upper Rooms, I Took my Goddaughter Charlotte Powney. it was very full. The Duke and Duchess of Devonshire and Family, and the French General Boger, who dined at her Grace's most days, he was permitted to come to Bath, though not to London and we rather wondered he had leave to come to such a public place as that, but he pleaded his health. Major and Mrs Plunket, his Lady, the Famous Novel Writer, Miss Gunning, an extremely plain woman were at the Ball just arrived at Bath.

7th, 8th, 9th – walk'd as usual all the morn, and p^d visits

10th – at a party at Mrs Cazalets Evening about 40, 5 Tables, walk'd and paid visits

12th – Mr Stafford Smyth preach'd, we staid The Sacrament.

13th – at the Dress Ball evening, walk'd all ye morning & p^d visits *15th* – […]

19th – Mr Salvador (Curate of Queens Square Chapel) read prayers, and preach'd a most excellent Sermon, he was Son of Mrs Salvador, The Jew but suppose he was not brought up to that Religion. A very fine Prayer for the King then ill

20th – at the Dress Ball, with D^r & Mrs Ord Mrs Lillingston, and I took Miss Arden who danced with Mr Oakes.

21st – At a party at Dr Ords Evening, The next four mornings walked and paid visits, and general had many call'd on us when out.

26th – did not set down who preach'd, think Dr Sibley.

March 1st—we had a party at home, walk'd and paid visits […]

3rd – a small party at Mrs Masons, the last time we saw her as She died soon after we left Bath.

4th – Mr Richards preach'd

52

5th – at the Dress Ball. *8th* – [...]
11th – Mr Drought did y^e whole duty, we drank tea at Mrs Lillingstons
12th – at the Dress Ball *14th* – [...]
16th – Friday morn after breakfast we set out at $^1/_2$ past Ten from Bath [...]

1805 *January 15th* – [...] we got to Bath to dinner by 5 to our Lodgings at Cowards N° 17 Bond Street.
16th – called on Miss A Schutz in the Grove.
17th – D^r M^rs & Miss Ord call'd on us we on them on y^e next morn
20th – Mr Sibley preach'd a Sermon for the Charity Schools, Queens Square, rain every day this week.
21st – died Mr Austin Uncle to our Son Cooper. as the mornings at Bath are always past in Walking and calling on ones Friends, I shall not each day set down ye visits received & paid.
24th – we went to the Cotillon Ball, Miss Talbot ye best Dancer and next her ye two Miss Freemans West Indians and Capt Miles a capital Cotillion Dancer. Snow in the night and lay on ye Ground, and intensely Cold
26th – at a small party at M^rs A Northys, but as evening parties are as general as morning visits, I shall not mention them.
27th – one of the Three Mr Ogles preach'd, a very good Sermon.
28th – at the Dress Ball upper Rooms, immensely crouded at ten, but the number of Card parties quite spoil the Balls, as tis fashionable to attend 5 or 6 before you go to the Rooms, it was endeavour'd to alter the hours, but fortunately for ye old people, and those who drink ye Waters, it was not permitted, and at eleven, if in the middle of a Dance, ye Music stops, but as I suppose tis reckon'd vulgar to come early, one sees nothing of the Dancing or Company for ye crouds, in short The Rooms are not half so agreeable as they were some years ago, when ye late London hours were not thought of, and how prejudicial must they be to ye health of all, is very visible in ye young as well in Old. formerly youth was seldom ill, now, from thin Clothing and late hours you hardly see a young Lady in good health or not complaining of Rheumatism as much as us old ones.
30th – The Snow hinderd us from walking out, hills & streets cover'd and every body violent Colds, seem'd a sort of Influenza. Sixteen Thousand Strangers at Bath in ye Seasons 1805
February 3rd – I was too ill to go to Church, had never been out since Monday and attended by Mr Sloper Apothecary.
7th – The Cotillion Ball.
10th – the same Mr Ogle preach'd, stay'd ye Sacrament, Snow & frost gone. [...]
11th – at the Dress Ball vastly full after Ten.

15th – I began the Waters, could not sooner as my Cold continued

17th – Revd Mr Richards preach'd

20th – The Fast day Dr Godfrey preach'd

24th – The same Mr Ogle preach 'd

March 2nd – at the Cotillon Ball, very full.

10th – Mr Sibley preach'd [...]

15th – at a party at Mrs Fiennes Trotmans Ten Tables, and so great a croud, that from ye numbers besides card players though very large Rooms, one could not stir about or procure a Chair to set down, and ye heat of the appartment was not bearable. Our Neighbours Coll & Mrs Inness came to Bath for his health, he has long been very ill.

17th – The Revd Mr Richards did ye Duty.

18th – at the Dress Ball, 23 at ye Cotillon 25 at the Dress Ball.

26th – and ye two following mornings were employ'd in seeing or leaving our T.T.L. Cards with our Bath Acquaintance.

29th – Friday we left Bath after Breakfast, [...]

1806 *January 17th* – [...] [we got] to Bath by 5 very luckily as it dark night and terrible stormy the whole day, went to our Lodgings Ballys No 11 Milsom Street.

22nd – returned many morning visits. *23rd* – [...]

26th – Mr Ogle preach'd an excellent Sermon we took a pew for ourselves and Servants at Queens Square Chaple.

27th – at the Dress Ball, Mr King was now master of the Ceremonies at the Upper Room, as Tyson had given it up. Snow

28th – Morn Mr Capper Miss Payne Mrs Powney and Mrs Bennet.

30th – at a large party at Mrs Hansleys. Snow. on this Evening died Mrs Lillingston[15] a very old acquaintance of ours, She was vastly well ye week before

February 1st – Snow'd very hard

  2nd – Mr Stafford Smyth preach'd, Snow thick on ye Ground.

  5th – Mrs John Gisborne morn and other visitors [...]

  6th – at the Cotillon Ball.

  7th – at a party of Miss Masons.

  9th – Mr Stafford Smyth preach'd, we staid the Sacrament

10th – I began the Waters at y^e Cross Bath. we drank at Mr Daniels and went with their party to y^e Dress Ball $^1/_4$ before Nine. Lady Hugh Smith Lodged opposite. She was Miss Wilson Daughter to y^e Bishop of Bristol.

11th – The only day without Snow or Rain since we came to Bath, near 4 weeks.

13th – at the Cotillon Ball.

14th – rain all day.

16th – Mr Richards read prayers and preach'd, my Servant Jones taken very ill in the night, sent for a nurse.

22nd – at the Play 'The School For Friends', the first time I had seen the new Theatre, a very nice one which was much wanted. I sat in Mr Bests Box.

23rd – Mr Stafford Smyth perform'd ye whole duty

24th – I call'd on Miss Best morn and She on me. at a large party at Miss Mason evening and a Dance for ye young people

March 2nd – Sr Thomas Broughton preach'd

6th – at the Play Mrs Didiers Benefit 'To marry or not to Marry', and The Farce 'a Tale of Mystery', a very fine day, only ye second without rain or Snow.

9th – Mr Stafford Smyth preach'd, we stay'd the Sacrament.

10th – at the Dress Ball with Mrs Wild & Miss Powney.

13th – at the Cotillon Ball with Mrs Charles Eyre

15th – at a party at Mrs Charles Eyres.

16th – Mr Richards did ye whole Service

20th – at a very large party at Mrs Daniels.

23rd – a Stranger preach'd, we dined at Mr Trotmans a M^r & Mrs Johnson, and a M^r & Miss Horseley. rain all day.

24th – at the Dress Ball.

26th – Mr Wilkins & Miss Devereause Sister to Lord Hereford married at ye Abbey Church

27th – at The Cotillon Ball.

29th – at the Play to see Cooke perform Sir Pertinax Macsycophant in 'The Man of The World', written by the late Charles Macklin Esq, and ye Pantomime of 'Harlequin Esop or Hymens Gift'.

30th – Mr Bowen did ye Duty

31st – paid a vast number of T.T.L. visits as were to leave Bath ye next day

April 1st – we left Bath at half past ten, changed Horses at Chipenham took on ye same chaise, dined and lay at Marlborough.

2nd – after Breakfast set out and changed Horses at M^r [blank] Speen Hill, our own coach met us at Reading and we got to Fawley to a late dinner. we had been much afraid Jones would not have been well enough to have come home with us, but fortunately after a six weeks Rheumatic fever, She was just able to Travel. I most luckily was charming well all ye time I was at Bath notwithstanding ye anxiety I was so long in about her illness, but no sooner were we returned to Fawley than from ye Intense Coldness of ye weather, or the Illness now every where term'd The Influenza, Mr Powys & myself were taken both very ill, his not his usual complaint of Bile, but a seizure one could hardly describe in short such a lowness and debility, it was most unpleasant. Mr Powys thank God, in about a week got Better, but I who have terrible Rheumatics was seized with such a violent pain in my face, I could get no sleep for many nights but at last by a Blister was perfectly cured of the most dreadful I think of all pains, but still felt very low and weak. and it seem'd a very general complaint round our neighbourhood.

1807 *January 14th* – [...] we got to Bath to dinner to our old Lodgings Ballys N° 11 Milsom Street. had very fortunately a beautiful day, though

15th – the next we had a deep Snow. The Streets and Houses cover'd, lay thick on the ground and intensely cold. [...]

16th – it thaw'd and got warmer, I got out and call'd on some of our Friends and we had many tickets left for us.

17th – Master Betty acted for his last night at Bath, and though we had no very great desire to see him, thought it would be foolish to lose yᵉ opportunity. he acted in The Play of 'Mahomet', and was just the thing we had expected, for though he certainly acts well, yet his Youth and Manner could never make one suppose him the character he represents, and his voice now is quite horrid. The Company at Bath did not seem the least sorry at his departure, and The Actors as one may suppose were much rejoyced. some years hence, I dare say he will be an excellent performer.

18th – on Sunday at Queen Square Chapel we heard an excellent Sermon for the Bath Charity School by Mʳ Ogle, we had many visitors after Church and we call'd on several & walk'd in yᵉ Cresant.

19th – This and several following days rain & Snow, but when possible to walk about received & paid visits as usual, had yᵉ pleasure of seeing my old Friend Lady Jane James, the present Lord Camdens Sister who was come for some weeks and 3 of her Daughters.

23rd – began the Waters at the Pump room after having been blooded, as usual one <u>small</u> Glass twice a day.

26th – at the Dress Ball with Lady Jane James her Daughters and Miss Ramsden.

27th – call'd on Mʳˢ Lutwidge who was return'd to their House in Bath from abroad.

29th – at The Cotillon Ball with a party. Mʳˢ Marriot & her Sister Miss Harris call'd on us as they went through Bath

February 2nd – I was at a morning Subscription Concert for the benefit of Miss Randal at the New Room York Hotel. She is only 6 years old and is indeed the most wonderful little creature. plays on The Piano in a most wonderful manner, and has a sweet voice; She is accompanied on The Harp by her Blind Father, and by her Uncle Mʳ Parry on the Flageolot, both reckon'd to perform each vastly well. It was a pleasing sight to see the little performer lifted on the Platform by her Uncle and placed at the Piano-Forte, and as She walk'd up and down the room She was spoke to by all She pass'd near and met with general applause. before she was 3 years old she could play 3 tunes.

2nd – at a party at Miss Masons in the Evening.

3rd – was at the procession of Mr Walter Longs Burial, which went from his House in Gay St and pass'd ours in Milsom St, he was buried at his Estate at Wrexham [Wraxall Manor], Wiltshire. The Cavalcade was very magnificent. first, seven men on Horseback then men with plumes of Feathers, his own mourning chaise & 4, Herse & Six, 1 Coach & Six Lord Hoods, 1 post Chaise & Six, 6 Chaises & pair and the concourse of people that follow'd were not to be number'd. he was 96 years of Age, and died worth Eight Hundred Thousand pounds, which he left to his Sister, then Ninety one, at her death to his Nephew John Long and at John's death to a Brother of Mr John, and at his death to a Mr Jones. he left above Fifty hundred pound Legacys.   *5th* – [...]

6th – at a party at Mrs Charles Eyres

9th – at a party of Mrs Daniels.

10th – at a small party at Lady Jane James.

11th – I call'd on Mrs Moore, The Late Archbishop of Canterburys widdow, who was just come to Bath.

12th – at The Cotillon Ball evening, every morn received & paid visits

13th – M^r P went to Mr Daniels to meet The Bishop of Ferne Dr Clever in the evening.

14th – I went to The Play (of 'Adrian and Orilla' and 'The Forty Theives') with Mrs Charles Eyre, we sat with Lady Wilmot in her Box. we were much entertaind as tis a good Play, and The Romance as tis call'd very amusing for once.

16th – we dined at Mr Lutwidges 12 of us M^r & Mrs Cooke of Worcestershire, M^r & Mrs Maccellan, Mrs Cookes Brother, Mr Collens related to Mrs Lutwidge and another Gentleman.

17th – Mrs Moore and Mrs Shafto paid visits morn.

19th – at The Cotillon Ball, with Mrs C. Eyre M^r & Mrs Eyre & Miss Ramsden

21st – we had a party in the evening, Sr Walter & Lady Jane James and their 3 Daughters & a Lady with them M^r & M^rs & Miss Pottenger Mr Marrel.

25th – The Fast day Mr Richards preach'd

26th – paid visits morn, at The Cotillon Ball evening with Lady Jane James & Family.

28th – at a party at Mrs Daniels The Bishop of Ferne & his Lady Mrs Clever &c &c.

March 3rd – at a small party at Mrs Moores, Mr Libinston M^r & Miss Benson Mrs Shafto &c.

5th – at The Cotillon Ball with Lady Jane James & Family and Miss Ramsden.

7th – at a party at Mrs Daniels The Bishop of Ferne Mrs Clever &c.

15th – The Bishop of Ferne preach'd at Queens Square Chapel, a most excellent Sermon, indeed he is a most amiable character, and his Lady equally so. We could not help feeling for what they sufferd in Ireland every time one was in their Company – their House tore down, all their furniture taken, and every place ransack'd, his loss above Ten Thousand pound, by the Irish Rebels; and what must have caus'd them infinite distress, most of their Servants were concern'd in the whole […]

17th – I went with Miss Cooke to The Play. we sat in Mrs Hollands Box, a most entertaining Play of Murphys 'All in the Wrong'.

19th – we dined at The Bishop of Fernes, M^r & Mrs Daniel Miss Hotham Mr Stroud. a party in the Evening, and we were highly entertain'd by the Miss Clevers who play and Sing with ye greatest Taste.

23rd – call'd on the Daniels left Bath ye next day. M^r & Mrs Cooke Miss Ramsden to Tea.

26th – at a party at Mrs Cookes, M^r & Mrs Stafford Smith, The Bishop of Ferne, M^r & M^rs & Miss Trotmans, The Rev^d M^r [blank]

28th – began to pay my T.T.L. visits

29th – we dined at Mr Trotmans, Mrs Johnston M^rs [blank] Dr Fletcher Mr Foster

30th – at Mr Kings Ball, master of the ceremonies at The Upper Rooms. many Hundred people, though Bath was reckon'd rather thin all The Season, owing as was supposed to the rise of every thing, but more particularly to the extravagant price of Lodgings, as numbers went to Bristol instead of taking them. I never saw so many to Let, and it was hoped, it might be a Lesson for them in future.

31st – paid all my visits as we were to leave Bath ye next day but one; had staid a week longer than we intended on account of the Cold Weather, as we were to go to so very bleak a situation at Fawley.

April 2nd – we set out from Bath at half past eleven a very fine day but terrible Cold morning and about two it begun to Snow. […]

1808 *January 15th* – […] we got to Bath about 4 to our Lodgings at Leedhams N° 1 New Bond St Bally did not Let his and Cowards were full, but we found these very and well Furnish'd. Mr Horne died at Bath, desired no expensive Funeral, was at Walcot, the Coffin carried by 8 men, no Herse or Coaches, Mrs Horne has taken Mr Waley's House in the Cresant.

20th – I call'd on Mrs Stirling Willm Gregory Grote Bennet &c &c, all return'd my visit the next day.

21st – walk to Mrs Powney Caroline Buildings and she to me so did not meet.

23rd – I walk'd up to Richmond Hill Landsdown to see my old Friend Mrs Pigou [? Pigot], a very long walk all up Hill, but I was only ³/₄ of an hour, and was happy to find her much better in health, for her long residence in Cornwall.

24th – at Queen Square Chapel Mr Rudge did the whole duty a Charity Sermon for the School. Snow'd

25th – many morning visits as usual. I call'd on Mrs Bloomberg* Eyre Fanshawe Hervy Stead Smith. *Mr Bloomberg made Clerk of the Closet. Mrs Powney Badderley and Mr Townshend call'd we were very much concern'd to hear Mrs Townshend was ill and at Bristol

31st – I had so very bad a Cold could not go out, Mr Bowles preach'd.

February 4th – I walk'd up to Camden Place to see Miss Nicolls *5th* – [...]

  6th – had been rain night and morn for many days a sad thing for Bath Walkers, particularly to me who never feel well if I cannot walk about all ye morning.

  7th – Mr Ofee preach'd.

  9th – I call'd on Mrs Moore ye late Arch Bishops Lady. continue rain.

10th – a frost, had many visitors

11th – Snow

13th – a great fall of Snow Intensely Cold.

15th – at the Dress Ball with Miss Ramsden.

16th – at a party at Mrs Stirlings

17th – The Fast day Mr Oliver preach'd a very good Sermon, Sr Henry Rivers read Prayers. The frost & Snow gone.

18th – at the Cotillon Ball. immensely crowded

20th – Dr Oliver preach'd

23rd – at a party at Mrs Lutwydges.

25th – at the Cotillon Ball, very full, many came ¹/₄ before 8.

28th – Mr Ogle preach'd a very fine Sermon. we dined at Mr Trotmans. The Revd Dr Greenhill Miss Thomson Miss Wills.

29th – The Dress Ball, but very few went to them this year.

March 1st – at a party at Mrs Charles Eyres.

  3rd – at The Cotillon Ball, immensely full; many came very early and numbers from Parties at half past 10

  4th – at a party at Mrs Moors. Lady Davis, M^r & two Miss Bensons and Mrs Wood, who we had met at Canterbury, &c &c. *5th* – [...]

  8th – we had to dinner M^r & Mrs Daniel, Miss Roles and her Aunt Mrs Jenkenson.

  9th – I went to Rauzzinis Concert to hear Madame Catalani, but was disappointed with numbers, as She came from the Opera in London all night, caught a violent cold & sore Throat. above a Thousand had been in the Concert room hours, some they said by 3 o Clock. we did not go till Six & had not a very good Seat; when at 8 when it was to begin Rauzzini came on yᵉ platform, to say how shock'd Mad: Catalani was at disappointing the Company but she was really too ill to Sing yᵉ Songs given out but She would try some others. we began to fear a riot as some hisses begun, however, Madame came, and I dare say did what she was able, but was quite unable to Sing & retired with numbers of apologies. The next morning hand Bills were given out that She could not sing that night as She had intended, as there was to have been two, but that she would come down yᵉ next Wednesday to Rauzinis Concert, and to those who had been on yᵉ evening before, She would Sing on the next Thursday morning so every one seem'd satisfied, till yᵉ Tuesday morning following, when Bills were again circulated, that She was still too ill to come down was impossible. so here it finally ended except to poor Rauzzini who behaved uncommonly generous desiring every one who was at the first concert or those who had Tickets for the second, to call to the Rooms, where each would be return'd their half Guinea for Either Night. so those on the first night (of which I was one,) had somthing of a Concert and the Sight of Madame Catalani at least.

10th – at The Cotillon Ball, The Lower Set, a remarkable good one, a French Emigrant who was permitted to be at Bath was reckon'd a remarkable good Dancer, and certainly was so, he had not been lately, as some Gentleman had said one night 'No wonder he Dances fine, why he was a Dancing Master', but they say that was only a joke.

13th – Mʳ Olive preach'd, we staid the Sacrament.

14th – at a party at Mʳˢ Willm Gregorys Poultney St

17th – at the Cotillon Ball, took Miss Powney, our man John Cornel taken ill of yᵉ Gout.

22nd – at the Play Mallinsons Benefit 'The School of Reform', I took Miss Ramsden.

23rd – had many morning visitors and paid many. The weather was Cold, and bad that hardly any body was well all the time we were at Bath, as to myself I was particularly Rheumatic of which every one complain'd.

24th – at the Cotillon Ball.

28th – call'd on Mʳ & Miss Masons

April 2nd – at a party at Mʳˢ Daniels.

4th, 5th – paid all my T.T.L. visits, rather warmer, the last week had been so cold we postponed our journey to the Cold Hills of Fawley, but I never remember Bath so Cold as this Time we were there.

6th – we set out after Breakfast, […]

III CONCLUSION

Caroline's accounts of her visits to Bath are largely concerned with the constant round of parties, concerts, plays, cards, and dances, the occasional visits of royalty, and other diversions of daily life, in late Georgian Bath long after the end of the strict régime of Beau Nash who died in 1761. We read of places of assembly for social, religious and theatrical purposes, such as the newly built Theatre Royal, opened in 1805; this was, she writes, 'a very nice one which was much wanted' (AJ, Feb. 22nd 1806). If Caroline makes little comment on the elegant architecture of Bath – other tour journals are ample evidence of her critical faculties – we should remember that here it provided the backdrop to the unremitting social round which was the primary purpose of the long visits.

Collectively, the day-to-day accounts give a vivid impression of the some-times overwhelming crowding of activities, as when, for example, she reports on the young lady who died because she was rushing madly from one event to another without protecting herself from the elements (AJ, Mar. 9th 1796), or when Caroline herself pleads with her friends to let her and Philip follow their 'old Fashion' ways (AJ, Mar. 10th 1798); the heat in the Rooms can be unbearable (AJ, Mar. 15th 1805); and young ladies nowadays look ill because they don't wear sensible clothes as they used to (Jan. 28th 1805). We need to remember, too, that almost all her visiting is done in late winter and spring, once even over Christmas, which was not her usual time for visiting Bath – perhaps she acquiesced to an invitation against her better judgment (AJ, Nov. 22nd 1796). Walking is most important to her: she does not feel well unless she can get out for long walks in the morning (AJ, Feb. 6th 1803), and yet, although she is apparently a country woman, Bath is her 'favorite place' (AJ, Jan. 12th 1797). Bath could be bitterly cold, with rain, wind, frost and snow, but these privations may have seemed more tolerable in this company than in the relative isolation of a country house.

Yet lodgings in Bath could be a serious problem: sometimes they seem to have been able to get in where they lodged the previous year, but one year they 'walk'd about for 4 hours before we could meet with any' (AJ, Mar. 30th 1799); in another they had to stay at an inn for three nights before they were lucky (AJ, Feb. 18th 1803). Their lodgings were all over the city, and not always convenient, such as Lansdown Place because of the distance.

Although Caroline's husband apparently benefited from the waters, the cure was not the first priority; nevertheless, they could rely on finding professional medical help if necessary (AJ, Apr. 14th 1799). Illness could also strike their servants: one year, a maidservant was so ill that they feared that she would not be well enough to travel home, and when they did get home, both Caroline, who had been 'charming well' for the whole of her stay in Bath, and her husband were dreadfully ill (AJ, Apr. 2nd 1806).

It is surprising that there is only one mention of Caroline herself taking a warm bath (AJ, March 7th 1803), but not infrequent references to taking the waters which are found to be beneficial. The company of friends was, of course, vital to their enjoyment, and many of the same names recur from year to year, and at the end of a visit there could be several days of the formal leave-taking, the 'T.T.L.' visits. Whatever trials there were, Caroline would not have spent three years of her life here in all her visits unless she had enjoyed the long periods away from home. This full transcript of selected later Bath journeys should help us to a better understanding of her pleasure, shared by so many other visitors over the years.[16]

Notes

1   Fourteen volumes of the manuscripts of Caroline Girle, Mrs Philip Lybbe Powys, are preserved in the British Library (Add. Mss. 42160–42173). These comprise the following works: three volumes of her Annual Journal with dated entries from May 1st 1757 to December 31st 1808 (vols I, II, III); nine volumes of journals of individual tours, the first in 1756, the last in 1800 (IV–XII); a small volume containing copies of two letters to friends (XIII); and a recipe book (XIV). These provide possibly 90% of the material published in 1899 (see note 2); the location of other tour journals, if they still exist, is not known; any information on their whereabouts would be welcome. These works are referred to as AJ, with date of the entry, for the Annual Journal and BL, with volume number, for the other works.

A detailed account of the manuscripts is contained in another article by the present writer, 'The Journals of Caroline Girle – Mrs Philip Lybbe Powys', in *The Powys Journal*, xii (2002), pp.102–25.

2   *Passages from the Diaries of Mrs Philip Lybbe Powys of Hardwick House, Oxon, A.D. 1756 to 1808*, edited by Emily J. Climenson (Longmans, Green and Co., 1899), referred to hereafter as Climenson. A thousand copies were issued, of which 150 were for subscribers. A long and appreciative review was published in *The Times* of August 16th 1899.

3   Richard Wilson and Alan Mackley, *Creating Paradise, The Building of the English Country House 1660-1880* (Hambledon and London, 2000), p.56; Ian C. Bristow, *Architectural Colour in British Interiors 1615-1840* (Yale University Press, 1996), Preface, p.xviii.

4   Caroline Girle's date of birth was December 27th 1738, Old Style, that is before the changes under the Act of Parliament (24 George II, c.23) which introduced the Gregorian calendar to England and her territories in 1752. Under the Act, any specific period of legal significance, including coming of age, had to complete the full number of days; this means that Caroline did not come of age until 11 days later than the original day of birth according to the Old Style calendar, i.e.

not until January 7th 1760, New Style. On nine occasions in her journals Caroline refers to her birthday occurring on January 7th, twice explaining the change from Old Style to New Style.

5   Climenson, p.vii. The house can be identified as No.1 at the north-west corner of Lincoln's Inn Fields, as shown by rating and other records in *Survey of London, Volume III, The Parish of St Giles-in-the-Fields (Part I.): Lincoln's Inn Fields* (London County Council, 1912), p.24. John Gyrle, as there spelled, is shown as in occupation from 1754 to 1760.

6   See W. Ison, *The Georgian Buildings of Bath* (rev. ed.,1980; reprinted Kingsmead Press, Bath, 1991), pp.142, 230. The 9 houses which Caroline Girle saw were part of the south-west segment between Gay Street and Brock Street.

7   Climenson, p.ix.

8   Philip Lybbe Powys was the grandson of Sir Thomas Powys (1649–1719), an eminent lawyer and judge, from whom were also descended an elder branch of Powyses created Baron Lilford in 1797, and the Powys family of Montacute which included the writers John Cowper Powys, Theodore Francis Powys and Llewelyn Powys, and the architect A. R. Powys. Details of the family connections can be found in a previous article by the present writer entitled 'An Earlier Diarist: Caroline Girle – Mrs Philip Lybbe Powys', in *The Powys Society Newsletter*, 43 (July 2001), pp.32-41; this includes a comprehensive 'bar chart' of the Powys family connections 1600-1900 and other information not in this article.

9   This quotation is given as it appears in Climenson p.24, as the original manuscript of the Derbyshire tour has not been found.

10 Mr and Mrs Powys took lodgings as follows: 1764, 1773, 1780 (no addresses); 1783, house in Russel Street; 1784, house in Gay Street; 1786 (no address); 1787, Gay Street; 1791, Portland Place, 'the new part of Bath'; 1794 (no address); 1796, 9 George Street; 1796-97, George Street, then house of friends in Laura Place; 1798, 34 Gay Street; 1799, Viners, 13 Bond Street; 1800, 32 Gay Street; 1801, 34 Gay Street; 1802, 11 Henrietta Street; 1803, Cowards, Bond Street; 1804, Balleys, 11 Milsom Street; 1805, Cowards, 17 Bond Street; 1806, Ballys, 11 Milsom Street; 1807, Ballys, 11 Milsom Street; 1808, Leedhams, 1 New Bond Street.

11 Jacob Spornberg, born in Finland in 1768 and trained as an artist in Stockholm, made a brief visit to Bath in 1785, and had returned by 1790. He is known principally as a silhouettist; his last known silhouette was done in 1813. He seems to have moved about, but established himself mainly in Bath. In 1840 he emigrated to the U.S. His silhouettes were achieved by what he called 'Etruscan profiles'; the sitter's features were painted against a red background with a black surround on the under surface of a convex glass. The portrait of Caroline is an example. Spornberg is represented in the Holburne Museum, Bath, by a double 'Etruscan profile' of Christopher Anstey and Ann Anstey (1793). For further details see Sue McKechnie, *British Silhouette Artists and their Work 1760–1860* (Sotheby Parke Bernet, 1978), pp.720-25.

12 The accounts printed here are from the three volumes of the Annual Journal. Initial capitals are exactly as in the manuscripts; punctuation, which is sparse and inconsistent, has been slightly amended for easier comprehension, especially in the occasional addition of commas and use of inverted commas for quotations and names of plays. Original spelling has been retained, but one or two obvious minor errors have been corrected. Text in square brackets has been supplied by

the present writer; and omissions of text from these extracts not relating to Bath are marked by ellipsis in brackets. Quotations in the text follow the same practice.

13   Queen Square Chapel, later St Mary's Chapel, on the north side of Chapel Row, was built in 1732–4 by a consortium of residents including John Wood the elder, with a fine classical temple front (see illustration in *Bath History*, Vol.VII (Millstream Books, Bath, 1998), p.131); it was demolished in 1875. Of the other two chapels regularly attended by Caroline Powys, 'Dr Randolfs new Chapel, Laura place'(Thomas Baldwin, 1795) was later demolished, and the Octagon Chapel (Thomas Lightoler, 1764) still exists but is no longer in ecclesiastical use.

14   James Leigh-Perrot, maternal uncle of Jane Austen, is mentioned on three further occasions. Six visits to or by the Austen family (spelled Austin), who had moved to Bath in 1801, took place on February 7th, 8th, 15th, 26th and March 6th 1802, February 24th 1803, and a visit by 'Mr and Mrs and Miss Austin' on January 18th 1804; the last could be either Jane or her sister Cassandra. Mr Austen's death is noticed on January 21st 1805. The families were already related, as in 1793 Caroline's daughter Caroline Isabella had married Jane Austen's cousin Edward Cooper; the closeness of the link is shown by the naming of two daughters successively Cassandra (1797) and Jane (1799).

15   See 'Genteel Widows of Bath: II – "A Persecuted Relation": Mrs Lillingston's Funeral and Jane Austen's Legacy', by Deirdre Le Faye, in *Bath History*, Vol. VII (Millstream Books, Bath, 1998), pp.92-106.

16   For further information on the journal entries of all 22 visits between 1764 and 1808, please enquire through the publisher.

THE NEW GAOL IN BATHWICK, 1772-1842

Chris Noble

> Ye men of Bath who stately mansions rear,
> To wait for tenants from the devil knows where,
> Would you a plan pursue which cannot fail:
> Erect a mad house and enlarge your jail !

Introduction

These lines of Christopher Anstey's epigram serve as an apt introduction to the history of the New Gaol at Bathwick.[1] They seem to be both relevant and prophetic. Anstey (1724-1805) lived in Bath from 1770 until his death, and his writing lampooned the city's society and manners. He implied that there was another aspect of Bath to that of fashion, genteel manners and prosperity. The men of Bath did replace, rather than enlarge, their gaol, but the New Gaol that they built resembled their stately mansions rather than the old gaol.

The Old Gaol before 1772

In the mid-eighteenth century, Bath had little need for a prison: the prisoners who had to be confined were a small number of debtors and those waiting to appear before the Justices for minor offences. The serious offenders, the felons, were sent to the County Gaols at Ilchester and Shepton Mallet. Bath's prisoners were held in the tower of St. Mary's Church, by Northgate (fig.1). St. Mary's had been redundant and in secular use since 1583, and the Northgate had been pulled down in 1755.[2] John Wood, writing in 1765, described the city prison thus:

> that structure is the very Tower of St. Mary's Church ; and, next to the Abbey House, is the oldest Building of Bath: it was an ancient Steeple even in Leland's time, who speaks of it as part of a Parish Church ; but no sooner had Queen Elizabeth ... by her Charter of A.D. 1590 Granted the citizens the privilege of a Prison, or Gaol, than they ... impiously turned the tower of it into a den for thieves ![3]

The City Chamberlain's records show examples of the modest expenditure which was required to run the old gaol. For example, in 1769 Mrs Sarah Sherston was paid £6.2s.7d for a year's supply of bread and cheese for the prisoners.[4] Her bill records her daily expenditure and on the basis of the allowance of

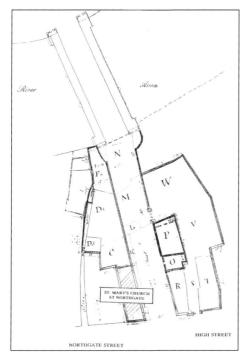

Fig.1 Extract from the plan from the Deed of Conveyance, Bath Corporation to William Pulteney, 1769, showing the site of St. Mary's church. (*reproduced by courtesy of Bath Record Office*)

two pence per head per day a daily gaol population of between one and eight is suggested by her accounts. Contemporary entries in the press suggested that the city did not choose to use its discretionary power to feed the debtors, who were dependent on their friends and families or appeals to charity:

BATH PRISON, 1771. Right Worshipful, – The Humble Petition of a Bro(the)r in extreme Distress, Confined almost a Twelvemonth, having no Allowance but from some Acquaintance, no bed to Lay on and often have not bread, nor victuals, nor money. Shall be Glad if my Bretherin will Consider my Deplorable Condition by Contributing something towards my Support, and as I am in a very Dissponding way hopes you will be Inclined to Reli(e)ve a Poor Unfortunate Bro(the)r.[5]

The city's responsibility for its prisoners is also shown by a 1767 bill for the burial of a 'Woman from the Prison' for £1.13s followed by one for 10s.6d for the expenses of her inquest.[6] This probably represented the failure of the Council to trace a parish from which to claim the cost.

Why build a New Gaol in Bath?

No contemporary source suggests any interest in replacing the city's ancient and decrepit gaol on utilitarian grounds, whether because of overcrowding or as the result of new and enlightened ideas of penal reform. What we see is a New Gaol built as a direct consequence of the interest of the speculators in developing their land for profit. By 1726, William Pulteney, later 1st Earl of Bath, had acquired nearly all of the 600 acres of the Bathwick estate, still a rural parish, open and undeveloped by building. Though close to the centre of the city it was separated from it by the river Avon, and accessible only by ferry. Pulteney, wanting to develop his land for profit, had, as they came to a natural end, converted the existing lifehold tenancies into short leasehold tenancies. By the time of his death in 1764, he had achieved direct control over three-quarters of his land either through its being subject to leasehold tenancy or through managing it directly.[7] However, Pulteney had failed to arouse interest in developing his land for housing because the only crossing of the river was by the bridge at Southgate, some distance from the city centre, and his two earlier attempts at securing a new bridge had failed.[8] The estate passed to his brother, General Pulteney, who in turn died in 1767. It then passed to Frances, the daughter of a cousin, and a new William Pulteney entered the scene. He was William Johnstone, who in 1764 had married Frances Pulteney, the niece and future inheritor. When she inherited the estate in 1767 he took the name Pulteney in addition to his own, becoming William Johnstone Pulteney. He is described as the senior and most important administrator of the Bathwick estate, and he set his considerable energy and skill to making it much more profitable, drawing up plans for a 'New Town' in Bathwick.[9] The first sign of his possible success was seen in the minutes of the City Council for 6th February 1768:

> Shall a committee be appointed to confer with Mr. Pulteney on his proposal for building a bridge over the river to Bathwick, and to report the same from time to time.
>
> Votes recorded: 15 in favour, 3 against.[10]

In 1769 Pulteney sent this proposal to the other trustees of the Bathwick estate:

> If a Bridge is built over the Avon somewhere near the City prison, it is expected that a good deal of the Ground near the Bridge will be taken by Builders for erecting Houses and that they will agree to pay considerable Ground Rents.[11]

This is the first recorded occasion on which there is a hint that the old gaol might have to be replaced. The Act of 1766 had given the Council powers to buy property compulsorily, and as it set about planning the re-development of the city centre around High Street and the old Guildhall which R.S.Neale describes[12], a proposal from the Bathwick side of the river must have proved attractive.

Nearly a year after the meeting in February 1768, on 2nd January 1769, the City Council minutes record:

> Shall Mr Pulteney have liberty to build a bridge from Bath to Bathwick at or near the present ferry, the corporation allowing him a way thereto from High Street provided he purchase at his own expense from the present possessors such houses and land as interfere with the said way and are not in the possession of the Corporation. This vote to take place only on

condition that the article here produced, dated 24th December 1768 and signed William Pulteney be complied with and on further condition that the corporation may have liberty to insert at their own expense such clause or clauses in the said bill for other purposes as they may think fit. Votes recorded: 14 in favour, 6 against.[13]

The old gaol was not mentioned, but as it was the one building that was in the possession of the Council, the inclusion of 'the corporation allowing him a way' can be taken to refer to its site: it stood on the approach to the planned bridge (fig.1).

The Council realised that in letting William Pulteney acquire the land that he needed for his bridge they would lose their prison, and so the 'further condition' was employed to ensure that the city would acquire a new site on which to build a new gaol. They resolved at the Council meeting on 26th June, 1769 that:

Shall the ground on which the City prison now stands be granted to Mr Pulteney upon condition that he shall promote under the authority of the late Act of Parliament concerning the late General Pulteney's estate in Bathwick, a conveyance to the city of a piece of ground eighty feet in length by sixty feet in breadth, next to the river and within 300 yards of the East end of the intended bridge for the purpose of building a new prison providing that the present prison shall not be removed in less than two years except a new prison be built before that time.

Votes recorded: unanimous in favour.[14]

Councillors ensured that the City was not to be left without a gaol. In exchange for giving up the site of St. Mary's church and their gaol the Corporation would gain a good sized plot of land in Bathwick which would be reached across the new bridge. The agreement can be seen as an early example of 'planning gain', a term introduced at the time of the post Second World War schemes of large-scale comprehensive re-development of town and city centres, to describe the supposed public gain in the form of car-parking space, housing units or open space, incorporated in the developer's schemes to secure planning consent. The site of the old gaol was the key to Pulteney's plans for a New Town for Bath in Bathwick. On the 25th August 1770 the Council appointed a committee 'to consider the plan of a new prison now produced' and on the 24th September 1770, they:

resolved that a new prison to be built, the committee to have power to draw upon the Chamberlain for money to pay expenses, and any member of the committee may attend the meetings on Tuesday evenings at 6 pm.[15]

At this time Thomas Warr Atwood was Mayor as well as architect to the city's estates, and the minutes also recorded the approval of his design for the prison.

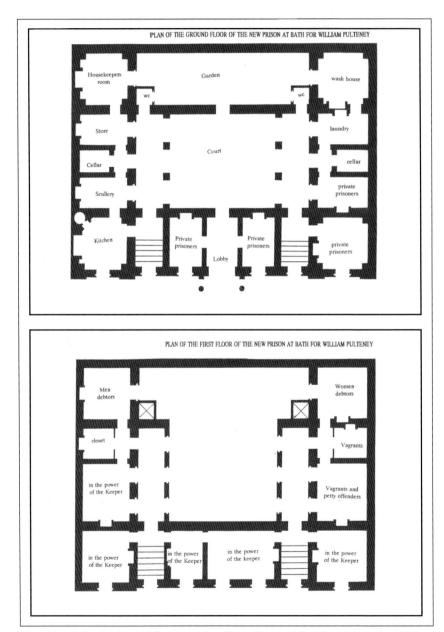

Figs. 2&3 Adam's plans of the ground and first floors of the New Prison for William Pulteney. (*reproduced by courtesy of the Trustees of Sir John Soane's Museum*)

Atwood's was not the only plan for a New Gaol. William Pulteney, who had engaged the architect Robert Adam to design the new bridge to Bathwick, also engaged him to prepare a design for the New Prison. Robert Adam's first plans for the prison, dated February 1771, may be seen at the Soane Museum (figs.2 and 3). They give an indication of what was then thought neccessary for a prison. They would use the whole site, eighty feet by sixty feet, and showed on the ground floor, four rooms for 'private prisoners,' a wash house, laundry, housekeeper's room and store rooms, a courtyard and garden. On the first floor was a small room each for men and women debtors, two rooms for vagrants and petty offenders and five rooms 'in the power of the keeper', presumably for his own accommodation. Adam's elevations have not survived. Robert Adam was paid £33.12s for 'a design for the west front of a new Gaol for the New Town of Bath, a design for the south front, a plan of ground floor and one pair storey,' and 'another plan of a smaller design'[16], but the Corporation favoured its own architect's design. Bath lost the opportunity to have a building which like Atwood's prison would probably have survived, but been much more widely admired. Pulteney Bridge remained Adam's only work in Bath. There is no evidence that the Bath Council were sympathetic to, perhaps even aware of, the new philosophy about imprisonment that was to lead to purpose-built gaols of separate cells in the small Sussex towns of Horsham, 1779 and Petworth, 1789, and in the city of Gloucester in 1791. On the evidence of the design chosen it could be suggested that the men who were elected to the Corporation of Bath would have seen only the need for a handsome building to fit in with the fashion in design, big enough to house the gaoler and his family, with communal rooms for a dozen or so prisoners.

The New Gaol at Bathwick

The gaol's newly-built appearance may be seen from early prints (figs.4 and 5 overleaf). At sixty feet by thirty feet, the prison built by Atwood covered less than half the size of the plot which the Council had requested from Pulteney. There is no explanation for the missing land. The foundation stone was laid by the Mayor, James Horton, on the 7th May 1772. The City Chamberlain's record shows regular payments of between one and three hundred pounds variously made to 'the Prison Committee', or 'Atwood for the Prison Committee', during 1772-1774. These payments total £2,400 plus a final sum of £78.6s.9d paid to Atwood. Building the new gaol represents the greatest single expenditure by the City during those three years.

Fig.4 View of the New Gaol, Bathwick, 1808. From the Chapman Collection. (*reproduced by courtesy of Bath Central Library, Bath and North East Somerset Council*)

Pevsner comments:

The building is from outside like any other Palladian mansion ... The interior was not designed specially as a prison either, that is without any effect of Howard's teaching yet.[17]

In fact the gaol pre-dates John Howard's work[18], although by only a few years, and it was obsolete as a gaol even as it was completed. The New Gaol, however, is a rare example of a public building erected at a time when most of the expenditure on building listed in the Chamberlain's records was on the Baths and the Guildhall.

The new thinking on both the purpose and proper conditions of imprisonment initiated by John Howard's writing were only a few years in the future. Bath's New Gaol showed so little of its original purpose that Meehan, writing in 1901, stated that 16 Grove Sreet was built as a private house for William Pulteney.[19] Drawings of the interior arrangements of Atwood's gaol have not been found, though the building itself survives, its appearance and proportions significantly altered by two major changes. John Howard had reported on his first visit of inspection in 1774, 'the ascent to

Fig.5 Rear view of the New Gaol, Bathwick, 1780. From the Chapman Collection. (*reproduced by courtesy of Bath Central Library, Bath and North East Somerset Council*)

this prison ... is by a fine flight of steps' and the closest to a contemporary plan shows a flight of steps leading up to a 'front court' from Grove Street (fig.6 overleaf). Subsequently Grove Street was lowered. Ison reported that 'the formation of Grove Street, intended for warehouses and made almost level with the river bank, has brought the original basement above street level, greatly detracting from the effectiveness of the design'. As may be seen from figs.4 and 8, the original front entrance was altered to become a window on the first floor and the basement level became the ground floor and entrance. Cotterell's large-scale map of the1850s for the City Council[20] shows the gaol (by then closed and identified there as the police station) on Grove Street with Grove Cottage standing opposite. The front court and steps have gone. The New Gaol was completed by 1774 but sat alone in the fields for more than ten years. The Bathwick estate was slow to develop and produce income. Neale comments that the gaol was

> the only substantial building built in Bathwick between 1774 and 1788. It sat incongruously ... a few hundred yards away from the pleasure resort of Spring Gardens, an organisation of space intended by no one![21] (see fig.7)

Development in Bathwick did not start until 1788, under the guidance of Thomas Baldwin, the city architect. Today Pulteney Street and Laura Place bear witness to the result of the 'Prison deal', and by the end of the century the financial returns were good. Through this property deal William Johnstone Pulteney became one of the most successful of Bath's developers.

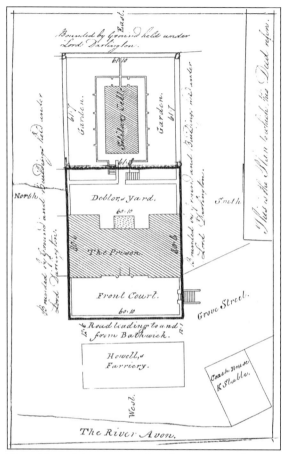

Thomas Warr Atwood (c.1733-1775), architect of the New Gaol, became a man of some importance and power during the third quarter of the eighteenth century in Bath. He was first elected a Common Councillor at a meeting of the Corporation on 20th September 1760. The office of Mayor was held by an Atwood for twelve of the years between 1724 and 1769, twice by Thomas Warr Atwood. For many years four Atwoods were on the Council: Thomas, his son Thomas Warr, Henry and James. One or more were usually Mayor, Chamberlain and a Justice: if they worked together they would have been a power to be reckoned

Fig.6 Plan of the New Gaol Bathwick, 1814, showing the front court and the block of solitary cells, built 1801. From the Conveyance, Lord Darlington to Bath Corporation, 1814, leases no. 2533. (*reproduced by courtesy of Bath Record Office*)

with. Thomas Warr Atwood was variously described as a plumber, builder, glazier, banker, surveyor and architect. He received generally favourable comment for his designs, but critical comment for the manner in which he was seen to succeed and profit as a developer. Later writers have echoed these judgements. Bryan Little describes him as 'Wood's competent rival' and considers that 'houses laid out under Wood's direction are rather tamer than those built by local plumber cum City Councillor Thomas Atwood, better placed than Wood to muscle in on the jobs available on Corporate land.' He comments: 'Atwood's prison of 1772 is a dignified work.'[22]

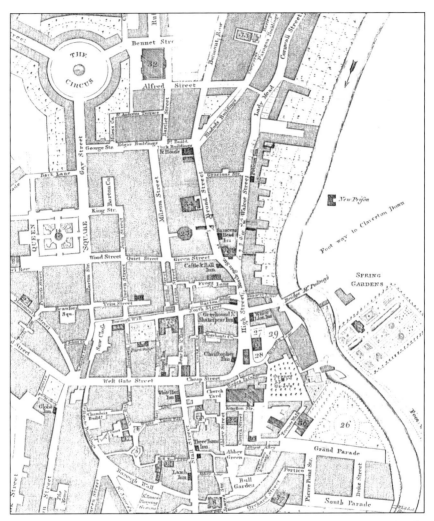

Fig.7 The Gaol stands alone in the fields. From a 'A New and Correct Plan of Bath' by Gilchrist, c.1776. (*reproduced by courtesy of Bath Record Office*)

Mowbray Green's view is that 'Attwood [*sic*] had far stronger feeling in his work than some of his contemporaries ... for his style and his mouldings are those of the elder Wood. Neither Attwood nor his building have ever received the attention which they deserve'.[23] Walter Ison considers the prison to be 'a scholarly essay in the Palladian manner, using the motifs commonly applied to domestic buildings erected at that time in the city.'[24] However on the critical side Atwood is seen by Gadd as the central figure in 'an extraordinary tale of vacillation and intrigue, behind-the-scene jobbery over contracts and acrimonious public controversy ... a leading member of the Building Committee as well as ... City Surveyor', but he goes on to observe that 'The new prison which he built for the Corporation across the river in Bathwick ... has ... an excellently designed Palladian frontage in an appropriately heavy idiom.'[25]

Atwood's influence on the building of Georgian Bath was substantial. Among the buildings which are wholly ascribed to him, built between 1755 and 1773, are the Paragon, Walcot Parade, and Oxford Row, and in partnership with Thomas Jelly or with Wood the Younger, Milsom Street (west side), Bladud Buildings, Rivers Street, and Axford Buildings. On the basis of this list Mowbray Green's plea is justified. But Atwood was a controversial figure, described as having enriched himself by obtaining leases of council property which he developed. His considerable success attracted criticism in the Bath press. A letter from 'Citizen' accused him of being scandalous, malicious, deceitful and dishonest. He is compared with MacHeath and Vitruvius.[26] The Council defended its fellow member from these allegations, resolving on 3rd July 1775:

> that the thanks of this Court be given to Mr Thomas Warr Atwood for his assiduity and attention in the management of such business relative to the public improvements of the city as had been entrusted to his care and that the plans already begun as well as those this day by him produced for completing the market and building the Town Hall be carried into execution, his employers being hitherto perfectly satisfied with his conduct therein, notwithstanding the scandalous and malicious insinuations in a paragraph in the Bath Chronicle, Twenty Ninth June last, reflecting on his judgement and integrity. Ordered, signed by the Town Clerk and for the justification of Mr. Atwoods character be inserted in both Bath papers.[27]

'Citizen', evidently undeterred, wrote again in September that year to complain of Atwood:

> For promoting the building of a Prison at enormous expense and in such an infamous situation that it cannot answer the end intended ... The present new prison is a disgrace to humanity, as it is often six feet deep in water, and a still greater evil is, that the unhappy objects confin'd in it do not experience the relief that was and often still would be administered to the sick and needy prisoners, if the cruelty of the people in power had not plac'd them in their present solitary situation; an instance scarce known but in the city of Bath.[28]

It is hard to reconcile this dramatic complaint with what the conditions must have been like for those confined in the old gaol housed in the tower of St Mary's church, but later accounts suggest that the comment of 'Citizen' was accurate as far as the problem of flooding was concerned.

Atwood was also embroiled in controversy over the building of the new Bath Guildhall, seemingly determined to promote his own design. The erection of the new Guildhall to his plans had actually started, but came to an unexpected conclusion with Atwood's death in November 1775 when part of a building collapsed on him. His part-built Guildhall was taken down and replaced by the design of his rival and successor, Baldwin.

The New Gaol in use

No daily records or journals, which might have been kept by the Keeper and later the chaplain and surgeon, have been found. They were not required by Government, and there may have seemed to be no purpose in keeping records beyond those of expenditure and warrants of committal. The City's good intentions for its New Gaol may be seen in an extract from the Bond of Indemnity, dated 5th October 1778, for John Fisher, Gaoler:

he shall well properly behave and demean himself as a gaoler ought according to law, the gaol to be clean, wholesome, in good order, no damage and the prisoners safely held without oppression, cruelty or hard usage, and not to permit escape.[29]

John Howard's journal gives not only the first, but the only full account of the Gaol. He records five visits between 1774 and 1782, and the third edition of his journal gives the following description:

The ascent to this prison, built in a meadow which is sometimes overflowed, is by a fine flight of stone steps. On the ground floor is the keeper's kitchen etc., and four rooms for petty offenders. Above are three stories; five rooms on each: one or two used by the keeper: the rest for debtors; one bed in a room, in which two prisoners sleep, they pay two shillings a week each; if one has it to himself, he pays four shillings a week. Two rooms on the second floor are free wards, one for men, one for women; on the upper floor is their workshop. There is a small court with offensive sewers. Keeper, a sheriff's officer: no salary: fees, if from the Court of Requests, 3s.6d. Debtors for large sums, 7s.8d. No table. Licence for beer. Allowance, to debtors, none (they are liberally supplied by voluntary donations); to offenders 2d a day. Clauses against spirituous liquors, and the act for preserving the health of prisoners not hung up. No chaplain or surgeon.[30]

This description suggests a total of fourteen rooms, excluding the Keeper's. Four rooms were for petty offenders and two were 'free wards'. Of the rest one at least was set aside for labour, leaving a small number which contained one bed which might be shared. The accusation of 'Citizen', above, was supported by John Howard's note of floods and offensive sewers, and by the carved inscription seen on the façade, three feet above today's street level: FLOOD LEVEL November 1, 1823.

Howard found that not all prisoners were being fed, and that the Acts of 1773 (13 Geo III,c.58, Appointment of Chaplains to County Gaols) and 1774 (14 Geo III,c.59, Health of Prisoners) were not being observed. Although he had arranged to have copies distributed to all gaols, Bath gaol was one of many where he found they were not displayed as required by the Act. There was no chaplain or surgeon.

Howard's table, below, listing the numbers of prisoners he found on each of his five visits, is a rare glimpse of how many were actually confined. This was very few in comparison with what was to follow in the next century.

	Debtors	Offenders	
1774: Aug 6	16	2	
1775: Dec 12	14	1	
1776: Dec 16	11	0	Deserters 3
1779: Feb 10	10	2	
1782: Feb 28	3	5	

A few years later, in 1785, the entry in Gye's *Pocket Guide in Cases of Arrest* repeats Howard's description verbatim, but adds:

> Several Regulations will shortly be made by the Corporation for the convenience of prisoners, by conveying a constant Stream of soft water by means of a feather join'd to the main Pipe which supplies the City. Also, it is intended that the keeper's room be at the right Hand on the entrance of the Gaol, as a security to prevent escapes.[31]

In contrast to the rest of the county, Howard gave the Bath Gaol a generally positive report in his survey conducted in 1789 when he wrote that:

> conditions in Somerset prisons are most unsatisfactory, there is no classification and debtors and felons are herded together. Bath City Gaol is an exception to the rule of general mismanagement. It is clean and quiet, with a separate room for debtors and a workshop for the employment of prisoners.[32]

However it should be noted that judging by Howard's own figures, Bath was holding mostly debtors, with very few criminal offenders. In the later 1770s items from the *Bath Chronicle* show that debtors were still dependent on family, friends and charity for their survival:

> debtors and other prisoners in Bath prison return their grateful and unfeigned thanks to Mr. John Palmer, Sheriff of the City, for bread cheese etc., which proved a very comfortable relief, many of the prisoners being in the most indigent circumstances and labouring under a long and tedious confinement. No donations had been sent to them for upwards of three months so that their situation is really deplorable.

And on Christmas Eve,1778:

> for the relief of our distressed fellow creatures who in this cold and unpitying season are shut out from the joys of society, and through the unfeeling hand of oppression are confined to a gaol and debarred the means of providing for themselves and helpless infants, a subscription is opened at Mr. George Chapman's in Cheap Street for the purpose of liberating all those in Bath Gaol whose debts may be compounded so as to restore them to their indigent families who require their daily assistance and to the public also which from their liberty may derive some benefit. To a sympathizing breast no motive can be more pleasing than having contributed to such good intentions.[33]

What is striking about these sentiments is the public sympathy expressed for debtors who many would have felt were the author of their own misfortunes and for whom gaol was seen as a necessary deterrent. What is also of interest is seeing that the City Corporation could act in an honourable and humane way, as may be seen some years later by a large payment authorised by the Corporation on 29th May 1801:

> Silvester White, lunatic vagrant, settlement unknown, found wandering, was confined by order of the Magistrates in the City Gaol, to the end that proper care might be taken of him, was placed in the care of Arthur Spencer for recovery in the expectation that costs would be paid, and the man being cured, agree to pay £48.15s.9d.[34]

Although in 1773 the Gaol Chaplains Act, noted earlier, had allowed the appointment of a chaplain to gaols, the cost to be met from the rates, Bath did not act on this until thirty years after the new gaol opened. In 1803 the Council minutes reported the decision 'to take into consideration the present state of the City Prison and to resolve on the propriety of appointing a chaplain and a medical man to attend to the prisoners confined therein and on what terms'.[35] The Rev. William Marshall, chaplain, and George Kitson, surgeon, were appointed, both on a salary of twenty guineas. The Chaplain's duties were 'to perform a service and read a lecture every Sunday'. In 1812, at the request of the Keeper, the Bailiffs reported on the 'bad state of the gaol', and found that it had many problems with both the building and the management of the prisoners. The ironwork was decaying and needed painting, the locks were defective, the water supply inadequate, 'with a cistern no larger than in a private house'. Turning to their wider responsibilities the Bailiffs reported that 'We conceive it to be as much the duty of those who have authority over it to promote the health and amend the morals of the prisoners as to provide means for their confinement'. They recommended a wall to divide the male from the female cells for:

> At present the most abandoned of both sexes are allowed to mix together and even enter into each others cells by which evil communication is kept up and opportunity offered of continuing that prostitution which has been the principal cause of their imprisonment. In vain will the Chaplain exhort while these things are permitted.[36]

In 1816 a report by the Bailiffs to the Mayor requested some very basic items: beds, mattresses, blankets, rugs, dresses, shirts, shifts and towels, and asked if two baths could be supplied. Through this period a budget of sorts can be determined by the regular appearance of sums in the Chamberlain's Records. The considerable expenditure that was anticipated through the 1823 Bill (which became 'Peel's Gaol Act' 4 Geo. IV c.64), so alarmed the Council that a campaign was mounted to lobby for the city's exclusion. Their reasoning was that 'in the peculiar circumstances of the city, including its liability to pay the county rate, the bill would not carry sufficient powers to enable the mayor and justices to put it into effect'.[37] The Council minutes for 16th March 1823 recorded that the town clerk, Philip George, had attended a committee of the House of Lords, and with the support of the city Recorder, the Marquess of Camden, Bath was excluded fom the Bill.

The New Gaol is outgrown

Events in its history suggest that the pressure to enlarge the gaol was two-fold: first from the realisation that individual cells were needed as opposed to rooms, and later from the sheer numbers of prisoners. The Council had decided in 1801 to build a block of separate cells on the ground behind the Gaol, the record stating that:

> Mr John Palmer, city architect, having prepared plans for solitary cells in the middle of the courtyard of the gaol of this city, to consider and resolve what is fit and ought to be done therein. Resolve that such plans be forthwith carried into execution under the direction of the committee.[38]

The block of cells was built but it appears only once on a plan of the gaol (fig.6) and no details of its appearance or capacity have been found. This building featured in subsequent reports when concern was raised about the ability of different classes of prisoner to see each other, converse, and worse.

It also featured again when George P. Manners, now the city architect, was asked in 1840 to prepare a plan and estimate for raising the cell block by adding two storeys.[39] It would have added 36 cells, which suggests that the existing block held 18 to 20 cells. Although the original gaol building survives, no trace of the block of separate cells can be seen for it was to be removed from Grove Street to the second new gaol, completed in 1842 in Twerton. The Gaol Governance Committee (set up as the Gaol Superintendence Committee in 1837), faced with the problem of providing hard labour, had resolved that it should be by breaking stone, and had instructed Manners to seek estimates for removing the cell block to Twerton, the stone to be used to build sheds where prisoners could work in conditions of separation.[40]

The freehold of land adjoining the Gaol was purchased in 1814[41] and in 1818 plans were produced at Council for enlarging the Gaol, and a committee set up to consider them. In 1819, four months on, the committee reported, the matter was deferred, and another three months on the committee was told its plans were too expensive. They were told to try again. Again the committee reported, only to be told that the matter was postponed to await the Government's reply to the Bath Justices' request for a Court of Quarter Sessions. The Government's response was clear and specific: such a court will not be proposed until a suitable court-house and gaol are ready.[42]

The last years: the pressure of numbers mounts

By 1837 the gaol population, though still manageable, was double the number seen by Howard on his first visit. The return compiled by the Prison Inspector in that year supplied statistics of which the following is a brief summary.[43]

Maximum number held on one day .... 42 of which 31 were male
and 11 female
Number of children held during year,
aged between 11 and 16 years .... 44 of which 24 were boys
and 10 girls
Annual Costs:
The total cost of running the gaol .... £1,140. 3s.1d.
The greatest cost was transport
to the courts and to the prison hulks .... £ 407.12s.4d.
The second highest cost was pay .... £ 225
The third highest cost was food......................... £ 177.10s.3d
or £   7.12s. per head
Total cost per prisoner per day ....   2s.8^{1}/4d

Bath was one of only eight gaols which had a daily cost per prisoner over two shillings. Among the 241 gaols listed, life was perhaps better at the Rutland County Gaol and House of Correction, Oakham at 3s.1d a day, and much poorer at Lincoln County Gaol at only 4 ^{1}/$_2$d a day.

By the late 1830s the evidence shows that the City Council was facing a crisis with its prison population. Between March 1833 and March 1835, 350 debtors were committed for debt, amounts ranging from £10 to 2s.9 ^{1}/$_2$ d. Committals were on a scale from twenty to two hundred days in gaol. Minor offenders received sentences from seven to forty days for offences such as breach of the peace, assault, keeping a disorderly house, and selling from the footway.[44]

Pressure from the numbers of inmates, and already existing pressure from government led the Corporation to decide on a whole list of strategies. They would see if neighbouring gaols would assist by taking Bath's prisoners if they were held there just for their trial; seek to alter the existing court-house to allow a Quarter Sessions to sit; and set up a committee to look for a site in order to build a new gaol to replace the one in Bathwick.[45] During 1836 the Council negotiated with the Shepton Mallet justices for the use of their House of Correction to take Bath prisoners, and at the end of the year agreement was reached at 11d. per head per day. In 1838 Ilchester and Shepton Mallet agreed to renew the contract, but at the rate of one shilling per day, plus one shilling on release for the return of prisoners. On 27th April 1840 the Council learned that Shepton Mallet declined to renew the contract.[46] Comments from Shepton Mallet gaol in 1835 gave a different perspective on Bath from that of the elegant and fashionable city:

> During this quarter a large proportion of prisoners have as usual been sent from Bath ... the boys from the vicinity of Bath are very numerous, Bath furnishes a never ending supply of juvenile offenders.[47]

The Council's letter to the Prison Inspectors in 1837 explained the problem. They were having to house an increasing number of prisoners. They had accepted the long drawn out demand to build a new gaol but were at a loss to know how to finance it. They were also anxious to raise the status of the city by getting their own Court of Quarter Sessions. The answer given to the financial problem was to issue bonds which must be signed by the mayor and two councillors or aldermen.[48]

The day-to-day evidence suggests that the considerable pressure being felt was leading to thoughts of desperate measures. In July 1838 the mayor suggested using the former Walcot Poorhouse as a gaol, the new Bath Union Workhouse at Odd Down having opened in May. In August, Manners, city architect, was asked to estimate the cost of adding accommodation for a hundred prisoners, and negotiations were being held with the Duke of

Cleveland's steward to purchase land adjoining the Grove Street gaol to enlarge it. In April 1840 the gaol committee wrote to Devizes whose new House of Correction had been opened in 1816. Their request, for the use of their old gaol to house 'a hundred prisoners', met with no response, and they wrote through the town clerk to Bristol to ask if twenty prisoners could be housed, and at what cost. Manners was once again asked to estimate the cost of housing more prisoners, by raising the block of separate cells behind the Grove Street gaol. As the Council moved towards the final stages of building a new gaol at Twerton the pressure on the Grove Street gaol was serious, and over-crowding must have made life difficult for all concerned. Early in 1841 the Bailiff, Edridge, reported to the gaol committee that the gaol was overcrowded, and that there were 'dangerous characters' who had made attempts to escape. He asked for an extra guard, and for increases in pay. It was agreed to raise the Gaoler's salary from £100 to £150, the principal turnkey's weekly wage from 21 to 23 shillings and that of the turnkeys from 18 to 21 shillings.

The first accurate piece of evidence since Howard's reports of the size and composition of the gaol population is to be found through the entry for the Bath City Gaol in the national census.[49] The return was completed on Sunday, June 6th 1841, by John Pike, Keeper of the gaol. His list commences with himself, his wife who is matron, and their six young daughters, together with two female servants. There is a principal turnkey, his wife, and two more male turnkeys. In summary:

Staff and family members: total: 14

Criminal prisoners, listed as follows:
   22 men aged 20 to 70 years
   31 boys aged 9 to 15 years.
   19 women aged 20 to 65 years
    2 girls aged 15 years   prisoners total: 74

plus the infant children of prisoners with their mothers   3

Debtors:
   12 males, one of whom is aged 15,
    1 female   debtors total: 13
           Total number living in the gaol: 104

The ages given seem somewhat arbitrary, for instance there are no prisoners listed who are aged between 16 and 19 years, although it appears that well

82

Fig.8 16 Grove Street, formerly Bath New Gaol. (© *Crown Copyright, National Monuments Record*)

over half of the sentenced male prisoners were aged 15 or less. All but 20 of the prisoners were listed as having been born in Somerset and the two originating from outside England were from Ireland. In 1841 unemployment was not a state identified in the census so all prisoners had an occupation recorded. Nearly three-quarters of the men were labourers, and the skilled men were all in the food or building trades. The proportion of unskilled women was lower at two-thirds, and the seven with skills were all in one of the clothing trades.[50] These figures conjure up a disturbing picture, the gaol population being more than twice that of four years earlier. While there is no evidence of the extremes of abuse and neglect that were being reported from gaols around the country, with the best will in the world and with the chaplain's best endeavours, it is hard to imagine how even the most primitive and elementary level of care, of privacy, hygiene and feeding can have existed for the ninety men, women and children held as prisoners in the last year of the gaol at Grove Street. In 1837 the council set up a Gaol Superintendence Committee whose first concern was the search for a site suitable for a New Gaol and the means to finance it.

The pressure from the Home Department was intense:

> four among the most defective jails so far as regards their construction and adaptation to the number of their inmates, namely ... the City Gaol, Bath ... are rebuilding and I believe that representations I have made to the Magistrates have contributed to that result[51]

The Gaol Committee set up a sub-committee to look at several other sites, limited by their belief that it must be within the City boundary. However once they were advised that this problem was overcome through Peel's Gaol Act of 1823, noted earlier, they finally recommended in September 1838 the purchase of land just outside the City, at Twerton, close to the Turnpike Road to Bristol, now the Lower Bristol Road. Mr Hale's land was described as offering:

> quiet seclusion, open, but not bleak or unprotected, with no obstruction to the free circulation of air. A kind of raised platform, where the neighbours stated that the water from the wells was good.[52]

It was to become the site of Bath's second New Gaol (1842-1878). Their positive assessment of the site was to prove ominously misinformed, but it must have been a moment of some relief when the agreement to build the new gaol was signed on 24th October 1840. The New Gaol at Twerton was completed and opened in 1842, a few months before the national penitentiary at Pentonville, on which design it was modelled. The gaol at Bathwick was to become a police barracks, later degenerating into 'sleazy tenements.' But it escaped the post-Second World War 'Sack of Bath'[53] and although nothing came of a proposal to convert the building into an Arts Centre,[54] it survived to become an attractive block of flats (fig.8).

The chance date of its origin, a direct consequence of William Johnstone Pulteney's ambitious plans for the development of Bathwick, led to the City building a gaol that although purpose-built according to the understanding of its time, was obsolete by the date of its opening. It was designed in the style of a Palladian mansion holding a collection of various sized rooms, whilst within a few years all new gaols would be utilitarian blocks of individual cells as the theory of separate confinement became universally applied. The Twerton New Gaol, opening in 1842, would be designed exactly as the Home Department demanded.

Notes

Sources listed in the notes:
> BCL Bath Central Library
> BPP British Parliamentary Papers
> BRO Bath Record Office, Guildhall
> PRO Public Record Office

1   BCL, *Bath Weekly Herald*, letter 18.7.1908, and Richard Phillips, *Public Characters 1802-3* (1803), quoted in his chapter on Anstey.
2   Meg Hamilton, *Bath Before Beau Nash* (Kingsmead Press, Bath, 1978), p. 50.
3   John Wood, *A Description of Bath* (1765; Kingsmead Reprints, Bath, 1975), p. 318.
4   BRO, Bath City Chamberlain's account, 1768-1769.
5   George Norman, 'The Masonic Lodges of Bath: Minute Book VII of the Lodge Meeting at the White Hart, No.49' in *Transactions of the Somerset Masters Lodge*, N0.3746, Bath (1922), p.404, quoted in Trevor Fawcett, *Voices of Eighteenth-Century Bath* (Ruton, Bath, 1995) p.156.
6   BRO, Chamberlain's Accounts, 23.12.1767.
7   R.S.Neale, *Bath, A Social History 1680-1850, or A Valley of Pleasure, yet a Sink of Iniquity* (Routledge and Kegan Paul, 1981), p. 227.
8   *Ibid*, p.227.
9   *Ibid*, p.228.
10 BRO, Bath City Council Minutes, 6.2.1768.
11 R.S.Neale, *op. cit.*, p.228, n.5, (from Pulteney Estate Papers, BCL).
12 R.S.Neale, *op. cit.*, p.230.
13 BRO, Bath City Council Minutes, 2.1.1769.
14 *Ibid*, 29.6.1769.
15 *Ibid*, 24.9.1770.
16 BRO, Chamberlain's Accounts, February 1st and December 3rd 1771.
17 N.Pevsner, *The Buildings of England: North Somerset and Bristol* (Penguin Books, Harmondsworth, 1958) p.136. The Italian architect Andrea Palladio (1508-80) recreated the style of the architecture of Greece and Rome. Eighteenth-century classical architecture in Bath (and elsewhere) was based on his buildings and his writing.
18 John Howard (1727-1790) prison reformer, appointed Sheriff of Bedfordshire in 1772. A conscientious man who on inspecting the Bedford County Gaol, was disturbed by the conditions that he saw. He visited neighbouring gaols to seek a

precedent for employing a paid gaoler at Bedford to improve conditions there. He then set himself the task of visiting every gaol in England and Wales, then throughout Europe, to describe the conditions that he found. His journals were published and achieved some local success in improving conditions. His theories of the purpose and proper practice of imprisonment, while less widely known than his descriptions, were more influential, becoming the basis for the first prison rules. He visited Bath New Gaol on five occasions between1774 and 1782.

19 J. F. Meehan, *Famous Houses of Bath and District* (Meehan, Bath, 1901), p.71.
20 BRO, Cotterell's map, prepared for the City Council,1852-54.
21 R.S.Neale, *op. cit.*, p 237.
22 Bryan Little, *Bath Portrait*, (Burleigh Press, Bristol, 1961) pp.60-61.
23 Mowbray A. Green, *The Eighteenth Century Architecture of Bath* (George Gregory, Bath, 1904), pp.172-174.
24 Walter Ison, *The Georgian Buildings of Bath from 1700 to 1830* (Faber, 1948), p. 88.
25 David Gadd, *Georgian Summer: Bath in the Eighteenth Century* (Adams and Dart, Bath, 1971), p.111.
26 BCL, *Bath Journal*, 21.8.1775. MacHeath was the villain in John Gay's *Beggars Opera*, first performed in London, 1728, and later in Bath on forty occasions between 1750 and 1805. The play was seen as an allegorical attack on the government, by portraying the villain, MacHeath, a highwayman, as a hero to be admired. Vitruvius, a Roman architect of the first century AD who 'desired that his name be honoured by posterity' *Encyclopedia Britannica* (15th Edn.,1993) was one of the influences on Palladio.
27 BRO, Bath City Council Minutes, 3.7.1775.
28 BRO, *Bath Journal*, 4.9.1775.
29 BRO, Schedule no. 4: 5.10.1778, Bond of Indemnity for John Fisher, gaoler.
30 John Howard, *The State of the Prisons in England and Wales* (Warrington, 1777), p.360.
31 BCL, W. Gye, *The Gentleman, Merchant, Tradesman, Lawyer and Debtors' Pocket Guide in Cases of Arrest* (Bath, 1785).
32 John Howard, *Account of Prisons and Houses of Correction in the Western Circuit*, 1789, p.37, in *Victoria County History, Somerset*, Vol.2, (1911, reprint Dawson 1969), p. 326.
33 BCL, *Bath Chronicle*, 17.7.1778 and 24.12.1778.
34 *Ibid*, 29.5.1801.
35 BRO, Minutes of Bath City Council, 3.10.1803.
36 BRO, Bath City Council Appointed Committees, report book, 1794-1837, Bailiffs report, 20.12.1812.
37 BRO, Minutes of Bath City Council, 5.8.1823. Peel's Gaol Bill prescribed the statistical returns required from gaols, allowed Justices to use revenue from the rates to fund gaols, and adopted Howard's four fundamental principles: sufficient and secure accommodation, a salaried keeper (now Governor), a reformatory regime and inspection by the Justices.
38 BRO, Bath Council Minutes, 2.1.1801.
39 *Ibid*, 2.7.1840.
40 BRO, Gaol committee, 16.8.1843.
41 *Ibid*, 8.7.1814.
42 *Ibid*, 3.5.1836, reporting letter from Lord John Russell.

43   Digest of Gaol Returns, Home Department,1837, private collection, Colin Mills.
44   John Wroughton, ed., *Bath in the Age of Reform (1830-1841)* (Morgan Books, 1971), p.101.
45   BRO, Bath City Council Minutes, 14.6.1836.
46   *Ibid*, 3.8.36, 25.10.36, 6.12.36, 24.12.38.
47   BPP, Report of the Select Committee, House of Lords, 1835, on the Present State of Gaols and Houses of Correction in England and Wales, 1835 (Irish University Press Series, Dublin, 1968).
48   PRO, HO: 20:4.
49   BCL, Census return for 1841.
50   R.S.Neale, *op. cit.*, p.56. Neale identifies clothing, housing and feeding as the most popular trades in the city at this time.
51   PRO, HO:45:127.
52   BRO, Gaol list no.16.
53   Adam Fergusson, *The Sack of Bath* (Michael Russell, Compton Chamberlayne, 1973) described the widespread destruction of the less prestigious areas of Georgian Bath by radical clearance of sites for re-development.
54   *Bath Chronicle*, 18 and 25.9. 1965.

THE LAST OF THE GEORGIAN ARCHITECTS OF BATH THE WORK AND TIMES OF JOHN PINCH

Robert Bennet

The architect John Pinch (1770-1827) has not so far received the attention he deserves. This article will attempt to provide a comprehensive analysis of the works of John Pinch set against the background of the times he lived in. It will conclude with a list of works attributed or partially attributed to Pinch in the most complete survey of his buildings so far.

The Pinch Family

The early life and training of John Pinch like that of many other Bath architects is shrouded in mystery. Proof that he was involved in the design of the buildings attributed to him comes from his neatly written signature on leases or 'skins', together with small drawings on the reverse of the document which identified the particular property to which the lease applied. We do not know what Pinch looked like but his drawings and carefully prepared notes give the impression of a capable but careful man, one who delighted in the work he did. The strong impression that emerges from a study of his career is that he was dependable and trustworthy. He was born in 1770 and died in 1827 at the age of fifty-seven.[1] There is no record of his birth in the Bath City archives but the *Bath Chronicle* for 14 March 1827 prints a brief obituary stating that he died in his fifty-seventh year. It is this report that alone gives some insight into his character for he is described as an affectionate husband and father, a warm-hearted and sincere friend.[2]

Recent work by the Bathwick Local History Society has revealed the whereabouts of the tomb of John Pinch, his wife Martha and two of his sons, John and Charles. In the burial ground of the Bathwick mortuary chapel, designed by Pinch, the tomb rests close to the southern wall of the chapel in the most favoured place. This important find helps towards a fuller knowledge of this family.

Records of the Pinch family begin with entries in the Walcot St Swithin's register for the 1790s. Eliza, daughter of John and Martha Pinch, was baptised on 23 March 1794. Another daughter Harriet and a son John were both baptised on 18 March 1798, the latter being two years of age. An earlier entry for 30 September 1795 for John, son of John and Martha Pinch, may provide an explanation for this delay. There is no later record of two Johns surviving in the family and we must assume that the first little boy died just after his baptism. When the second boy was born in 1796, he was given the patronymic John but the family waited for two years before having him baptised. Finally, in the same parish record for 26 May 1800 there is an entry for the baptism of Laura, daughter of John and Martha Pinch.

The Poor Rate book for Chatham Row, a property owned by William Johnstone Pulteney, shows that in July 1795 the Pinch family arrived to live at number 12.[3] This is the end property high above the river Avon, purchased by Pulteney with a view to a possible site for a new wharf. John Pinch lived there with his family, using the house as his business address for his work as an architect.[4] The Poor Rate books show that he paid rates on that property until 1803. He may however have had to move to another location before that date, for after bankruptcy his stock of building materials was advertised for sale in 1804.[5] In the throes of a severe financial crisis, it is likely that Pinch took his family to his Spring Gardens yard, possibly John Eveleigh's old premises where they lived in whatever shelter that site provided.

Browne's *Bath Directory* for 1809 gives Spring Gardens as Pinch's business address. On this site there still stands a small building that has obviously been used as a storage yard at some time in its history. Called the 'Boathouse', it is occupied by several small businesses. A painting by Samuel Grimm dated 1789 shows this as Mill Cottages, just behind the building on the waterfront.[6] The next directory to be published, Gye's *Bath Directory* for 1819, records 'Pinch and Son Messr's Architects and Surveyors 27 St James Parade'. From this information, it may be assumed that the bad times in Spring Gardens were behind the family. Keene's *Improved Bath Directory* of 1824 also showed Pinch and Son at that address. By 1826, as shown in Keene's *Directory*, the family were living at 2 Duke Street and had their business premises there.[7] This was part of the elder Wood's Parades development, still regarded as high status housing for important people. After the death of John Pinch senior in 1827 his son John did not remain in Duke Street but moved to 21 Henrietta Street, presumably returning to Darlington estate property where the rents may have been more favourable. This address appears in the 1837 *Directory*,[8] and again in 1849,[9] the year of John junior's death, when both his and his son Charles' names are included as occupants. Interestingly, it was Charles Pinch who appeared in the list of professional men as architect, indicating that John may have been a sick man by that time and unable to work.

It is not the intention in this study to include the works of John Pinch junior apart from observing that he succeeded his father as architect and surveyor to the Darlington estate.[10] Some of the works attributed to the younger Pinch have been severely criticised by later generations but this is also the case with many architects. He designed in the Greek Revival style and was responsible for a number of important buildings in Bath and elsewhere.[11] Eliza the eldest daughter was still alive in 1876 at the age of eighty-two and is referred to in the Calendar of Probate as approving the wills of her deceased sister Harriet who died that year. She is also mentioned in 1875 as performing the same service for Louisa Susannah Pinch, who may have married into the Pinch family. The 1851 census for Bath records two separate households bearing the name of Pinch, the first consisting of Charles aged forty-four, Louisa aged forty-nine and Eliza aged fifty-five. The second household could have been the family of John Junior (d.1849). It records his widow Elizabeth aged forty-one, an eldest son William aged twenty-one and seven other children aged between sixteen and two years. The Ordnance Survey *Historical Map of Georgian Bath* attributes the building of Rochford Place to William Pinch, and the *Bath Directory* for 1868 gives number 4 Rochford Place as his address. The *Directory* for 1854 had shown that Charles was living at that address.

Historical and Social Background

Why were there so many opportunities for the construction of fine buildings in Bath in the eighteenth century? The answer lies in the patronage of the grandees, the royalty and aristocracy, from the early years of the century.

The visit of Queen Anne in 1703 attracted a vast concourse of visitors. In succeeding years Richard Nash as Master of Entertainment was able to build on this popularity, making Bath the principal centre for fashionable life in England. Because Bath was alone in offering hot water bathing, its season became a long nine-month period from September to May. London continued to retain its popularity for the summer season. By the 1760s the excessive numbers, the crowded public rooms and the dilution of the quality by the quantity were arousing comment.[12] By the end of the eighteenth century the days of the 'Season' were almost over. The nobility had departed to the newly fashionable resorts of Cheltenham, Brighton and even the Dorset coastal towns. The new patrons of the baths at Bath were now the visitors coming for the curative properties of the Spa. The population of the City of Bath was increasing, in part because the earlier demand for seasonal accommodation was changing to a demand for houses where people might take up permanent residence.

The century ended with a severe crisis as revolutionary France declared war on Britain in February 1793. Financial insecurity in England was such that on 21 March 1793, the Bath City Bank closed its doors to join the Bath and Somersetshire Bank in bankruptcy. As the banks broke, public and private building came to an abrupt end. Builders toppled like ninepins. One of the principal moneylenders, Richard Bowsher, never did produce the money he promised and Pulteney and the Corporation brought their fine schemes to an end.[13] Architects also faced ruin. Thomas Baldwin's bankruptcy and dismissal in disgrace as city architect caused him also to withdraw from the employ of Sir William Pulteney. Pinch took over from Baldwin as surveyor for the Pulteney estate in 1793, and it may have been the support received from this source that enabled him to survive bankruptcy and stay in business as an architect. The Pinch signature on deeds for 17 Pulteney Street earlier than 1793 show that he had been acting as Baldwin's assistant while still in his early twenties.

These profound changes in Bath gave John Pinch his opportunity to be the last of the Georgian architects in the city. He may have learned his lessons from the great architects that had preceded him (the Woods, Baldwin, Palmer and Eveleigh), but what he built was quietly revolutionary, matching the spirit of the times. Initially, Pinch completed the unfinished work that reflected Baldwin's neo-classical style. Gradually however as his confidence and opportunities increased it is possible to detect the development of designs that were within the accepted *métier* yet entirely of his own devising

John Pinch's own bankruptcy did not occur until after 1800 and does not seem to have seriously affected his activities. He continued to work for William Pulteney and his daughter Henrietta Laura Pulteney. At the latter's death in 1808, there was a lull in building activity until the right to the succession had been legally decided. This was eventually settled upon William Henry Vane, third Earl of Darlington and first Duke of Cleveland, who had however signed the lease documents for New Sydney Place as early as 1808.[14] In 1810, he began his own development of what was now called the Darlington estate. Fortunately for Pinch, who had to exist without his estate salary in the interim, it is recorded that Lord Darlington, on his acquisition of the Bathwick estate, stimulated renewed building activity. He also authorised the payment of John Pinch's salary, indicating that Pinch must have survived up to that time on the occasional payments received via James Goodridge, Lord Darlington's local agent.[15]

It is important to point out that the final design of the Bathwick estate was drawn by Pinch as surveyor to the estate, and not by Baldwin, though his influence may be sometimes detected. But it is clear from the number of variations to the Bathwick site plan prepared in later years by John Pinch that Baldwin's ideas did not meet with the approval of a later generation.[16] During the early years of the nineteenth century numerous changes were made in the further development of the Bathwick estate. The grand ranges of terraced houses were not extended and instead smaller houses and villas were built up on Bathwick hill. Where terraced housing was built, as in Raby Place and Darlington Place, it was on a more modest scale and aimed at the expanding middle class. The building of the Kennet and Avon canal (1810), which passed through the Bathwick estate, introduced a commercial element resulting in the building of wharves, warehouses and a temporary road from the Sydney Gardens to the river Avon. In 1799 the central arch of Pulteney Bridge collapsed, revealing the inadequacy of the original piling work.[17] It was Pinch, as surveyor to the estate with an active involvement in all these affairs who repaired Pulteney Bridge, rebuilding the northern side including the shops that remain today. If we regard the starting point of John Pinch's career as the sale of New Sydney Place buildings in 1808 then there were just nineteen creative years ending in 1827, the year of his death. For that period of Pinch's life it is possible to plot the career of a moderately successful man, whose fame spread from Bath to bring him work in Somerset, Wiltshire and Berkshire for houses, monuments and churches.

The Development of John Pinch's Style

The architectural historian Walter Ison has observed of the buildings completed and the new work commenced in Bath after the restoration of the peace with France in 1815, that 'Some of the finest of these new buildings were designed by John Pinch ... The domestic buildings of the elder Pinch are the logical outcome of Baldwin's work, to which an effect of extreme elegance has been added by generally attenuating the proportions of the fenestration, and using sharply-cut mouldings and minor detail of refined delicacy, particularly in the metalwork of fanlights, balconies and verandas'.[18] What were those characteristics that made a crescent, a terrace or villa built by Pinch different from the buildings of other architects? It may be argued that the influence of Robert Adam upon architects such as Baldwin, Palmer and Eveleigh led them into developing a far less ornate style of architecture than the work of the Woods. This is what influenced John Pinch, and it is visible in all of his major terraces and especially his only crescent. It is only in works like the United Hospital that we see him make full use of the classical orders. Unlike some architects in the city, there was no slavish following of the designs of the Woods, but a subtle variation to the earlier designs that commentators have recognised as a unique personal style. His work has been described as essentially the last expression of the grand urban-Palladian tradition, fine in detail and balance but intensely conservative in style.[19] An example of this, the full height corner bow pavilion used by John Wood senior in the north-east corner of Queen Square is also used by Pinch at both ends of his New Sydney Place. This bow feature appears in others of his buildings such as Sion Hill Place and the semi-detached villas of Winifred's Dale. It is also to be found in some of the country mansions that are attributed to John Pinch.

It is now possible to attempt to define those forces that would have exerted so much influence upon Pinch's work. Unlike John Wood who arrived in Bath with a grand plan already in his mind and the ideal space to realise it, Pinch was, at the beginning of his career, an inheritor of other men's work. If we detect influences of other architects such as Adam and Baldwin or Palmer in his buildings it is because they were men of repute who were invited to present the genesis of design for a new site. At the beginning of his career, Pinch had to continue to design and build on those sites in the same *métier*. Where his own style emerges it does so quietly, with a fine detail and a light touch. The house building business was changing too. Not so many high-status houses were required. Instead, it was dwellings for the middle classes that were in demand. John Pinch, designing houses for this new class of customer, was not called on to produce flamboyant classical splendour for grandees but could instead indulge his own liking for neo classical architecture within the price that the new class of client could afford.

Bath was built upon a gradually rising south-facing hill, that extended from the Old Bath Bridge over the river Avon to the slopes of Lansdown, and from Pulteney Bridge upwards through Walcot to Beacon Hill. When John Pinch commenced his career as an architect it was the steeply sloping sites in these upper parts of the City that were available, and part of his characteristic style sprang from his designs for unified terraces on a sloping site. The strategy he adopted was to use concave quadrant ramps to lift the sill bands, the stringcourse and decorative bands and finally the cornices, smoothly from one house to the next. The resulting buildings have an elegance that distinguishes Pinch's work from that of others who have also built on these hillsides. The idea of using ramped detailing may have come from Baldwin in a design he produced for Abingdon Buildings but his disgrace and removal from the post of surveyor to the Pulteney interests meant that this design was not then used. Instead, it was Pinch who took it to its ultimate refinement as can be seen from his Cavendish Place, begun in 1808 but not

Fig.1 Front elevation to Cavendish Place with (inset) detail of the Vitruvian decoration on the curving plat band. (*photograph by R.J.Bennet*)

finished for another eight years (fig.1). The enlarged portion of the Vitruvian decorative band illustrates how Pinch treated the change of angle at the top of the curve. Certain of the ground-floor façades in John Pinch's buildings follow the style already created by earlier architects, with V-jointed rustication in the case of Cavendish Place and in New Sydney Place a ground-floor storey arcaded throughout the range. In this latter example, each house has a group of three arches where in all but the end pavilions the left-hand arch is wider than the others and of segmental form to contain the doorway.[20] New Sydney Place is John Pinch's finest creation. This is perhaps surprising, considering this was possibly his earliest complete design for the Pulteney family and was being built at a time when the outcome of the war with France was uncertain. Work began in 1804 and the newly completed terrace was offered for sale during 1808. Unlike other ranges of buildings it was constructed in a special way with the stone brought from one quarry and the houses raised gradually together tier after tier, thereby forming one compact building in which not the least flaw or settlement or different shades of colour can be seen. A contemporary account praises the structure as a specimen of the architectural perfection that may be formed of Bath stone.[21]

Walter Ison is full of praise for this beautiful building and comments that 'The stone has weathered to a beautiful tawny golden colour, and the building merits the highest praise for its subtle design and the excellent craftsmanship it displays'.[22] New Sydney Place attracted many high-status residents. In 1817 Queen Charlotte stayed in the upper pavilion, and the future William

IV at the other end of the terrace in the lower pavilion. Noble visitors in his houses helped Pinch's career by bringing his name before many potential clients among the affluent. Pinch first used the concave ramping of the horizontal detailing in New Sydney Place. The piers between the colonnaded windows and the imposts from which the door and window arches spring reflect the same upward curve from house to house. The impost moulding is a lighter copy of the string course. Ison's authorative description of this elegant range of buildings does not neglect the attic storey: 'The plain wall face is horizontally divided by an entablature-like string course at first-floor level; a moulded band carved with Pompeian scrolling at second-floor level; a moulded sill underlining the second-floor windows; and by the boldly profiled main cornice below the attic-storey, this last being finished with a secondary cornice and plain parapet'.[23] Pinch, unlike so many other Bath architects, did not build his attic storey into the mansard roof but gave full space to his attic rooms by bringing the windows forward to form a fourth storey to the façade. This feature, which gives the impression of monumental scale, is used in many of his buildings.

John Pinch was a master of fenestration. It is tempting to speculate that his original trade was that of joiner for in his houses joinery reached a high standard. The notice of sale at his bankruptcy does describe him as Carpenter. Pinch achieved great height for his first-floor windows by taking the sills to floor level and using six panes over nine. It was later the fashion in other parts of the city for owners to lower the sill height, but in these houses by Pinch the evidence from the original balconies with their delicate ironwork shows that the windows were designed to descend to floor level. Illumination of rooms at this date was expensive and because the occupants of these houses wished to use them for parties, there was a clear advantage in allowing maximum daylight into the room. Pinch produced the designs for Cavendish Place immediately after completing those for New Sydney Place, but the sashes for the former were replaced in Victorian times, clearly shown to be of a later date by the horns to the side stiles of the upper sash. The progression in numbers of panes from ground floor to attic storey is today, twelve, eighteen, twelve and six panes. It is generally thought unlikely that Pinch designed the windows of the *Piano Nobile* (the principal storey of a house) to have eighteen panes, rather the more common six over nine. When the sashes were replaced in Victorian times the joiners made the upper and lower sash the same size, and when in recent years the Georgian glazing bars have been reinstated it was into these equal-sized frames. Thus each individual pane is slightly smaller than it was in Pinch's time and there are eighteen rather than the original fifteen.[24] 'The three rectangular windows to each upper storey are

Fig.2 New Sydney Place showing the horizontal detailing and fenestration of the northern face. (*photograph by R.J.Bennet*)

spaced at equal centres but graduated in width and height, and though all are without architraves that in the centre of the first-floor tier is emphasised by a frame of reeded pilaster strips, with fluted and foliated consoles supporting a return frieze and straight cornice.' This style of cornice is not unique to Pinch, but where he used it the stonework with all of its detail is crisply modelled. This responds well to effects of weathering and light or shade.[25]

The treatment of the glazing bars in the round-headed windows of New Sydney Place is a copy of those used by Baldwin in Great Pulteney Street, but the feature unique to Pinch is the delicate and complex fanlights (fig.2). It is impossible to say whether these and the glazed side panels, were made specifically to his order or were chosen from the pattern books that were available to him.

Delightful and delicate balconies enliven the façades of most of John Pinch's work in Bath. Did Pinch design these or did he order them from the pattern books of the Coalbrookdale and the Carron Company ironworks? The complete answer will never be known but surviving drawings prove that Pinch designed the ironwork for some of his buildings, for example the gates, overthrow lamp holder and railings for the church of St Mary's Bathwick, and the ironwork balconies to New Sydney Place (fig.3 overleaf).

Fig.3 Detail from the skin prepared by John Pinch for New Sydney Place. (*reproduced by kind permission of The Building of Bath Museum*)

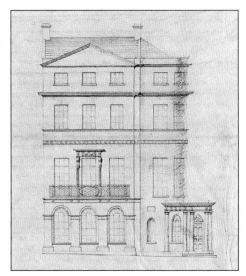

Whether John Pinch designed interiors and how much of what remains today can be attributed to him is a matter for debate. Undoubtedly he produced designs for the interior of St Mary's Church, Bathwick, showing both the longitudinal section and the cross section, and including the detail of the painting on the reredos in colour.[26]

Conclusion

John Pinch's qualities as a family man and tutor are suggested by the fact that his eldest son John successfully succeeded him as surveyor to the Darlington estate. In 1827 and for two years after, John junior may have completed work started by his father; however, estate plans bearing the inscription '*J Pinch architect*' dated 1833 were certainly by the younger Pinch. The houses that John Pinch senior designed are, however, his most enduring testimony. They were built for people to live in and to use for entertaining their friends. There was a new need for space on the first storey for large groups of people to gather, in a house built at an affordable price. Pinch met this challenge with his tall well-lit first storey salons. He provided interconnecting doors to give the owner a choice of one large room or two separate rooms. Other rooms were equally well designed and comfortable to live in. Externally Pinch's buildings give the impression of great height and elegance, of vertical emphasis achieved by careful use of the fenestration. The whole effect is completed by the strategy of bringing the attic storeys forward to share the façade of the house and in doing so, provide the entablature of the Orders represented by the whole structure.

The many visitors to the city will not have come especially to look at Pinch's work but during their walks they will have derived much quiet pleasure from his contribution to the buildings of Bath. John Pinch gave the final shape to the Georgian architecture of Bath yet was a restrained revolutionary, reflecting in his work the rapid change in the social life of the city.

Appendix: List of Buildings

Northampton Street
Built between 1791 and 1805. Commenced by Thomas Baldwin, continued by John Pinch and completed by George Phillips Manners.[27] The only independent development by William Johnstone Pulteney in the city, the lower, narrower part of the street contains several houses by John Pinch, confirmed by his signature and drawings on the deeds.

Richmond Hill
Built in 1795 with deeds signed by John Pinch.[28] Terrace of eight houses with a uniform front three storeys high, having the end houses stepped forward to form pavilions. Each house is three windows wide with the exception of number one which is just two.

Johnstone Street
A short street, seven houses in a terrace to the left and six to the right. Built in 1805, leading southwards from Laura Place which was part of Thomas Baldwin's earlier work from 1790. Built in the time of John Pinch as surveyor to the Bathwick estate. His shared involvement with Baldwin in its design and construction can be deduced from both exterior and interior details.[29]

New Sydney Place
Built during 1807 and completed for sale by March 1808. Signed leases with drawings by John Pinch exist for some of these properties.[30] Terrace of eleven houses with a balanced composition, the large house at each end and that in the middle treated as pavilions set slightly forward of the main face of the building.

Rockfield House, Nunney, Somerset
Built *circa* 1805 by John Pinch and listed grade II*.[31] Country house of two storeys with three bays, the central bay being in the form of a segmental bow.

Cavendish Place
Terrace of thirteen houses designed by John Pinch and built on the steep slopes of Lansdown between 1808 and 1816.[32] There are many similarities between this building and that of New Sydney Place.

Park Street
Built in 1808, parallel with Cavendish Place having Park Place as a connecting road. The properties forming the upper two-thirds of the street were designed and built by John Pinch.[33]

Park Place
Attributed to John Pinch and built in 1808.

Daniel Street
Built in 1810 by John Pinch and named after Daniel Pulteney. A double terraced street of thirty-six houses and a public house.[34]

Winifred's Dale

Built in 1810 and attributed to John Pinch, this pair of semi-detached villas may well have been the first attempt by a Bath architect to achieve two dwellings in what was designed to appear as one elegant structure.[35]

Bishopstrow House, Warminster, Wiltshire

Built in 1817 for William Temple to plans by John Pinch.[36] This country house closely resembles Rockford House with its central bay and plain flanking wings.

Corsley House

Built *circa* 1814 for Nathaniel Barton, an attorney practising in Warminster. This small but well-proportioned country house is attributed to John Pinch.[37]

Cavendish Crescent

The only crescent designed by John Pinch. Building work commenced in 1815 but was not completed for many years owing to the bankruptcy of the developer, William Broom, a speculating builder.[38]

Sion Hill Place

Construction of this nine-house terrace, the last of Pinch's designs to be built on the Lansdown slopes, began in 1818 and was completed in 1820.[39] Although built over a period of time the terrace was constructed to a prearranged design.

Claremont Place

Consisting of four pairs of small semi-detached houses built in 1817 to designs attributed to John Pinch.[40] Each pair of houses has a plain ashlar front and is two storeys high.

St. Mary's Church, Bathwick

The plans were drawn up by John Pinch in 1814 and today rest in the Somerset County Record Office at Taunton. Although the foundation stone bears the date 1814, the church was not consecrated until 1820.[41]

Raby Place

Building began in 1818 and was completed in 1825. The plans for the terrace of fifteen houses were drawn by John Pinch.[42] The terrace, originally called Church Street, is slightly angled to follow the curve of Bathwick Hill, the apex of the angle being at the mid point.

Cleveland House (*right*)

Built in 1820 on a bridge over the Kennet and Avon canal, originally as the canal offices. The deeds of this building prove it to have been designed by John Pinch.[43]

Sturford Mead, Corsley, Wiltshire

Built in 1820 for Henry Austin Fussell of Frome and attributed to John Pinch.[44] Occupied by the Thynne family of Longleat from 1854 to 1954.

Spa Villa, 9 Bathwick Hill

The plans for this two-storey house bear the signature *John Pinch Bath*. The ground plan shows that the building was to be an irregular octagon having three long faces, four short faces and a two-storey front set forward in the direction of the city.

Camden Terrace with Lower Camden Place

These two terraces built after 1820 on the steep slope of Beacon Hill and attributed to John Pinch are examples of the architectural distinction given even to small houses.[45]

The United Hospital

John Pinch prepared three sets of plans for this hospital which opened its doors to patients in 1826.[46] Ison comments that the front is 'bold in scale and severe in expression', appropriate for a prestigious public building surrounded by the works of earlier architects.

Prior Park Buildings

Built *circa* 1825 and with the design attributed to John Pinch, this terrace of nineteen houses has slightly projecting centre and end pavilions, with a pediment to the central pavilion.[47]

Fig.4 Cleveland House, built in 1820. (*photograph by R.J.Bennet*)

Willow House, 6 Bathwick Hill

(fig.5 right, photograph by R.J.Bennet)

Plans for this house were drawn by John Pinch just prior to his death in 1827.[48] The original design did not include an attic storey and a hipped roof was planned rather than the end gables that exist today.

Cumberland Villa

No.2 Bathwick Hill, built in 1824 to drawings by John Pinch, in the collection of the Lord Barnard at Raby Castle in Northumberland.[49] The style of this villa with its hipped and deeply-eaved roof is similar to that of Spa Villa built four years earlier.

Nos 1, 3, 4 & 5 Bathwick Hill together with 1, 2 & 3 Sion Place

The drawings for these buildings are from the Darlington estate office where John Pinch worked, and bear his signature. Use of his initials only may indicate that he was not the designer but had initialled his approval as Surveyor to the estate. Reasonable certainty of his authorship is given elsewhere by his full signature or the designation *John Pinch and Son(s) architects.*

St. Saviour's Church, Larkhall

Although this church was not consecrated until 1832, the process of gathering funds and designing it had begun in 1824. John Pinch junior was responsible for overseeing the building work but there is no doubt that it was his father who drew up the plans for this elegant building.[50]

Darlington Place

Built in the period from 1813 to 1824 to plans by John Pinch.[51] Of four storeys, the ground-floor of which is rusticated with two flat-arched windows.

St. Mary's Buildings *(right)*

This small cul-de-sac on the slopes of Beechen Cliff is well hidden and therefore relatively unknown. Deeds possessed by owners of houses in the terrace have John Pinch's signature and his manner of using ramped horizontal detailing has certainly been employed here on this short terrace of nine houses.

1-6 Cambridge Place

The four detached and two semi-detached villas built in 1820 on this steep slope at the foot of Widcombe Hill were considered by Ison to have been designed by John Pinch.

Pulteney Bridge repairs

Although the original Pulteney Bridge began to collapse in September 1799 and severely so in 1800, it was not until after 1802 that John Pinch was able to complete the rebuilding of the damaged north side of the bridge.[52]

Assembly Room and Stables adjoining the George Inn, Frome, Somerset

Drawn and signed by Pinch but never realised.

St Lawrence Church, Hungerford, Berkshire

Built in the Gothic style, between 1814 and 1816.

Gothic Mausoleum, Stourton, Wiltshire

Built in 1819 for Sir Richard Colt Hoare, Bart, in the churchyard of St Peter's Church, Stourton.

St Michael's Church, Twerton, Bath

Enlarged by Pinch in 1824 but rebuilt by Manners in 1839.

Fig.6 St Mary's Buildings (*photograph by R.J. Bennet*)

102

Notes

1   H. M. Colvin, *Biographical Dictionary of British Architects 1600-1840* (Yale University Press, 3rd edn., 1997), p.756.
2   *Bath Chronicle* 14 March 1827, obituary of John Pinch senior.
3   Bath Record Office, details taken from the Poor Rate records. The Pinch family had been living in the same parish before that date as shown by the record of Eliza's baptism.
4   Robbins' *Bath Directory* 1800.
5   Walter Ison, *The Georgian Buildings of Bath* (1948; revised ed. Kingsmead Press, Bath, 1980), p.20.
6   M. Rowe, *viva voce*. For the location of Spring Gardens, see Fig.7, p.73.
7   Keene's *Improved Bath Directory* 1826.
8   Silverthorne's *Bath Directory* 1837.
9   Charles Clark's *Bath Annual Directory* 1849.
10 M. Rowe and W. McBryde, *Beyond Mr. Pulteney's Bridge* (Bath Preservation Trust, 1987), p.16.
11 Colvin, 1997, p.757. Thirteen separate works are credited to John Pinch junior including six churches and several buildings in Bath, the principal being the central block on the west side of Queen Square.
12 T. Fawcett, *Voices of Eighteenth Century Bath* (Ruton, Bath, 1995), p.49.
13 R. S. Neale, *Bath, A Social History 1680-1850, or A Valley of Pleasure, yet a Sink of Iniquity* (Routledge and Kegan Paul, 1981), p.262. See also Stephen Clews, 'Banking in Bath in the Reign of George III', *Bath History*, Vol.V (Millstream Books, Bath, 1994), pp.104-124 and Jane Root, 'Thomas Baldwin: His Public Career in Bath, 1775-1793' in the same volume, pp.80-103.
14 J. J. Self, private archive.
15 Rowe and McBryde, p.15.
16 Rowe and McBryde, p.10.
17 J. Manco, 'Pulteney Bridge'. Reprinted from *Architectural History*, Vol. 38 (Bath Preservation Trust, 1995), p.137.
18 Ison, pp.20-21.
19 B. Cunliffe, *The City of Bath* (Alan Sutton, Gloucester, 1986), p.146.
20 Ison, pp.184-5.
21 Quoted but not attributed by Ison, p.183.
22 Ison, pp.183-4.
23 Ison, p.184.
24 Self, archive.
25 Ison, pp.185-6.
26 Somerset County Record Office, Taunton (Ref. D/B/BATW.M 8/2/1).
27 T. Fawcett, F. Kelly, *Northampton Street, An Outline of its Historical Development* (Bath, 1999), p.4.
28 Bath Preservation Trust, interiors survey. All owners of houses surveyed are asked whether they have the original deeds or skins for their properties.
29 Self, archive.
30 Building of Bath Museum. The drawing for part of New Sydney Place carrying John Pinch senior's signature has been part of the permanent display in the museum.

31 Mendip District Council listing specification.
32 Ison, p.185.
33 Ison, pp.2-3.
34 *Ibid*.
35 N. Pevsner, *The Buildings of England: North Somerset and Bristol* (Penguin Books, Harmondsworth, 1958), p.131.
36 Wiltshire Buildings Archive, Devizes.
37 H. Grice, *Corsley House, A History* (1999), p.23.
38 Ison, p.186.
39 Pevsner, p.131.
40 Ison, p.191.
41 Ison, p.66.
42 Rowe, Raby Castle Archive.
43 Bath Preservation Trust, interiors survey.
44 Grice, p.23.
45 Ison, pp.191-192.
46 Ison, p.78.
47 Ison, p.192.
48 Rowe and McBryde, p.48.
49 Rowe and McBryde, p.45.
50 Ison, p.67.
51 Rowe and McBryde, p.43.
52 Manco, p.140.

EDWARD SNELL'S DIARY: A JOURNEYMAN ENGINEER IN BATH IN THE 1840s

John Cattell

Edward Snell (1820-1880) is a relatively obscure figure who is best known in this country for his two watercolour views of the new locomotive works and railway village in Swindon in 1849.[1] But he was so much more – engine erector, civil engineer, surveyor, draughtsman, inventor, artist, traveller and adventurer. His greatest contribution to posterity, perhaps, was as a diarist and chronicler of the social scene in England and subsequently in Australia. He wrote two diaries, both profusely illustrated by charming pen and ink sketches, the first covering the period 1842-49 in England, the second covering his adventures in Australia between 1849-58 and his return to England.[2] The period 1842-49 in this country was a time of great industrial expansion fuelled by the growth of the railways and accompanied by fluctuating economic conditions. It was also an age of immense social upheaval and reform characterised by migration from the country to the towns, by a drive for self-improvement among the working classes, particularly the educated artisan class of which Snell was a member, and mass emigration. His English diary provides a very personal and colourful insight into these and other aspects of life at the time, and as such is of very considerable historical interest.

Snell had a special affinity with Bath. The diary was intended as a record of his working and social life following the completion of a seven-year apprentice-ship at the Newark Foundry of his relative, the prominent Bath engineer, Henry Asprey Stothert. The first part of the diary covers in considerable detail his life and adventures in the city between 16th March and 20th May 1842 prior to moving to Bristol and later to Swindon to take up employment as a fitter in the new railway works. Throughout the 1840s many of his days off were spent on return trips to Bath to visit his foundry friends and relatives, and it is clear that he regarded Bath as his second home after his native North Devon.

He was born in Barnstaple on the 27th November 1820 the grandson of William Snell, a serge manufacturer of Crediton, and the son of Edward Snell, a silversmith, jeweller, watch and clockmaker with premises in High Street, Barnstaple.[3] The latter married Elizabeth Stothert, the daughter of Abel Stothert, a cutler of Shaftesbury, at St Peter's Church, Barnstaple on 24th June 1820.[4] The couple had four children, Edward, the eldest, and three daughters, Rose Emily (known as Emily), Emma and Elizabeth (known as Lizzie). Edward Snell senior died at the age of 33 in 1827, probably of typhus fever, when his son was aged only six. The sale of the business, the High Street shop and the family's house above it realised £1500 which was left in trust for his wife and family.[5] This appears to have placed Elizabeth and her four children in some immediate financial difficulty and they moved to smaller premises in Newport on the southern outskirts of Barnstaple.

The first page of the English diary gives a brief account of the young Edward's early upbringing, his education at the local schools and in particular his love of the sea: 'I always had a strong inclination for the sea, which inclination was always thwarted and crossed by my over anxious mother; in consequence I began to be, and have remained up to the present time what a seaman would designate, "a land lubber"'. He was to retain a strong interest in the sea throughout his life, visiting coastal areas as well as the shipping at Bristol and London docks and elsewhere whenever possible. He described himself as a 'Mammy's Darling', and as the eldest child and only son his future career and fortunes were closely linked to those of the whole family. With this in mind his mother used her family connections to secure for her son an apprenticeship with the Stotherts in Bath. Elizabeth Snell's father was the brother of George Stothert who established the Stothert ironmongery business in Bath in around 1785.[6] She was thus first cousin to George Stothert's son George junior (1786-1858) who set up a foundry in Horse Street in 1815.[7] This was run as a separate business from his father's No. 11 Northgate Street ironmongery establishment, and would later come to form an engineering firm of national and international importance.

The premises at Nos. 16 and 17 Horse Street, later renamed Southgate Street, were acquired by George senior from 1799 as part of his ironmongery business and subsequently extended through to the rear (east) with buildings fronting Philip Street, renamed Newark Street from around 1829.[8] By 1821 the main entrance to the engineering complex, then under the management of George junior, was from Philip Street and with the change of street name the works became known as the Newark Foundry. George junior retired in 1827 and the foundry was taken over by his younger half-brother and partner Henry Stothert under whose management the business expanded further.[9] Two other sons of George Stothert senior, John and William continued their father's Northgate Street ironmongery firm.

George Stothert junior took a close interest in the fortunes of Edward Snell, being his friend and patron and using his influence to obtain employment for his young cousin throughout the period covered by the English diary. It was probably he who facilitated Snell's apprenticeship, perhaps reckoning, rightly as it turned out, that a training of this kind would stand him in good stead at a time of rapid advancements in the fields of civil and mechanical engineering.

106

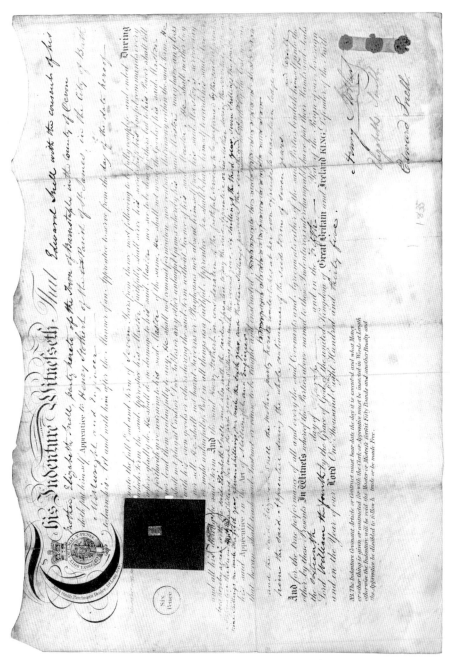

Fig.1 Edward Snell's apprenticeship indenture. *(private collection)*

He began his apprenticeship at the age of 14 on 16th March 1835, the date recorded on his indenture of apprenticeship (fig.1). His move to Bath was the first time he had left Devon and was a traumatic experience, arriving in an unfamiliar city, away from his family and school friends and removed from his hitherto largely rural existence. His initial unease is apparent from the following passage at the beginning of the diary: 'At length on the 11th of January 1835, I left my dear native town & came up to Bath to be apprenticed, and I think the first 6 months of my apprenticeship the most miserable I ever spent'.

He was apprenticed as an engineer and millwright, and the agreement entered into between Edward, his mother and Henry Stothert appears by today's standards to be very draconian, but was probably fairly typical by the standards of the time. Snell was required to serve his master faithfully, obey his every command, and not waste his goods or lend them to anyone unlawfully. He was not to 'commit fornication nor contract Matrimony'. He was also forbidden to 'play at card or dice tables or any other unlawful games', to 'buy nor sell', to 'haunt taverns or playhouses' or to absent himself day or night without his master's permission. It is perhaps little wonder that, after a brief account of his childhood, the first entry in the diary, dated 16th March 1842, reads 'Hurrah! Emancipated at last …'. On the following evening he celebrated his new status at the *Engineer's Arms* public house with a group of his 'shopmates' and 'our most respected foreman Old Bluebottle', the nickname given to the Foundry's managing engineer George Rayno who in 1844, with Robert Pitt, became co-partner with Henry Stothert in the engineering business.[10]

There is relatively little information in the diary on the work undertaken during the seven years of his apprenticeship except that he was confined to the pattern shop for the first five years and spent much of the remainder of the time in the millwrights and fitting shops. The pattern shop was almost certainly located above the foundry building at the rear of the Horse Street premises on the site of the old smithy, while the millwrights and fitting shops were possibly accommodated in the newer part of the complex entered via the main entrance on Newark Street.[11] Snell also records making two apprentice models: 'during my apprenticeship I made two small High Pressure Steam Engines, one a beam, and the other an oscillating Engine, the stroke of the former being 2 inches & that of the latter 1 inch'.

Although following his 'emancipation' Snell concentrated on recording his social activities, presumably regarding much of his work and the foundry as too humdrum to be worth describing in any detail, it is still possible to get a good impression of the kind of tasks he undertook. On 9th April 1842 he was 'At work in Bathwick Tunnel fixing a cast-iron cistern up to my neck in mud and dirt'.[12] Later that month he mentions repairing a sugar mill for

108

Francis Asprey, a tea dealer and grocer of No. 17 Southgate Street and a relative of Snell and the Stotherts by marriage.[13] 'The sugar mill I repaired had about a pound of sugar sticking between the cracks and it was astonishing to see the voracity with which it was devoured by some of our foundry chaps'(fig.2).

Fig.2 Snell's sketch of Newark Foundry workers eating sugar left in the cracks of a sugar mill he had repaired. He wrote: 'I refrain from mentioning names but … the generality of the foundry gents are not at all squeamish about sucking a dirty finger or two poor Devils!'.

Two days later he was busy fixing a chimney to the boiler of a steam dredging machine. This may have been one of the steam dredgers designed by Brunel in the 1830s to drag the mud from Cumberland Basin in Bristol.[14] This task took him two days including a half hour spent in the boiler of the 'mud boat' reading Cobbett's *History of the Protestant Reformation* in protest at Henry Stothert's decision to reduce his wages (see below). Shortly afterwards he was told to hold himself ready to go to Newbury to fix an old mud engine in a new boat, although in the end he was not asked to perform this task. On 5th May he mentioned repairing a pump to go to Batheaston and then being sent to '… Watson's Corn Mill in the Lower Bristol road to repair the engine'.[15] He sketched the engine (fig.3) and described it as 'A regular ricketty old puffer with a leakage in every joint, and the boiler in such a state that in the course of the night the leakages almost empty it'. Two days later he was still at the mill trying 'to get the engine started before night' and endeavouring to fill the boiler by dipping buckets into the river from an open window. On 12th May he was busy drawing 'steam apparatus' for the new City Gaol at Twerton East opened in 1843. He also produced drawings for a Mr Daniels of Twerton, possibly Joseph Clissild Daniell, the inventor and improver of machinery who worked for Charles Wilkins the owner of the two large woollen mills at Twerton.[16] He also drew some 'manure machinery' for Barrett who was employed at the 'Twerton Factory', perhaps one of the woollen mills or a separate engineering business.[17] Snell obtained Rayno's permission to copy drawings of a marine engine illustrated in 'Tredgold on the Steam engine and Steam Navigation', which he described as 'a capital work' and one which he 'should like to have'.[18]

Taken together these jobs amount to a wide and fascinating range of engineering work under-

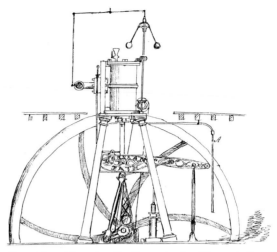

Fig.3 The old engine Snell repaired at Watson's Corn Mill off the Lower Bristol Road.

taken by a local foundry. Much of it was concentrated in and around Bath but occasionally, as the Newbury job shows, it involved working further afield.[19] It was also hard physical work often carried out in difficult conditions. Snell commented that his '… fist which was once as delicate as a lady's is now as rough as the paw of a bear with fingers as stiff as pokers and fit to handle nothing but a 16in pipe' and 'we do get most horribly black to be sure and I think it would not be a bad spec. to send some of our old clothes to the Monmouth St mendicity society to be boiled into soup for the poor'.

On average he worked six days per week and eight hours per day not including meal breaks, recording in the diary the total number of days worked per week and any additional hours. Sometimes he worked for less than the six days and occasionally a few hours more. On 17th April he refers to a notice put up in the foundry stating that the men had to be at work by 6.05am or lose a quarter day's wages. Also those working outside the foundry were now required to work two and a half hours per quarter day, in other words a ten-hour day, instead of the usual eight hours. The notice also stated that they could continue to work two-hour quarters, in which case the daily lodging allowance when working away would be reduced from one shilling to 6d. Snell thought 'this a great encroachment on the men and as soon as I can afford it I shall bid old Bluebottle goodbye and let him tyrannize over the rest'.[20]

Snell's indenture stipulated that he be paid three shillings a week in the first year of his apprenticeship rising to 13 shillings in the seventh year.

However it seems that he was being paid over 20 shillings per week by the time he had completed his apprenticeship, as on 18th April he was informed by Henry Stothert's clerk that he was being overpaid and that his wages were to be reduced to 20 shillings. Snell was most indignant at this 'rather queer intelligence' and began making preparations to leave the foundry while trying to think of ways of making extra money: 'Think I shall take one or two of my pictures & endeavour to sell them at the shops, any scheme to get money. Money! The want of which is the root of all evil – had I but £5 in my pocket how soon would I bid farewell to old Bluebottle and the whole lot of ragamuffins at Newark Foundry'. His inability to save was probably made worse by the relatively high cost of procuring lodgings in relation to his wages.[21] Being of a fiercely independent character with a strong sense of natural justice he was determined not to let the matter rest, writing a fairly stiff letter of complaint to Henry Stothert:

> Sir – As I have seldom a chance of seeing you I take the liberty of remonstrating by letter against the excessively low wages which you have thought fit to give me and as I cannot discover wherin I am so greatly inferior to the rest of the men I see no reason why such an immense distinction should be made between our respective wages. That I am of some use in Drawing I have sufficient proof by being sent for so often by Mr Daniels of Twerton, and though I dislike praising myself yet do I not find but that I can do my share in the other branches of the business and in the whole course of my Apprenticeship I do not remember ever to have had a job given me which I was unable to accomplish. But setting self commendation aside it is at best but a spiritless and unmanly thing for a person to underwork his fellows and for my part I consider the practice highly reprehensible inasmuch as it is calculated to bring down the price of labour and thus involve hundreds of persons in misery and destitution, so I shall leave the matter to your generosity especially as I think it high time I should begin to do something for my Mother who stands in great need of my assistance …

The letter was bound to have annoyed Stothert who made no move to increase Snell's pay presumably reasoning that at a time of general economic malaise he would fare no better elsewhere. Snell seemed to recognise he had little option but to accept the cut: 'I feel quite ashamed of working for less than the rest but what can I do. Its all very fine for a fellow to throw himself out of employment but starvation wont altogether suit my constitution so I suppose I must put up with it till Mr Henry Stothert returns from Wales …'.[22]

His dissatisfaction with a pound a week prompted him to contemplate emigrating: 'Begin to think by Jove that I must bid Adieu to Old England for a short time and emigrate to the United States or New Zealand unless I can get a berth in some Steam ship, and Mother must console herself for my absence in the best manner she can'. However concern for his mother's feelings seems to have been the main reason for not pursuing the idea of emigration at that time: 'should have no objection to go to America myself but I know my mother would make a bother about it so I suppose I must stay at home'.

Fig.4 No. 2 Great Stanhope Street, Snell's lodgings in the late 1830s-early 1842.
(*photograph by James O. Davies*)

In early April, in an attempt to increase his savings, he decided to leave his lodgings at No. 2 Great Stanhope Street and move to cheaper accommodation at No. 12 Brougham Hayes Buildings, Twerton, south of the river. No. 2 Great Stanhope Street was Snell's second lodgings. He moved there in the late 1830s from No. 7 Paragon Buildings where he had stayed with John Lambert.[23] No. 2 is an ashlar, three-storey and mansard terraced house of the late eighteenth century (fig.4). In the early 1840s it was occupied by Mrs Sarah Thornthwaite, a 40-year-old lodging housekeeper of independent means who lived there with her four sons and daughter Susan. All were present on census day in 1841, along with three lodgers: Miss Hanna[h] Brooke, of independent means; John Harris, aged 20, ironmonger; and Edward Snell, listed as an apprentice coach maker. Three of Mrs Thornthwaite's children, Miss Brooke and Snell were evidently having some fun with the enumerator, all giving their ages as just 14 or 15 although they were all older. Snell claimed to be 15 when in fact he was 21.

No. 12 Brougham Hayes formed part of a terrace of much smaller two-storey, single-bay houses, probably of early nineteenth-century date, on the southwestern outskirts of the city (fig.5 overleaf).[24] The terrace was later cut in two by the creation of Lorne Road. No. 12 was run by Mrs Mary Coopey, whom Snell described as '... a quiet, clean and tidy woman & withal a most excellent cook'. In 1841 she was aged 55 and of independent means. The house probably had two rooms on each floor, accommodating as well as Mrs Coopey, a lodger called Hall whom Snell described 'as being twice in America'; and a chum from Newark Foundry called Zenas Hall who shared a room with Snell. Noting that 'I think on the whole I am not too badly quartered', Snell produced a sketch plan of his room, carefully annotating each item of furniture as well

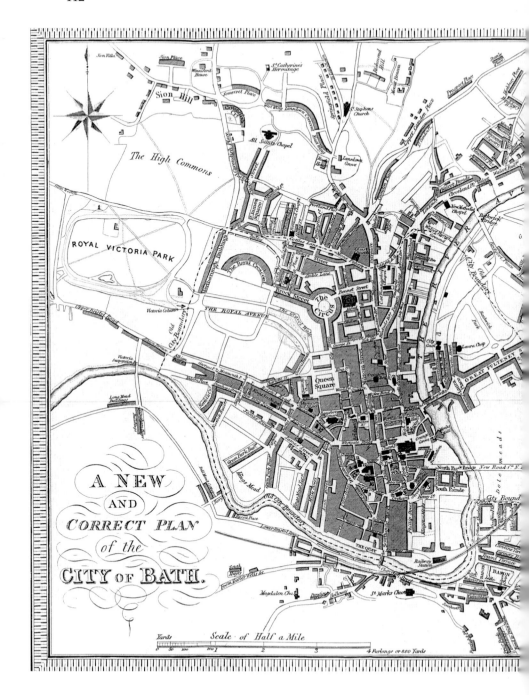

A NEW AND CORRECT PLAN of the CITY of BATH.

Scale of Half a Mile

Reference

1 *Abbey Church*
2 *St Michaels Church*
3 *St James's Church*
4 *St Johns Chapel*
5 *Roman Catholic Chapel*
6 *Quakers Meeting*
7 *Unitarian Meeting*
8 *Blue Coat Charity School*
9 *Pump Room*
10 *Kings & Queen's Bath*
11 *Cross Bath*
12 *Hot Bath and Swimming Bath*
13 *Hot Bath Pump Room*
14 *Kingston Bath*
15 *General Hospital*
16 *City Dispensary & United Hospital*
17 *Society's Office for the Suppression of Vagrants*
18 *Theatre*
19 *Upper Rooms*
The Names of the other Public Buildings are in their respective Places

Fig.5 A map of Bath in the 1840s, from Samuel Gibbs, *Illustrated Bath Visitant or New Guide to Bath* (Samuel Gibbs, Bath, n.d, c.1847?). Brougham Hayes Buildings where Snell lodged in early 1842 is the block immediately above the word 'new' in the map title.

as the two occupants of the bed (fig.6 overleaf). This must be one of very few such illustrations of the interior of a lodging room of the period. A great observer of his fellow man he devoted considerable time to describing the antics of Zenas Hall.[25] His entry for 14th April reads:

> Staid at home all evening reading. Zenas Hall came in slightly fuddled and began to show symptoms of a scrimmage – but the effervescence of his spirits soon passed off and he sat down quietly playing his flute till bedtime … [When] Zenas … staggered into the room this evening … the first indication of his not being 'compis mentis' was communicated to me in the shape of a punch on the head. Owing however to the difficulty he experienced in preserving his centre of gravity the said 'punch' was no more than a love tap and did not in the least ruffle my truly amiable temper.

Following a similar display from Hall, Snell '… began to think him rather an ardent devotee of Bacchus or to speak more correctly though less classically of John Barleycorn.' Snell drank relatively infrequently although on one occasion he described an incident involving a glass of whisky:

> Miss B[rooke] desired me to brew myself a glass of whiskey and water and as I was not aware of the strength of the 'cratur' I mixed a jolly good tumbler of half and half swallowed it and soon found myself unable to preserve my centre of gravity and as great as a lord in my estimation. Can't very distinctly remember all the little absurdities I was guilty of. I had a notion of trying to walk in a straight line from one lamp post to another but I have a strong suspicion that I did not succeed. I have likewise a faint recollection of making love to Mrs Coopey, attempting to preach a sermon, then spouting Richard the 3rd, singing a Psalm & then toddling up stairs to bed with a great many injunctions from Mrs Coopey to be sure & take care of the candle and not set any thing on fire.

114

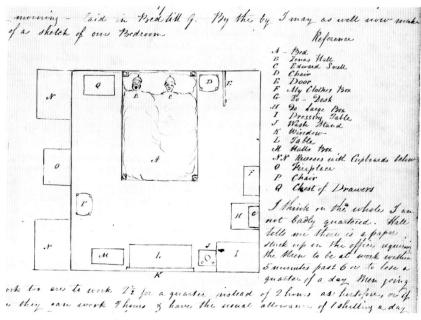

Fig.6 Snell's sketch of his room at No. 12 Brougham Hayes Buildings.

The diary is peppered with amusing anecdotes and sketches illustrating his life as a lodger. He seems to have got on well with his room mate Zenas Hall despite the occasional minor falling out. One such incident involved an argument over whether or not to open a window:

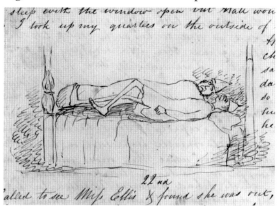

Fig.7 Snell (foreground) being advised to 'shut his head' by his co-lodger Zenas Hall.

Went home to bed – found it plaguey hot & wanted to sleep with the window open but Hall wouldn't consent to it so I took up my quarters on the outside of the bed and kept Hall awake by chattering till he got so savage I thought it dangerous to persist so in compliance with his advice I 'shut my head and went to sleep' (fig.7).

Snell records staying in bed until twenty minutes to six, '… which is as long as we possibly can with safety. Great and manifold are the grumblings too before we do turn out …'. Their route to the foundry was probably via Dredge's suspension bridge (Victoria Bridge) (fig.8) and along the Upper Bristol Road to Monmouth Street, Westgate Street, Stall Street and Orchard Street.

His diet seems to have included staple items such as bread, butter and cheese together with copious quantities of pork: 'Zenas is pecking away at a ham bone most voraciously but I can't find much fault with him for I have eaten so much pork lately that I am getting quite bristly in the face'. He makes no mention of vegetables except for enjoying some 'brocoli' with bacon, suggesting the former was something of a novelty.

Fig.8 Victoria Bridge, an improved type of suspension bridge designed by James Dredge c.1837, to provide a crossing between the Upper and Lower Bristol Roads. (*photograph James O. Davies*)

Snell spent much of his spare time socialising with work mates and friends he had made at his various lodgings in Bath. He also went to the theatre and visited the hot baths.[26] One of his closest friends was John Gully, a fellow apprentice at the Newark Foundry in the 1830s.[27] His father, Philip Gully, ran an ironmongery business at No. 11 New Bond Street and was probably a friend of the Stothert family.[28] John Gully worked at the Bath Savings Bank, Trim Street, from the late 1830s until 1846 when he went into partnership with his father. Gully and Snell shared a great interest in art, Gully being a painter of considerable ability who emigrated to New Zealand in late 1851 and became one of that country's most important landscape painters. Snell was a regular visitor at the Gullys' house at No. 12 Argyle Street and relished 'overhauling' John's latest works. The latter gave Snell a lesson in crayon drawing on Christmas Day 1844.

His social activities also included frequent visits to the houses of the Stotherts and their relatives the Bartrums and the Aspreys. He was evidently a favourite of the Stothert women who, judging by various references in the diary, seemed to take their young relation under their wing. Snell's kinship with the Stotherts placed him in a privileged position, allowing him access to social circles closed off to many of his fellow foundry workers, who, despite being highly skilled artisans, were essentially working class. The Stotherts were by the early 1840s prominent members of Bath's middle class. This increasingly influential section of society was dominated by successful manufacturers, reflecting the growing industrialisation of Bath at that time.[29] A liberal and Nonconformist, Henry Stothert supported the election of the Radical candidate John Arthur Roebuck to Parliament in 1832 and shared his enthusiasm for reform and greater freedom for Dissenters.[30] The increasing influence of Stothert and others like him resulted from success in business evident, in the former's case, by the expansion of the Newark Foundry and the establishment of the large Avonside Ironworks in Bristol in 1837. Other members of the Stothert family were influential in business and social circles. They lived in comfortable circumstances, often on the then outskirts of the city. George Stothert junior, a retired bachelor with a second house in London, resided at No. 2 Richmond Hill with his unmarried sister Ann whom Snell referred to in the diary as Miss Stothert. This house, which has a three-bay ashlar façade, forms part of a terrace of three-storey houses dating from 1790-1800. The houses are set well back from the street and have splendid prospects out over the city below. Henry Stothert and his family lived at No. 4 Priory Place, Lyncombe, while his brother William, who had retired from the family ironmongery business in around 1837 and who by 1842 was listed as among the gentry, resided nearby at Southcot House, Lyncombe.[31] The ironmonger, John Stothert, was a city councillor and resided at No. 23 Bathwick Hill, while another brother, Richard, was a solicitor.[32]

Throughout the 1840s Snell made return visits to Bath as often as he could. Initially he obtained accommodation with Mrs Coopey at his old lodgings but later stayed either at No. 2 Richmond Hill or at Belmont, Hay Hill, the residence of George Stothert senior's second wife Elizabeth Stothert, née Asprey (c1765-1855), stepmother of George junior and mother of Henry. Belmont is a three-storey plus mansard house with a bowed single-storey entrance section fronting the narrow pedestrian passage making up Hay Hill. Snell spent the Christmas of 1844, 1845 and 1846 with the Stotherts in Bath. His diary entry for Boxing Day 1844 gives a good impression of the fashionable and cultivated lifestyle enjoyed by the family:

> We met at Mr HS [Snell's shorthand for Henry Stothert] the same company we saw the night before with the addition of Mr Laufiere & Mr & Mrs William Stothert & family. Spent the evening gloriously – every delicacy of the Season – beautiful girls, music, dancing, etc. Obliged to leave them at 12 tho. Went into the Full Moon with Mr Laufiere & Mr Pitt & had a glass of brandy & water & cigar.

Snell possessed a keen and often impish sense of humour devoting considerable space in the diary to recounting and sketching the various practical jokes perpetrated by his fellow foundry workers, some of these accounts giving useful insights into his working conditions:

> This morning old Bluebottle came up into the pattern shop grumbling about our shutting the door and trigged it open himself, but had barely reached the bottom of the ladder before it was shut again, by that fountain of all mischief Bill Glass.[33] This contempt of his authority acted upon old Bluebottle's excitable temper to such a degree that he was constrained to blow off steam, which he immediately did in the shape of a volley of oaths and imprecations quite dismal & heartrending to listen to, but we excused it as we thought without a vent of some kind he must inevitably have burst his boiler. When the tempest of his wrath had in some degree subsided, he mildly swore by God he'd have the door off the hinges, which was accordingly done by old Sam Hook, so that the pattern shop is now most admirably ventilated, though unfortunately instead of pure air of heaven, 'wot poets call zephyr breeze' the Sulphuric vapour from the furnace finds it way into the shop, and by half suffocating the unfortunate inmates gives them a slight foretaste of what they may expect in the next world, when consigned to the tender mercies of the gentleman whose name should never be mentioned in the hearing of 'Ears polite'.

On another occasion a group of noisy ragamuffins playing a game of pitch and toss just outside the foundry walls had a bucket of clay wash thrown over them by one of the workers. This '... covered them completely & served the vagabonds right' (fig.9). In the tricks he he played on his friends Snell occasion- ally went too far. One incident involved Silas Lambert who was presumably the son of his first landlord and later became a Baptist preacher. About a year earlier he had fallen desperately in love with Snell's sister Emily when she had visited Bath, although she had not the slightest interest in Lambert's advances. Snell,

Fig.9 Ragamuffins outside the Newark Foundry wall being doused with a bucket of clay wash by a foundry worker.

118

however, seeing the potential for a practical joke, told Lambert that his sister was interested in him. Lambert then wrote to Emily via Snell to express his feelings for her to which Snell forged a rather unsympathetic reply. He then persuaded Lambert not to give up and write again. The next letter forged by Snell was a much warmer one, encouraging Lambert to begin a correspondence lasting three months, the latter blissfully unaware that all the replies were written by Snell. Eventually things got so serious that Snell concocted a letter from an imaginary rival in the hope of discouraging Lambert. This failed and when Lambert started talking about visiting Mrs Snell in Barnstaple to request Emily's hand in marriage Snell was obliged to tell him the truth. As a result Silas became sick and refused to speak to Snell for six months before shaking hands and making up. Snell's recounting of the tale suggests that he was ashamed of the whole episode and the act of describing it in detail in the diary seems to have served as a form of absolution.

Perhaps not surprisingly, given the high proportion of females to males in Bath at that time,[34] Snell enjoyed the company of a number of young women. Most appear to have lodged at Mrs Thornthwaite's in Great Stanhope Street. He seems to have struck up a friendship there with a Miss Ellis, on one occasion inviting her and a Miss Baker to his new lodgings to take tea. On 22nd April he recorded calling '… to see Miss Ellis & found she was out. This is probably the last time I shall ever see her as she leaves Bath for Glamorganshire tomorrow & will not return till the winter, & before that time I shall, I expect, have quitted Bath for London'. Two days later he wrote:

> In the afternoon took a walk with a Miss [Susan] Thornthwaite to Sham Castle where she left me to flirt with a tailor and 2 counterjumpers and if I had any regard for her I should have taken offence at it. As it was it made me look rather silly and I'll warrant I don't walk her out again for some time to come …After Chaple [sic] took a walk with Miss Ellis and after I left her took another with Henrietta.

It is not known who Henrietta was, although she was evidently quite a close friend judging by his frequent use of her first name. Immediately prior to leaving Bath for Bristol he described having a 'parting interview with Henrietta too and left her like Niobe all tears but at length comforted her with a promise of seeing her again. NB she's deceived though'. At times he seems to behave remarkably freely with his female friends and acquaintances, although it is difficult to judge the extent to which this was out of the ordinary without knowing the precise circumstances surrounding these relationships or the backgrounds of the women in question. That he was not exactly shy in his dealings with the opposite sex is evident from an encounter with a young woman on the platform of Bath Station:

While there observed a nice looking girl waiting as well as myself so got into conversation with her but was soon interrupted by the arrival of the engine puff, puff, puffing away. Laid hold of her hand took her across the rails to the opposite platform, handed her in and took very good care to sit on the next seat to her. All Right – off she goes – cutting along like a sky rocket. In going through the tunnels the engine fellow set the confounded screeching whistle a going which so terrified my fair companion that I was obliged to put my arm around her waist to comfort her and being in total darkness thought there could be no harm in giving her a kiss or two but the tunnel was so confoundedly long at Brislington that by Jove I could hardly make a hundred last all the way through.

He met the 'railway maiden' twice more by chance, but did not see her again.

His life at that time was very much that of a young bachelor determined to enjoy himself to the full, which, in Bath, he was able to do. Snell's attitude to marriage reflected the popular Malthusian belief that settling down was unwise without first having accrued sufficient financial resources: 'Marriage … is a deuced expensive thing and wont suit me yet these 10 years unless some pretty young lady with a handsome fortune would be kind enough to fall in love with me and then I should have no objection to do the Hymeneal instanter'. He would later find life in Swindon very different with its initial lack of recreational and cultural facilities and the almost complete absence of unattached female company. His unhappiness with his single state would in 1847 be expressed in a poem 'The Bachelor's Complaint' written in the album of a friend, Miss Sarah King.[35] He eventually married Charlotte Elizabeth Bayley in Geelong, Victoria, on 23rd June 1853 and the couple had nine children, all but the first, Emily Charlotte, surviving to adulthood.[36]

Snell's attitude to religion was somewhat ambiguous. His parents were Nonconformists and although he was baptised in St Peter's Parish Church in Barnstaple his sisters were all christened at Cross Street Chapel.[37] While in Bath he attended a number of chapels including the Methodist Chapel on King Street (rebuilt 1847 by architect James Wilson), the Walcot Methodist Chapel, and the Argyle Chapel of the Independent Congregationalists. He seems not to have been a regular at any one chapel and on occasions was content to attend both Anglican and Roman Catholic Churches. He disliked the prevalent evangelical style of preaching and at times found the delivery of fire and brimstone sermons highly amusing (fig.10 overleaf). Nevertheless his faith was sufficiently strong to engender feelings of guilt when he was unable to attend Chapel: 'this is sad sinful work though – here I am on Sunday morning writing in this journal instead of being at Chaple. Must positively turn over a new leaf & attend more regularly'.

Fig.10 Snell's sketch of the preacher at the Welsh Independent Chapel, Bristol, delivering a fire and brimstone sermon in Welsh to a congregation of four.

However in common with many other Dissenters, including the Stotherts, Snell was very much a free-thinker and liberal, and as such was open to new ideas. At the Avonside Ironworks in Bristol he was to meet Edward Prowse (1824-62), whom Snell called 'one of the respectables'. Prowse introduced Snell to the writings of Thomas Paine and almost succeeded in converting him to deism, prompting something of a crisis of faith. In the early 1870s Snell would gain local notoriety for his conversion to spiritualism, a movement which had spread from America in the 1850s and gained popularity among the middle class and well-educated members of the working class.[38]

During his time in Bath Snell made a number of local excursions, including a two-day Whitsuntide trip to Bristol and a one-day river journey from Bath to Bristol and back. Prior to setting out on the former, Snell wrote: 'While dressing heard two fellows in the street talking very hard about starvation so has 'em in to breakfast with me and seeing one of them minus a shirt gave him one of mine'. He took the train to Bristol where he was met by an old school friend John or 'Jack' Gillard and the two embarked on a rapid tour of the city's churches. After dinner they took a walk around St Vincent's Rocks, Snell commenting that 'the weather was intensely hot and brought out the Bristolians in their finest toggery like butterflies'. The next morning he got up early and walked to Cook's Folly where he pulled out his telescope and obtained views of Denny [Island] and the Monmouthshire Hills. He sketched the view towards Bristol including the abutments of the incomplete Clifton Suspension Bridge, as well as the view in the other direction toward the Bristol Channel. After breakfast he went down to Cumberland Basin to see the shipping, catching a glimpse of the 'Mammoth', the 'large Iron steamer building by Acraman' that was later to be named the *Great Britain*.[39] He talked his way onto an old steam packet, the *Nora Creina*, and also got on board the *Queen* and the *Hero*, observing 'I am certain I learnt more of Marine engineering from inspecting those two or three steamers than I should from reading Tredgold in a month'.

In the afternoon he visited Bristol Zoo, noting 'The collection of animals is not very extensive, but they are all kept in capital order'. He also had a ride on an elephant: 'The Elephant was brought out into the lawn and I had a ride on his back which was as rough as a hedge and his <u>walk</u> was nearly as fast as I can <u>run</u>' (fig.11).

Fig.11 Snell riding an elephant at Bristol Zoo

The next day back in Bath he got up at six and went with two foundry mates Bill and Fred Glass to a boathouse near Bathampton to fetch a rowing boat. They rowed down to Pulteney Bridge and after lifting the boat over the weir proceeded to Dredge's suspension bridge (see fig.8) where they stopped for breakfast at Snell's lodgings. Back on the river they passed through the various locks arriving at the outskirts of Bristol by about 2.00pm (fig.12).[40]

Fig.12 Fred and Bill Glass with Edward Snell (at the oars) among the shipping in Bristol while on a 'pull' from Bath to Bristol, Whitsun 1842.

Reaching a point near Temple Meads Snell recorded that:

> Every thing now was subject of wonder & astonishment to Fred Glass [who had never been to Bristol]; the height of the chimneys, the hum of machinery, and the glimpses we got of Engines at work & wheels in motion through the windows of the various factories were constantly subjects of remark, but when we got into the thick of it he was surprised indeed. We had a narrow escape of getting crushed through passing a bridge at the same time as a large Iron barge but luckily escaped without accident. This bit of a job gave Bill Glass the horrors again and he became as nervous as a Toad under a harrow...

On the way back they got into trouble for avoiding the toll at Hanham locks, the irate lockkeeper chasing them for six miles before eventually giving up and treating them '... to a tolerable sample of Bristol abuse'. They got back to Bath at midnight, Snell reckoning he had rowed '... 45 miles ...[and that he was] cold, wet and almost fatigued to death'.

On 18th May 1842 he received a message from Henry Stothert telling him to get himself to Bristol ready for work at the Avonside Ironworks on the following Monday. Snell duly set off on the back of a waggon, noting: 'This was my first removal from Bath and I may say MY FIRST STEP IN LIFE'. The Avonside Ironworks was established in 1837 by Henry Stothert on Avon Street in the industrial area of the city, St Philip's.[41] This heavy engineering works specialised in the production of stationary and marine engines as well as locomotives such as those supplied to the Great Western Railway between 1841-2.[42] Snell hoped to procure a position as a draughtsman but was instead put to work in the erecting shop. After the more relaxed and friendly atmosphere at Newark Foundry he took an immediate dislike to the gruff manner of the managing engineer Edward Slaughter, who became a partner in the firm in 1840, and particularly to what he viewed as his tyrannical management style, which included a severe system of rules, regulations and fines. He wrote: 'By Jove Rayno was right when he told me I should find a difference when I went into another shop and I should never have believed had I not seen it that in 'Happy England' tyranny was carried to so great an extent'. Leaving after just three weeks in protest at the regime and low wages (20 shillings per week) he returned home to North Devon where he stayed until February 1843. He was unemployed during this period except for a short spell as a 'quill driver' (clerk) at a bank in Barnstaple. His rapid departure from the Avonside Ironworks resulted in a 'blowing up' from both Henry and George Stothert. However the latter used his influence with Daniel Gooch, the Locomotive Superintendent of the Great Western Railway, to obtain a position for Snell at the Swindon Works on 28th February 1843. Apart from a four-month stint at Penn's marine engineering works in Greenwich in 1844 Snell remained with the GWR at Swindon until 18th May 1849, by which time he had become deputy works manager in charge of several hundred men and with responsibility for a major new building campaign. When the GWR sought to cut his pay during the post railway mania crash of 1848-9 he left and decided to emigrate. Having settled on the United States he changed his mind at the last minute and instead sailed with his friend Prowse for Australia.

His adventures on the voyage out and his life in Australia and on the Victorian gold diggings are vividly recounted in the published Australian diary (see note 2) the original manuscript of which is now rightly regarded as one of the treasures of the State Library of Victoria. Snell was subsequently appointed Surveyor for the Melbourne-Geelong Railway and built a large railway works at the Geelong terminus. Although he was to make his fortune from this appointment, enough in fact not to have to work for the rest of his life, the post exposed his short-comings as an engineer.[43] Under something of a cloud he sailed with his family for England in 1858, where he settled in Saltash and died there in 1880 aged 59.

Snell's English diary offers fresh insights into the true nature of life for many of Bath's inhabitants in the 1840s. His account of a busy working life is strikingly at odds with the usual descriptions of genteel Bath society, and reflects the changing nature of the city at that time. It puts flesh on the bones of the histories of the period in a way that amounts to a veritable goldmine for the social historian. Above all it is the personal and highly entertaining story of an articulate young artisan eager to make his way in the world. That it is told with wry humour and illustrated by such amusing sketches, at times approaching caricature, only adds to its appeal.

Notes

1   The more detailed of the two paintings forms part of the collection of Swindon Museum, Bath Road, Old Town, Swindon. The other version is a slightly later copy held by STEAM: The Museum of The Great Western Railway, Kemble Drive, Swindon. For an account of the origins of the two paintings see John Cattell and Keith Falconer, *Swindon: The Legacy of a Railway Town* (HMSO, 1995; revised ed, English Heritage, Swindon, 2000).

2   The 1842-49 diary (the English diary) is in the possession of Snell's great grand-daughter and is being edited for publication by the author of this article. The diary is 253 pages long and is 8" x 8" square with cloth boards. The 1849-59 diary (the Australian diary) was lavishly published by Angus & Robertson in 1988 with an excellent introduction. Edward Snell, *The Life and Adventures of Edward Snell: The illustrated diary of an artist, engineer and adventurer in the Australian Colonies 1849 to 1859*, edited and introduced by Tom Griffiths with assistance from Alan Platt (Angus & Robertson, North Ryde, NSW, 1988). The diary was purchased in 1935 by the State Library of Victoria, Melbourne, from a book dealer in Exeter (information from file in Bath Reference Library, accession no. D802236, class B620.0092).

3   Edward Snell, *The Life and Adventures …*, pp. 408-9 includes a family tree with details of Snell's ancestors.

4   North Devon Record Office (NDRO), Barnstaple Parish Registers.

5   NDRO, Index of Barnstaple wills, ref. S 986.

6   Hugh Torrens, *The Evolution of a Family Firm: Stothert and Pitt of Bath* (Stothert & Pitt Ltd, Bath, 1978), p.2. See the detailed account of the origins of the Stothert ironmongery and engineering businesses.

7   *Ibid.*, p.23.

8   For a description and plans of the Newark Foundry see Mike Chapman and Elizabeth Holland, 'Stothert's Foundry, Southgate Street, Bath', *BIAS Journal*, 30 (1998), pp.34-38.

9   Torrens, *op.cit.*, p.26.

10 *Ibid.*, p.32. Following Rayno's retirement in 1855 the firm Stothert, Rayno and Pitt became Stothert & Pitt, the name by which the firm is still known. Pitt and Snell were fellow apprentices at the Newark Foundry in the late 1830s-early 1840s.

11 Chapman and Holland, *op.cit.*, pp.35-36.

12 It is not clear whether this refers to the GWR tunnel at Bathwick or the Kennet & Avon Canal tunnel west of Sydney Gardens.

13 *Royal National and Commercial Directory and Topography* (Pigot & Co., London and Manchester, 1842).

14 L. T. C. Rolt, *Isambard Kingdom Brunel* (Penguin edn, Harmondsworth, 1974), pp.95-96.

15 There is no mention of a mill of this name in trade directories although a William Watson, baker and flour dealer, is listed in the *Bath Directory* (Silverstone, Bath, 1841). One elevation of the mill adjoined the river.

16 K. H. Rogers, *Wiltshire and Somerset Woollen Mills* (Edington, Wilts., 1976), p.171. See also Nicholas von Behr, 'The Cloth Industry of Twerton from the 1780s to the 1820s', *Bath History*, Vol. VI (Millstream Books, Bath, 1996), pp.88-107.

17 The Barrett mentioned by Snell may have been James Barrett, Old Crown Inn and Millwright, Twerton, *Hunt & Co.'s Directory and Court Guide for the Cities of Bath, Bristol & Wells* (1848).

18 Thomas Tredgold, *The Steam Engine, its invention and progressive improvement. An investigation of its principles and its application to Navigation, Manufactures and Railways* (revised and enlarged edn with a section on Steam Naval Architecture, edited by W. S. B. Woolhouse, 2 vols., John Weale, 1838).

19 The Newbury job may have been for the Kennet & Avon Canal Company, the Stothert's having connections with the canal from the late eighteenth century, Torrens, *op.cit.*, p.11 ff.

20 Despite this comment about Rayno the two men enjoyed a cordial relationship. On return trips to Bath Snell often called at the foundry to talk to Rayno and the two travelled to Swindon together on Snell's first day at the GWR Works.

21 Snell makes no mention of the cost of his accommodation in Bath but for a week's lodgings at 21 Langton Street in Bristol in May 1842 he paid 13 shillings.

22 For more information on Stothert's business interests in Wales see Torrens, *op.cit.*, pp.31-32.

23 *The Bath Directory* (Silverstone, Bath, 1837).

24 This terrace survives largely intact although its street elevation is much altered.

25 Snell was also fascinated by his fellow lodgers in the Swindon railway village and made a number of amusing sketches of them in his diary.

26 Henry Stothert was responsible for a number of engineering works at the Hot Baths in the 1830s, for an account of which see Torrens, *op.cit.*, pp.30-31.

27 For more on Gully see J. S. Gully, *New Zealand's Romantic Landscape: paintings by John Gully* (Wellington, New Zealand, 1984).

28 Philip Gully was staying at the house of William Stothert, the retired ironmonger and brother of Henry, at the time of the 1841 census.

29 See Graham Davis and Penny Bonsall, *Bath: A New History* (Keele University Press, Keele, 1996), pp.87-114.

30 R. S. Neale, *Bath 1680-1850: A Social History or a Valley of Pleasure, yet a Sink of Iniquity* (Routledge & Kegan Paul, London, Boston and Henley, 1981), p.347.

31 Torrens, *op.cit.*, p.26; *Royal National and Commercial Directory and Topography* (Pigot & Co., London and Manchester, 1842).

32 Davis and Bonsall, *op.cit.*, p.128.

33 William and Frederick Glass are listed as engineers and millwrights, 36 Thomas Street in Hunt & Co.'s *Directory and Court Guide for the Cities of Bath, Bristol & Wells* (1848). The brothers accompanied Snell on a boat trip down the Avon to Bristol and back.

34 Davis and Bonsall, *op.cit.*, p.69.

35 This album, which has only recently come to light, includes a number of poems by Snell and his sisters. Private collection.

36 Marriage certificate in family papers; Edward Snell, *The Life and Adventures* ..., pp.408-9.

37 NDRO, Barnstaple Parish Registers, Baptisms, 1813-1979; Edward Snell, *The Life and Adventures* ..., p.xi.

38 Edward Snell, *The Life and Adventures* ..., p.xii; S. F. Cooper and P. Atterbury, 'Religion and Doubt', in John M. MacKenzie ed., *The Victorian Vision: Inventing New Britain* (V & A Publications, 2001), p.142.

39 Snell's reference on 16th May 1842 to the *Great Britain* being built by Acraman's is perplexing, since according to Charles Wells, *A Short History of the Port of Bristol* (Arrowsmith, Bristol, 1909), p.76, the Great Western Steamship directors built the *Great Britain* in their 'own yard at Wapping [Bristol] because "no existing" ship-builders in the port would tender for the construction of an iron ship nearly three times the capacity of the *Great Western*'. In fact the directors had to provide a yard for this purpose at a cost of £52,000. Snell's attribution is therefore erroneous or refers to some works (the fitting of the engine perhaps?) by Acraman's as sub-contractors. The ship was launched on 19th July 1843, Snell obtaining time off work to attend the event.

40 For the history of the Avon Navigation see Brenda J. Buchanan, 'The Avon Navigation and the Inland Port of Bath', *Bath History*, Vol. VI (Millstream Books, Bath, 1996), pp.63-87.

41 For an account of the Avonside Ironworks see John Cattell, 'Avonside Ironworks, Bristol', *BIAS Journal*, 30 (1998), pp.13-24.

42 In 1842 Stothert & Slaughter supplied 'fixed engines' for the new locomotive works at Swindon, Cattell and Falconer, *op.cit.*, p.27. See also Torrens, *op.cit.*, p.39.

43 Edward Snell, *The Life and Adventures* ..., pp.xx-xxi.

Acknowledgements

I would like to thank the following who have kindly assisted with the preparation of this article: Dr Brenda Buchanan, Gilly Burrough, Keith Falconer, Professor R. Angus Buchanan, James O. Davies, Peter Williams and Ian Leonard.

WILLIAM BECKFORD AND FONTHILL ABBEY : A VICTORIAN SHOWMAN'S ACCOUNT

Steven Blake

Travelling shows were a familiar sight in Britain's towns and cities throughout the nineteenth century – everything from menageries to waxworks, and including such oddities as 'the pig-faced lady', a whale's skeleton and a troupe of 'industrious fleas'.[1] One of the largest and, in its day, best known, was John Bellamy's British Model Gallery, a collection of cork and card models of historic British buildings that toured the country in a number of caravans between 1837 and 1893. The models, which were on a scale of one tenth or one twelfth of an inch to one foot, were the work of a Gloucestershire-born model maker and travelling showman named John Bellamy (1808-93). Unusually for such individuals, Bellamy wrote an account of his life, which contains considerable detail about his own career as well as information about many of his contemporaries, including William Beckford.[2]

Bellamy's memoirs record that after an early career in agriculture and domestic service he began making models for sale, and then staged his first public exhibition of models at Southampton in March 1834. The exhibits comprised Queen's Lodge in Bushey Park (the residence of King William IV while Duke of Clarence) and Netley Abbey in Hampshire, models which he had made in 1831-2 and 1833-4 respectively, plus other models borrowed from purchasers of his work in the Southampton area. During 1834-6 Bellamy added another five models to his collection, and his second exhibition was held at Cheltenham during June and July 1836. The additional models were Raglan Castle, Flaxley Abbey, Tintern Abbey, Cheltenham's Pittville Pump Room and Fonthill Abbey, the latter being described in an advertisement for the exhibition in the *Cheltenham Free Press* for 25 June 1836 as 'that splendid and most magnificent edifice … as it appeared previous to the falling of the High Tower'. The advertisement claimed that 'the above models have been inspected by Sir Geoffry [sic] Wyattville and Mr Nash, Architects to the Royal Family, and are pronounced by them and other scientific gentlemen to be the most accurate and beautiful specimens in the kingdom', and that the Fonthill model, which was on a scale of one tenth of an inch to one foot, had taken Bellamy twelve months to make. In order to create his models, Bellamy certainly visited each of the buildings, although in the case of Fonthill he also had to rely on published views to recreate the tower and central part of the building, which had collapsed in 1825.

During the winter of 1836-7, while his collection was being shown in one of the upper rooms at Cheltenham's Pittville Pump Room, Bellamy modelled Berkeley Castle. He also had two caravans built to house and transport his collection, which opened at Gloucester in May 1837. He was to tour his exhibition throughout Britain for the next half century, and by February 1845, when it arrived in Bath, the British Model Gallery had already travelled over 900 miles and had been shown in at least sixty-five different towns in the Midlands and southern England. Models of the castles at Dudley, Kenilworth, Goodrich and Warwick were added to the collection in 1837-9, and in 1841 Bellamy began work on the exhibition's *tour de force* – a model of Windsor Castle, which, though still incomplete (lacking St. George's Chapel), was included in the exhibition by the time of its second visit to Bath, in 1847. Heralded in Bellamy's handbills as 'the greatest achievement of the nineteenth century', the Windsor Castle model eventually measured 90 square feet and had no less than 2,128 windows.

Bellamy's exhibition was shown in the Royal Victoria Park, Bath in both 1845 and 1847. It first opened on 5 February 1845 on a site 'adjoining the Park Dairy' and remained there until early September, when it left for a sixteen-month stay at Clifton. It reopened at Bath on 1 January 1847 and stood 'opposite the Upper Gate, Victoria Park', also described in Bellamy's memoirs as 'at the bottom of the High Common on the Weston Road', until late June or early July, when it moved on to Trowbridge.[3] On both occasions the exhibition was open from 10 a.m. to 9 p.m. daily, admission one shilling, with a reduction to sixpence for children and servants. Handbills for the exhibition were produced, and a copy of one of these, for his 1847 visit to Bath, is now in the John Johnson Collection at the Bodleian Library in Oxford (fig.1 overleaf). Although this handbill fails to list his model of the Pittville Pump Room (which one must presume was still included in the exhibition), it does provide evidence that further models had been added by then, including Godstow Nunnery and Cumnor Place, both near Oxford.

During both visits to Bath, the exhibition was advertised, and received some editorial coverage, in the local press. On 19 March 1845, the *Bath and Cheltenham Gazette* noted of the models that,

> As mere works of art they may be pronounced unique, while for fidelity to nature they are deserving the highest admiration. The crumbling wall, the 'ivy-mantled tower', the graceful slender arched window, the spacious hall, the massive donjon and the 'glassy moat' are all brought before the eye as faithfully as in a visit to the ruins of some time worn specimens of departed strength and beauty which are scattered throughout our land.

FOR A LIMITED PERIOD.

The Greatest Achievement of the Nineteenth Century is
Bellamy's Stupendous Cork Model
OF
WINDSOR CASTLE:

Its Court Yard, State Entrance, Sovereign's Entrance, St. George's Hall, Corridor, the magnificent Keep or Round Tower, Norman Gateway, the Winchester, Henry the III's, Edward the III's, York, Lancaster, Augusta, Victoria, Clarence, Chester, Prince of Wales', Brunswick, Cornwall, George the IV's, and King John's Towers; State and Private Apartments; Castle Hill, Slopes, Terraces, Gardens, Statues, Fountain, &c., &c.

Mr. BELLAMY respectfully intimates to the Nobility, Gentry, and Public of Bath and its Vicinity that after SIX YEARS indefatigable study he has completed the above GIGANTIC MODEL, which is without parallel in the three Kingdoms, a task in itself so herculean never before attempted.

From the very distinguished patronage which he was honoured with during his visit to Bath two years since, he has been induced to open his Exhibition again for a limited period, feeling assured that the addition to his Collection of a Model of a building of such vast national and historical importance, will afford the highest gratification to those who may be pleased to honour him with their patronage.

Mr. Bellamy would state that the above ELABORATELY FINISHED MODEL has been executed from drawings and actual measurements of the Castle taken by himself with especial permission; in order to give some idea of the Grandeur of this Model, it may not be out of place in stating that the surface of the frame on which it stands exceeds 70 square feet, being executed on a scale of 1-10 of an inch to a foot. The Royal Pile and Terraces, to which in every particular this Splendid Model conveys the mind, stands on more than twenty-four acres of land, it is the largest and by far the most

Majestic Castellated Palace

in the known world; containing, as represented in this chef-d'œuvre of modelling, 1428 WINDOWS, executed with that precision as to set criticism at defiance.

Antiquities of Windsor Castle.

During a period of nearly 800 years, Windsor Castle has been distinguished as the most favored residence of the Sovereigns of England. Tradition has assigned its origin to King Arthur, and assembled here the Knights of the Round Table. The earliest authentic notice of Windsor occurs in the reign of Edward the Confessor, who granted Wyndleshore with all its appurtenances to the Abbot of Westminster; it was however re-annexed to the Crown property in the first year of William the Conqueror. It is not until the reign of Henry the First, by whom it was entirely rebuilt, that Windsor Castle assumes any importance in History, and from this period it becomes conspicuous as a Royal Residence, and as one of the principal fortresses of the kingdom.

To enter into a lengthened account of the Antiquities of this interesting Castle, and the many remarkable occurrences connected with a building of such vast importance, is past the limits of a bill.

THE COLLECTION ALSO COMPRISES CORK MODELS OF

Warwick Castle.

Including the Mount, the Court Yard, and the River Avon. This Model contains 350 Windows.

Ruins of Kenilworth Castle.

Embracing Mervyn's Tower, in which Amie Robsart was concealed, Lun's Tower, Mortimer's Tower, and the surrounding Walls.

Ruins of Ragland Castle,

Monmouthshire, the property of His Grace the Duke of Beaufort.

Ruins of Dudley Castle,

Worcestershire, the property of Lord Ward.

Flaxley Abbey,

Gloucestershire, the residence of Sir Thomas Crawley Beovey.

Ruins of Goodrich Castle,

Near Ross, Herefordshire.

Ruins of Netley Abbey,

Near Southampton.

Goodstow Abbey, Cumner Place, &c., near Oxford,

Berkeley Castle,

Gloucestershire, the residence of Lord Segrave, which is the most ancient and perfect Castle in the kingdom.

To the correctness of this Model, the following is Earl Fitz-Hardinge's testimonial;—

"Cheltenham, April 3rd, 1837.
"I have examined, with great satisfaction Mr. Bellamy's Model of Berkeley Castle, it is most correct both in detail and proportion.
"SEGRAVE."

Bushy Park, Middlesex,

Residence of the Queen Dowager. This Model has been inspected by Her Majesty the Queen Dowager, and His late Majesty King William the IV, which obtained their patronage.

Ruins of Tintern Abbey,

Monmouthshire, which is one of the most magnificent Ruins in the kingdom.

Fonthill Abbey,

Near Salisbury, as it appeared before the falling of the High Tower

Open daily from TEN until NINE, at the
BRITISH MODEL GALLERY, Opposite THE UPPER GATE, VICTORIA PARK.
Admission to the whole 1s.; Children & Servants half-price.

*** The Exhibition Room will be found well aired, as fires are constantly kept.

Fig.1 Handbill for Bellamy's exhibition at Bath, 1847.
(reproduced by courtesy of the Bodleian Library, University of Oxford: John Johnson Collection; Dioramas 1)

Bellamy's memoirs include some comment on his 1845 visit to Bath, where he 'did pretty well most of the time. Nearly all the Nobility and Gentry of Bath visited the Exhibition. Fine afternoons we were generally busy, but rainy days, nothing to do, as the Bath people are very fussy, always afraid of taking colds'. Visitors to the exhibition were provided with a magnifying glass with which to study the models, and might also be given an historical account of the various buildings, by Bellamy himself. While reporting a visit to the exhibition at Wolverhampton in 1850, for example, a reporter for the *Wolverhampton Chronicle* assured its readers that 'an intelligent *cicerone*, we can promise, will be found in the proprietor of the exhibition. With the historical events and architectural details connected with the models shown he is thoroughly acquainted'.

Some idea of the information that visitors might have received about the Fonthill Abbey model may be found in the only published catalogue of the exhibition to have come to light, for a showing at Glasgow's Egyptian Hall in 1873.[4] The catalogue provides a numerical list of the principal parts of the building at Fonthill, implying perhaps that the model itself was numbered in some way. The twelve features listed were : 'The Oratory, or Chapel; King Edward's Gallery; Great Octagon Tower, 270 feet high; The Grand Entrance to the Hall; The Cloisters; St. Michael's Gallery; Oak Dining-room; The Grand Drawing-room; The Entrance to the south end of the Building; The Baronial Hall Windows; The Octagon Turrets, 120 feet high, copied from St. Augustin's [sic] Gateway at Canterbury; Kitchen Yard'. The catalogue also provides a descriptive account of the building, which reads as follows:

> This magnificent Abbey was built by the late William Beckford, Esq., as his private residence; he was the only son of William Beckford, Esq., who was twice Lord Mayor of London, in 1763 and again in 1769, and great-grandfather of the present Duke of Hamilton. After the death of his father he became the richest commoner in England. In 1795 he commenced the building of Fonthill Abbey by erecting a high wall six miles in extent round the park, with lodge-gates at each entrance, through which no strangers were allowed to pass within the estate. The building of the Abbey was continued so rapidly, that in November, 1800, nearly 500 men were employed to expedite the work by day and by torch-light at night; at one time 450 men were taken from the works of Windsor Castle to work at Fonthill, the building of which is said to have cost Mr. Beckford upwards of £300,000. It was universally acknowledged to be the most magnificent private residence in the kingdom of modern erection. The paintings and furnishing decorations of the interior were

more costly and excelled in splendour any of the royal palaces. In 1822 he sold the Abbey and its valuable contents to John Farquhar Esq. On December 21, 1825, the great tower fell, which destroyed all the centre of the building. Soon after the falling of the tower Mr. Farquhar sold the remains of the Abbey and the estate to John Bennett, Esq., M.P. for Wiltshire. The Marquis of Westminster is now the owner of the estate; he has removed nearly the whole of the remains of the Abbey.

Fig.2 Model of Fonthill Abbey, completed by Michael Bishop in 1981, now vested in the Bath Preservation Trust as sole trustee of the Beckford Tower Trust, by whom the model was commissioned. (*reproduced by courtesy of Michael Bishop*)

John Bellamy appears to have had a particular interest in Beckford and Fonthill, for of all the models it is the only one to have a full account within his memoirs, including many personal details about Beckford, gleaned, at least in part, from stories about the man and his buildings that Bellamy had heard during his travels. As a previously unknown contemporary account of one of Bath's most celebrated residents, his account of Beckford is worth quoting in full.[5] Bellamy notes that he had visited Fonthill during the summer of 1834 and had begun work on the model during the winter of 1834-5, while staying with relatives in Birmingham. He wrote in his memoirs that,

> … the centre part of the building was all gone. When the great tower fell some years before, it carried all the middle part down with it. Fonthill Abbey was built by William Beckford Esq. It was one of the grandest places in England. It is said to have cost three hundred thousand in building. Mr. Beckford first built a wall 16 feet high, six miles in circumference round the Park with Lodges to prevent any persons getting in except the workmen employed. When finished George the Fourth sent to him saying he should like to see the Abbey. Mr. Beckford sent him an answer that when he made a show of his house, His Majesty was welcome to see it. I was anxious to get a model of such a noted place. The middle part of the Abbey I made from architectural drawings. Mr. Bennett at Liverpool have got that model with my old collection.
>
> Fonthill Abbey is situated near Hindon, Wiltshire, sixteen miles from Salisbury. Mr Beckford was the son of Alderman Beckford of London, a great slave owner in Jamaica. After he had built Fonthill his income became greatly reduced in consequence of the Government emancipation of the slaves in Jamaica. He said the paltry sum that the Government granted him for the loss of his slaves was not enough to keep up his establishment at Fonthill. It was now offered for sale with its contents, which was of the most costly description. During the early part of his life he lived abroad, where he collected everything that was rare in paintings, cabinets, china and all things of vertu. All this was arranged in Fonthill Abbey, but the things he prized most he removed to Bath. There was loads of valuable things brought down from London by the auctioneers in place of them. The catalogues of the sale were one guinea each and no one was admitted to see the Abbey without one. This set all the fashionable world mad to see this wonderful Fonthill. People flocked from all parts abroad. All had to travel by coach or post horse. All the towns within miles of the Abbey was filled with sightseers.

Beds let at a guinea a night each and everything else in proportion. The sale of Fonthill caused more consternation than any sale ever known in this Kingdom. A rich stock-broker the name of Farquar [sic] ultimately bought the Abbey and Estate. Gave an enormous sum for it and soon after he bought it the centre tower fell, destroying all the centre of the building. The tower was 270 feet high. At the time it fell Mr. Beckford lived in Lansdown Crescent, Bath. He had two houses in the Crescent, with a roadway between them, and a passage under the road from one to the other. His servants lived in one house and he at the other. He also had a beautiful garden and pleasure ground on the top of Lansdown Hill, and a tower with splendid rooms in it, in which he spent a deal of his time. From the top of this tower, on a clear day, he could see Fonthill Abbey which stood on a hill nearly four hundred feet above the level of the sea. It so happened that the day the Fonthill tower fell he went to the top of his tower on Lansdown and missed the Fonthill tower, when he exclaimed, by Jove, it's down at last. I would have given any money to have seen it come down. I was sure it would fall. It made curtseys in my time and now it has bowed down.

Beckford was one of the most eccentric men of his day. He was author of many works, was very charitable. At Bath he subscribed almost to every charitable cause. His £50 or £100 could always be depended on, but never put his name on the list. He was said to be the proudest man living. He always prided himself as acting like a Prince in all his movements. He resided at Bath all the later part of his life. When walking about Bath he always had two menservants walking behind him and several dogs, carried a sort of huntsman's whip in hand. If anything took his fancy in the shops he would take it. The shopkeeper had to send the bill for it, price was not asked. He was a great man for flowers. If he saw any new sort of flower in the seed shops he would pluck it off and put in his coat, if it destroyed the sale of the plant it did not matter to him, the seedsman had only to send the bill for it. While building Fonthill it was said he never looked over the bills at the different items, only the sum total, and paid it. When I was at Andover in 1844 with my Exhibition, the landlord at the Star Hotel told me that Mr. Beckford, on his way to London, always stayed to breakfast at the Star. He always travelled with four horses to his carriage, with an out rider in advance and two footmen behind, altogether five men in attendance. He always brought a large hamper of delicacies from Fonthill. This was set out on a sideboard and the landlord always provided the choicest things he could from London for his breakfast. Sometimes he would partake entirely of what he brought. No bill must be given in. After he had left, the landlord would find a £10 note on the table for the breakfast of himself and servants. Many years before his death he had his tomb made of an enormous block of red granite in which a space was made for his coffin to fit in. Over the coffin another large block of granite was fixed which formed the lid, with pillars at each corner. It was all of polished granite. This tomb was fixed in his pleasure ground at the tower on Lansdown Hill, where he intended his remains to lie.

He died at his residence at Bath. His daughter, the Duchess of Hamilton, was prevented carrying out his wishes in placing his remains in the pleasure ground as the ground was not consecrated, therefore she had the tomb removed to Bathwick Cemetery where he lay a few years. In the meantime the tower and ground were sold by auction. An inn keeper in Bath bid for it and as there was not many bidders, it was knocked down to him at half its worth, but he was in a fix to know what to do with it. In fact he did not want it, however he decided to open it as Tea Gardens for pleasure parties, entertainment etc., which came to the knowledge of the Duchess of Hamilton who was quite upset to think of her father's favourite place should be turned to such a purpose. She now appointed a person to make the publican an offer for it and she succeeded in getting possession of it again by paying a good price for it, she then gave it to the city of Bath on condition that it was converted into a Cemetery, which was done. She then removed the body and the tomb from Bathwick Cemetery to the tower on Lansdown Hill.

The Duchess of Hamilton herself is known to have been among the visitors to the exhibition, in either 1837 or 1838, for Bellamy records in his memoirs that 'it was at Leamington that the Duchess of Hamilton, daughter of Mr. Beckford of Fonthill Abbey came, accompanied by a Mr. Hamilton. While looking at the Fonthill model and pointing out the windows belonging to certain rooms, Mr. Hamilton made the remark "this model, Duchess, must bring to your recollection many things". She replied, "indeed it does. Some very pleasant and others distressing to think of"'.

Bellamy's exhibition continued to grow steadily after 1847. The Windsor Castle model was completed, with the addition of St. George's Chapel, by 1851, on 28 April of which year the collection was viewed at Windsor by Queen Victoria and Prince Albert, following which Bellamy renamed his exhibition the Royal Model Gallery. The Royal family revisited the exhibition

Fig.3 Queen Victoria, Prince Albert and members of the Royal household visiting Bellamy's exhibition at Windsor, 1857. (*anonymous pencil drawing, reproduced by courtesy of Mrs Pat Fairfax*)

on 9 November 1857, an event that has given us our only view of the entrance to the exhibition, in an anonymous pencil drawing (fig.3). By then the exhibition occupied five caravans and in 1860 these were adapted for travel by rail, so that Bellamy was able to reach increasing numbers of destinations each year, although there is no evidence that he ever revisited Bath. Further models were certainly added to the exhibition, and no less than thirty-two different models have been identified from surviving handbills, catalogues and newspaper advertisements.

The model of Fonthill Abbey remained part of Bellamy's exhibition until sometime between 1878 and 1881, when, along with seventeen other models, it was sold to William Bennett of Heysham Tower in Lancashire. According to his obituary in the *Gloucester Journal* for 28 January 1893, Bellamy 'afterwards made a smaller collection and travelled through the west of England, and had been in Wales for the last twelve months, still travelling, though in very delicate health'. He died at Cardiff, in his caravan, on 14 January 1893, and was buried six days later at Westbury on Severn, in west Gloucestershire, where members of his family had lived since the seventeenth century. The burial register entry records him as 'John Bellamy who for many years past has travelled the Country with Architectural Models made of cork, and is said to have been the oldest showman in England'.[6]

Fig.4 Bellamy's card model of the Pittville Pump Room, Cheltenham, 1835. (*reproduced by courtesy of Cheltenham Art Gallery & Museum*)

Sadly, none of the models purchased by William Bennett, including that of Fonthill Abbey, appear to have survived. In 1882-4, Bennett donated them to the Walker Art Gallery at Liverpool, of which city he was an Alderman, and although the models were audited in 1917 they can no longer be traced and are assumed to have been destroyed during the Second World War.[7] A number of others have, however, survived, including that of the Pittville Pump Room, which is now in Cheltenham Art Gallery & Museum (fig.4). Made of card in 1835, it is the only model that was included in the two Bath exhibitions that has yet been located, although neither Queen's Lodge nor Flaxley Abbey were sold to Alderman Bennett, so they too might just have survived somewhere. So far, ten models that may confidently be attributed to John Bellamy have been located, in public or private collections, but there must have been many more, as he undertook private commissions and made models for sale or raffle throughout his career.[8] One can only hope that, one day, more might come to light, to add further to the story of 'the oldest showman in England'.[9]

136

Notes

For background information on travelling shows in general, see Thomas Frost, *Old Showmen and the Old London Fairs* (1874); Edward Bostock, *Menageries, Circuses and Theatres* (Chapman & Hall, 1927); Richard Altick, *The Shows of London* (Harvard University Press, Cambridge, Mass., 1978) and David Kerr Cameron, *The English Fair* (Sutton Publishing, Stroud, 1998).

I am most grateful to Mrs Pat Fairfax for kindly providing access to, and permission to quote from, Bellamy's manuscript memoirs, on which much of this account is based. I would also like to record my thanks to Mrs Fairfax, and to Mrs Marion Hodson, for access to other relevant material, and for their help and encouragement during my research into John Bellamy's career. In order to assist modern readers, quotations from the memoirs have been punctuated, something which is completely lacking in the original manuscript, and Bellamy's poor spelling and erratic use of capital letters has been corrected. Additional information about Bellamy's career has been obtained from a small number of surviving handbills and exhibition catalogues, and from extensive searches through the British provincial press between 1837 and 1893. Comparable published autobiographies of travelling showmen include David Prince Miller, *The Life of a Showman to which is added Managerial Struggles* (1849); G. Van Hare, *Fifty Years of a Showman's Life or The Life and travels of Van Hare by Himself* (W. H. Allen, 1888) and George Sanger, *70 Years a Showman* (C. A. Pearson, 1914).

.   For the history of the Royal Victoria Park, see Robin Whalley, 'The Royal Victoria Park', *Bath History*, Vol.V (Millstream Books, Bath, 1994), pp.147-169, which includes plans of the Park in 1829 and 1879. The article also reproduces a photograph (*c*.1900) of the surviving Park Farm, near the Victoria Gate, which is titled 'The Dairy Victoria Park, Bath'. Bellamy's exhibition must have stood close to here in 1845. The location of the exhibition in 1847 appears to have been on the High Commons, opposite the Upper or Weston Road Gate to the Park. A map of Bath in the 1840s, including the Park, may be found on page 112.

Catalogue in the possession of Mrs Marion Hodson.

Modern published accounts of William Beckford (1760-1844) include James Lees-Milne, *William Beckford* (Compton Russell, Tisbury, 1976); Brian Fothergill, *Beckford of Fonthill* (Faber & Faber, 1979) and Timothy Mowl, *William Beckford. Composing for Mozart* (John Murray, 1998). Beckford's Bath connections, including an account of the purchase of his two houses in Lansdown Crescent, the building of Beckford's Tower and the laying out of the connecting gardens, are discussed in Philippa Bishop, 'Beckford in Bath', *Bath History*, Vol.II (Alan Sutton, Gloucester, 1988), pp. 85 -112. See also Jon Millington, *Beckford's Tower, Bath : an illustrated guide* (Bath Preservation Trust, Bath, 7th edition, 2002).

Westbury on Severn burials (Gloucestershire Record Office P354 IN 1/17).

Personal communication with Mr. Timothy Stevens, Director of the Walker Art Gallery, Liverpool, 1984, and confirmed by Mr. Julian Treuherz, the present Keeper of Art Galleries with the National Museums & Galleries on Merseyside, 2002.

Apart from the model of the Pittville Pump Room, several others have been located: three are in the collections of Tullie House Museum & Art Gallery, Carlisle, namely Penrith Castle Keep, the Fratry, Carlisle, and a model of a Carlisle cockpit; and six in private ownership, namely St. Martin's Church, Canterbury, the Abbot's Kitchen, Glastonbury Abbey, Holyrood Abbey, Edinburgh, and three private houses – Much Fawley Court, Herefordshire, The Cliffe at Warwick and a model labelled 'Horstway House', although no such house has been identified. Card models of Flaxley Abbey and Church, of which Bellamy is known to have produced several models, also survive in a private collection and are perhaps by Bellamy.

9   It is interesting to note that Bellamy's model was not the only one of Fonthill. An original *papier mâché* model of the Abbey, attributed to its architect, James Wyatt, still survives in a private collection and was displayed in exhibitions about Beckford in 1966 (Bath) and 1976 (Bath and Salisbury). The model is discussed and illustrated in John Wilton-Ely, 'A Model for Fonthill Abbey', in Howard Colvin & John Harris eds., *The Country Seat. Studies in the History of the British Country House* (Allen Lane: The Penguin Press, 1970), pp.199-204, and in John Wilton-Ely, 'Beckford, Fonthill Abbey and the Picturesque', in Dana Arnold ed., *The Picturesque in late Georgian England* (The Georgian Group, 1994) pp.35-44. A more recent model of the Abbey, made over two years by Michael Bishop and placed on display in Beckford's Tower in 1981, was included in the 2001-2 exhibition *William Beckford 1760-1844 : an eye for the magnificent* (New York and Dulwich); a photograph of Mr. Bishop's model is shown as fig.2 on p.130.

WALTER RICHARD SICKERT (1860-1942) PAINTER OF THE BATH SCENE

Philippa Bishop

During his long career as a painter Sickert twice visited Bath. The second occasion was in 1938, immediately before the outbreak of war, when as an old man he came with his wife Thérèse Lessore to spend his final years here. The first occasion was twenty years earlier, towards the end of another war, during the summers of 1917 and 1918. Already by then he had reached his late fifties, with a substantial reputation and a body of work that encompassed a variety of subjects. He was known for his penetrating character studies, which made him sought after as a portraitist. Also his love of the theatre drew him to paint the interiors of the old music halls of Camden Town and Islington. At this time, too, he was producing a number of atmospheric townscapes; and the locations where he found most inspiration happened to be abroad, in France and Italy.

He always felt at home on the continent, perhaps because he came of mainland European stock. His grandfather and father, both artists, were Danish in origin. His father, Oswald Adalbert Sickert, after working in Germany, decided to settle in England in 1868 with his English wife. Sickert himself felt proud of his foreign heredity which – paradoxically – he claimed contributed to his Englishness. At a dinner party during the Great War he startled the assembled company by declaring 'in a voice loud enough for the whole table to hear: "And no one could be more English than I am – born in Munich in 1860, of pure Danish descent"'.[1] He might also have mentioned the fairly exotic background of his mother Eleanor. She was illegitimate, the offspring of a liaison between an Irish dancer and a distinguished Cambridge astronomer, the Revd Richard Sheepshanks. In order to conceal as far as possible the fact of her existence she was despatched abroad for her education to an English school at Neuville-lès-Dieppe. Whether or not prompted by this family association, in 1885 Sickert chose to honeymoon at Dieppe with his first wife Ellen Cobden. In any case, through his work as pupil and etching assistant to the cosmopolitan artist James McNeill Whistler, he was inevitably being drawn into the circle of painters attracted to the influential French school which migrated to Dieppe from Paris during the spring and summer. The Café des Tribunaux – one of Sickert's favourite subjects – became the meeting ground where the English avant-garde such as Whistler, Sargent, and Sickert himself mingled with their French counterparts such as Degas,

Pissarro, Renoir, Monet and Jacques-Emile Blanche. As Blanche remarked, 'Eight months out of the twelve, Paris and the universe arrived in Dieppe'.

In addition to the practising artists, wealthy cultivated patrons were an important part of this social mix. At one of Blanche's dinner parties Sickert was introduced to Celia, Lady Noble,[2] the granddaughter of Isambard Kingdom Brunel, who commissioned him to paint her portrait. Much later, when she was living in Bath, she presented this portrait to the Victoria Art Gallery. It shows how, under the influence particularly of Degas, his art was developing a much greater lightness and freedom of touch. At about the same time that Lady Noble sat to him Sickert was entranced by a couple of models he used in London: 'I am deep in two divine coster girls – one with sunlight on her indoors'.[3] A similar treatment of light and shadow on her half-averted head is apparent in the portrait of Lady Noble.

He chose to settle in Dieppe from 1898 to 1905, a period that was only broken by visits to Venice. In both places the architecture and the settings inspired him to begin the first of his townscapes. Although he returned to live more permanently in England in 1905, he was drawn back each summer to France. The outbreak of the Great War in 1914 brought this most agreeable phase of his career to an end. With London now as his permanent base, he worked mainly in two studios in Fitzroy Street. One – known as the 'Frith', at No 15 – he had for his own use, while in the other – the 'Whistler', at No 8 across the street – he instructed his many students.[4] Inevitably, as the war dragged on into its third year, the Zeppelin raids began to have an effect on civilian morale. The critic Roger Fry, in a letter written in the autumn of 1917, described how the warning would send everyone down to the basement:

People have been much shaken – Walter Sickert … is however much pleased, as the place where he teaches has good cellars where he sits and smokes and drinks with his pupils and gets a guinea for doing so.[5]

Possibly Sickert was more shaken by the bombing than this insouciant character sketch would suggest. He was in any case concerned for the health of his wife Christine,[6] and had already decided that Bath would provide the ideal peaceful retreat. Their initial visit in the summer of 1917 proved such a success that they returned the following summer. Their address was The Lodge (fig.1 overleaf), a house situated high on the slopes of Entry Hill, with extensive views over the city and surrounding countryside. It had originally been built in about 1828-9, with the name of Entry Hill Villa, and designed by the architect Edward Davis as the first of a group of neo-Tudor houses to occupy an idyllic wooded site among open fields.[7] Although the house had changed its name several times since then, the setting had hardly altered. One could get down into Bath by taking what was virtually a country walk.

All Sickert's expectations were fulfilled. In May 1918 he sent an ecstatic telegram to Nina Hamnett in London – 'Bonjour Nina. Bath spiffing' – and followed it up with a letter:

> I am dying all obvious selfishness apart, for you to come to Bath. It will rest and amuse and refresh you, and week for week will cost you less money than in London. The beauty of the place is incredible. My walk down after breakfasting à l'Anglaise in the kitchen at about 6 is like a German woodcut of the views down through beech trees on the elaborate town … You could walk in these gardens and orchards in perfect peace. Such roofs, such roses, such contorted walls ... such bracing air.

Though not strictly one of his pupils Nina Hamnett was one of a number of aspiring young artists in whom he detected promise. With characteristic generosity he had given her permission to use the studio at 8 Fitzroy Street for her portrait painting while he was away. Now, because he felt that Bath would benefit her, he bought one of her paintings for £15 so that she could afford the fare, and found her lodgings in a row of workmen's cottages half-way down Beechen Cliff: 'From the bed it looks as if someone had chucked the roofs of the whole town in at the two windows, with the Abbey in the middle and the towers of your old school on the horizon. It takes ones breath away'.[8]

Bath provided a tonic and an inspiration. In accordance with the regime he had established during his time in Dieppe, Sickert would get up at 6 am to make his drawings and colour studies before going down to his studio in the city where he would settle to the serious business of painting. At noon he would break off for a swim, then have lunch, and a nap in the afternoon; followed by tea at 4 pm, and more work. At 7 he would return home to Entry Hill, where Christine would be waiting with their

Fig.1 View of The Lodge, Entry Hill Drive, Bath, from the northwest.
(*reproduced by courtesy of the present owner*)

maid Marie to serve dinner. Nina Hamnett, who had responded to his invitation to come to Bath, was privileged to hear his views on art, though she hardly seems to have received them with a great deal of respect. She would go along to his studio in the late afternoon, and listen to him discoursing on his methods as he painted sketches of the river and Pulteney Bridge. She wrote to Roger Fry:

> He … spends at least two hours daily at teatime in holding forth. I always say 'yes' and go home and do the opposite. He admits he can understand nothing of modern art. I understand that he doesn't, but why he doesn't I don't see. I am giving him all the available literature on Rimbaud which thrills him.[9]

The way in which Nina dismisses the outpouring of technical advice lavished on her from Sickert's years of experience reveals the gap between their generations. Did she adopt the same brusque contemptuous tone if ever allowed to interrupt his monologue with a few words of her own? She certainly felt able to express her opinion of his work with brutal frankness in another letter to Fry: 'W.S. now paints on four small panels a day and paints them in ink colour black and tan boots colour, the architecture is getting more and more minute and laborious. I sit beside him in a garden in the last sitting after tea. How silly he is!'[10]

Sickert, if he had been made aware of her critical resistance to his advice, would doubtless have acknowledged it with a certain tolerant amusement, and made allowance for the fact that it expressed the point of view of the youthful avant-garde. He too had been avant-garde in his time, as a pupil of Whistler and above all as a disciple of Degas: the lessons he had learnt from them formed the basis of his technique painstakingly worked out through his development as a painter. Following Degas's dictum, 'On ne donne l'idée du vrai qu'avec le faux' ('Only by artificial means can reality be revealed'), Sickert advocated the use of photography as an essential preliminary to the creation of a picture. From 1892 onwards he was using photographs in support of his portraiture, and to an even greater extent in his pre-war Dieppe townscapes. The practice continued in Bath. As Clifford Ellis recalled:

> The photographer would come in the morning, find a message from Sickert: 'Go to Camden Crescent, third lamp-post on the right, take a photograph facing so-and-so when the sun is facing in the right direction'.[11]

Duncan Grant, who attended a lecture given by Sickert in 1938, summarised the way in which the painting would gradually evolve from there: 'Sickert's method … is this. He sees a subject … [and] has it photographed, he squares out the photo, he draws it in charcoal on the canvas'.[12] Grant might also have noted the number of pen or charcoal drawings and sketches in oil (often on board) which Sickert made to assist in the creation of the finished work. It was ideas like these for Pulteney Bridge that Nina Hamnett mentioned with such disfavour in her letter to Roger Fry. Sickert was clearly fascinated by the contrast between the fixed classical immobility of the bridge itself and the movement of the river beneath; and the tension between these two is beautifully conveyed in the several finished versions of the subject.

For such finished compositions the canvas itself would have been carefully prepared beforehand with a basic underpainting that he termed a 'camaieu.'[13] In one of the many letters he wrote to Nina Hamnett on the subject, Sickert outlined the next stage of the operation with the boast: 'I have certainly solved the question of technique … It is extraordinary how agreeable undiluted paint scrubbed hard over a coarse bone-dry camaieu … becomes. It tells semi-transparent like a powder or a wash'.[14] This was the basis for the final touches, which would appear 'fatter and more opaque'. Helen Lessore (his future sister-in-law), commenting on Sickert's work after his death, remarked that he 'attached great importance to what I think he called the cooking side of painting'.[15]

Apart from his fascination with the river bank by Pulteney Bridge, he was also captivated by the streets and views on the upper slopes of Lansdown. As Clifford Ellis remembered, the services of the photographer would often be needed at Camden. There the house on the corner of the Crescent, with its distinctive semicircular balcony, had a special family interest for Sickert since it had belonged to his great uncle, the brother of the Astronomer Royal.[16] Just as he had done with the subject of Pulteney Bridge he produced several finished versions of Mr Sheepshanks' House, Camden Crescent. While he was working in that area his eye was also taken with the possibilities of the view down the hill and across to Beechen Cliff. Before completing two finished versions of this he worked at a number of preliminary drawings as well as doing a small study in oil on board.[17] From a viewpoint on the curve of the pavement at the top of Belvedere he looked down to where the street appears to narrow at the bottom, and then allowed his gaze to rise over the roofs of the houses to the massed bluish-green cloud of trees on Beechen Cliff opposite (fig.2). In the finished versions he enlarged the composition on the right, to include a homely everyday detail of a horse and cart just coming into view, with the horse's legs stuck out stiffly in front to prevent it slipping on the hill.

Bath struck him as a place of 'incredible beauty', the phrase he had used in his letter to Nina Hamnett. She for her part found the place utterly boring and stagnant by contrast with her lively Bohemian existence in London. There was nothing in the townscape of Bath that appealed to her as a subject to paint. After five weeks of listening to Sickert discoursing at length in the afternoons, and occasionally going to dinner with him and Christine in the

Fig.2 *Beechen Cliff from Belvedere, Lansdown, Bath*, 1917-18, by Walter Richard Sickert (1860-1942). Oil on board, 35.6 x 25.4 cm. A preliminary study for the painting now in the collection of Tate Britain, London.

(*reproduced by courtesy of the Victoria Art Gallery, Bath and North East Somerset Council*)

Fig.3 *Paradise Row, Holloway, Bath*, 1917-18, by Walter Richard Sickert (1860-1942). Pen and ink drawing on squared paper, 24.8 x 20.7 cm. A preliminary drawing (which shows Sickert's method of 'squaring up') for the painting now in the collection of Manchester City Art Gallery. (*reproduced by courtesy of the Victoria Art Gallery, Bath and North East Somerset Council*)

evening, she packed her bags and returned to London. Sickert, on the other hand, clearly found the old part of Bath where she had lodged a great source of inspiration; and the result was his painting of *Paradise Row, Holloway* (fig.3). He must have noted this picturesque convergence of the little narrow streets when he was on his morning walk down from Entry Hill to the 'elaborate town' on the further bank of the river. The house behind the garden wall on the left is Paradise House, built in the early eighteenth century with a terrace of attached houses known as Paradise Row.[18] In Sickert's day it was a flourishing artisan area, lived in by painters and carpenters among others. Just up the hill, at No 94 Holloway, was an 'oil, colour and hardware store' which would certainly have stocked items useful to artists in their work.

It would be interesting to know whether any of the views that Sickert completed in Bath over the course of his two-year stay found an immediate or ready market. Denys Sutton[19] mentions that the collector Montagu Shearman wrote to Sickert saying that he liked what he was doing; but it is unclear whether Shearman bought any paintings from him at this point, or later. Probably Sickert's best move would have been to leave them with his dealer at the Leicester Galleries in London.

As soon as the War was over Sickert and his wife returned to France to settle in their favourite spot near Dieppe, at Envermeu. Bath had served its purpose while he was prevented from working on the Continent. They may also have considered that the climate and conditions in France would somehow help to improve Christine's health. But she was now in the advanced stages of tuberculosis, and died in 1920. Sickert, who hardly seems to have realised how ill she was, felt overcome by a mixture of guilt and misery. He shut himself away in his loneliness, and produced very little work. Various close friends from his London circle of art students and pupils came out to Envermeu to be with him, and try to comfort him. Thérèse Lessore was the one who eventually filled the void left by Christine's death.

Lessore, like Sickert, was descended from two generations of foreign artists. Her father Jules, a Frenchman, had settled in England in 1871 and made a name for himself as a painter and etcher. Thérèse, following in his footsteps, had begun by exhibiting with groups such as the Allied Artists. Sickert later claimed that he had noticed her work in their show of 1913, and had been 'profoundly elated' by her picture of a vegetable market. In his review of the exhibition of 'Twentieth Century Art' at the Whitechapel Art Gallery in 1914 he wrote:[20] '... she [Lessore] will always appear to be the most interesting and masterful personality of them all ... First and foremost she has human interest, without which art on this planet probably cannot exist'. Two years later, reviewing the London Group exhibition,[21] he confessed:'The artist who

has always thrilled me in these and kindred groups is Thérèse Lessore …
[who] has the gift of stimulating perpetual curiosity and leaving it unsatisfied'.
Undoubtedly she stirred him to admiration of her looks and personality as a
whole. Something of her quiet elusive charm was conveyed in his comparison
of her to a Persian miniature. Before the War he enjoyed meeting her and her
then husband Bernard Adeney at their house in Hampstead. When the
Adeneys moved to become close neighbours in Fitzroy Street, there is a
suggestion that Christine Sickert felt some jealousy of her husband's
increasing involvement with Thérèse.

After Christine's death, and Thérèse's divorce from Adeney, their
relationship became close, both personally and artistically. When Sickert
decided to return to England in 1922, he still continued to isolate himself and
keep the doors closed even against old friends. It was Thérèse who managed
to overcome the barrier; and she did so through the art they both practised.
By this time she was not only using paint on canvas but also on ceramics.
Her sister and brother-in-law Louise and Alfred Powell worked as decorators
and designers for the firm of Wedgwood, and it was probably through them
that Thérèse began decorating the blanks from the kiln. She in turn introduced
the artists of the Omega Group – Duncan Grant, Vanessa Bell, Roger Fry, and
inevitably Sickert himself – to the same line of work. Her designs were
pictorial, often on a contemporary theme. Sickert is known to have painted,
and signed, three teapots with a view of Pulteney Bridge, which remained
one of his most enduring memories of Bath. Two of the teapots were lost in
the kiln; the third he kept, until on his death it passed to Thérèse.[22]

After his marriage to Thérèse in 1926, Sickert was not to revisit Bath for
another twelve years. In the intervening time, however, he would be
represented here by some of his paintings of the city from his earlier stay. A
number of them were shown as part of the three important Festivals of the
Arts organised in Bath in 1930, 1935 and 1936. The first Festival of the
Contemporary Arts was held from 20 March to 5 April 1930, under the joint
aegis of the Bath Spa Committee and the Library and Art Committee. An
impressive programme of concerts, lectures, theatre, and even an avant-garde
novelty such as the first provincial performance of William Walton's *Façade*,
was put on. In addition, the generous space allotted to literature and every
conceivable branch of the visual arts and crafts would doubtless astonish
the organisers of the Festival today. The displays scattered throughout the
whole complex of rooms and corridors in the Pump Room must have been
quite staggering. On the walls were hung paintings, drawings, prints and
woodcuts by a wide variety of established artists such as Sickert himself,
James Pryde, William Nicholson, in company with some of the slightly

younger generation such as Augustus John, Henry Lamb, J.D. Innes, Roger Fry and Duncan Grant, Mark Gertler and Harold Gilman.

The Festival was widely publicised as part of the Mayor's successful campaign to raise money for a new hospital, and received good coverage in the press both locally and nationally. On the same day[23] that the *Daily Herald* noted how well the contemporary paintings and sculpture looked in juxtaposition with reminders of Bath's historic past, the special correspondent to the *Morning Post* picked out Sickert's painting of *Mr Sheepshanks' House, Camden Crescent*[24] in order to praise it for its 'local touch and some charming local colour ... incidentally [showing] how a modern electric light standard can take its place beside eighteenth century architecture'. Sickert might also have appreciated the discerning appraisal of this picture by the critic of the local *Bath & Wilts Chronicle* who commented on its

> architectural originality ... Most contemporary artists are becoming more original in their points of view, and are bringing out that originality on their canvases. But it is rational originality. It strikes the medium between the first modern movement and the cubist. Particularly noticeable and delightful are the blendings of tone and the perfect balance of colour.[25]

It was a critique which appreciated the careful preparation of the canvas and application of the paint in order to produce that 'perfect balance of colour'. Nina Hamnett had impatiently rejected Sickert's exposition of his methods of painting, and had found him unreceptive to the most avant-garde forms of art. But here the critic sums up Sickert's position very accurately, midway 'between the first modern movement and the cubist'. It also applies to the other artists of the Camden Town Group who were influenced by him and whose works were shown alongside his in this exhibition of 1930 at the Pump Room.

Bath had to wait another five years for the Second Festival of the Contemporary Arts, held from 24 April to 8 May 1935, when Sickert was again represented in the exhibition in the Pump Room by his painting of Sheepshanks' house. Without further detailed evidence as to its size, and without knowing if it was painted on canvas or panel, it is impossible to be sure whether this was the finished work on the subject (sold just before the Second World War to Durban Museum and Art Gallery, Natal, South Africa), or one of the four or so smaller preparatory oil studies which Sickert is known to have done. Another painting of Camden Crescent by Sickert was also included in the 1935 exhibition, as well as a picture of his titled in the catalogue simply as *Beechen Cliff, Bath*.[26] Could this have been a version of the picture already described, taken from Belvedere on Lansdown and looking across to Beechen Cliff, or was it a view just of Beechen Cliff itself that has somehow escaped further notice? Again, the question has to remain open.

The Festival for the following year took a different title – 'The Art of Three Centuries'- and was of rather a different nature. In the Victoria Art Gallery there was an eclectic exhibition of paintings and drawings covering the eighteenth century to the twentieth. Sickert's contribution consisted of a view of *Dieppe Harbour* (no. 280, priced at £21), and two views of Bath including his favourite *Camden Crescent* (no. 279, lent by the National Art Collections Fund).[27]

By the time that works like these of Sickert's were being sought for exhibitions, admired by the critics, and acquired by public institutions as well as by enlightened private collectors, he himself was no longer regarded as the *enfant terrible* he had been in his younger days, but rather – now that he was in his mid-seventies – as the grand old man of British contemporary painting. Meanwhile he and his wife continued their careers, first in Islington, then at Margate, and then at St Peter's-in-Thanet where they moved in 1934. While they were in London he had opened the last of his private schools at 1 Highbury Place; and when they had settled at St Peter's he taught at Thanet School of Art. He delighted the students with his now famous eccentricity of dress and behaviour. They also revered him for his art and the evident pleasure he took in passing on what he had learnt over the years. He was always generously encouraging of young talent. Basil Jonzen, then living in London, later wrote an affectionate tribute[28] describing in vivid detail the Sickert ménage at this time:

> Four of us had been invited to visit him next Sunday at his house near Broadstairs. He had even promised to meet our train. What hospitality from an old man … 'Of course', said his niece when I told her, 'you will never recognise Uncle Walter. He changes so. Last time I saw him he had shaved off all his hair except for a fringe and behind that, perched on his head, sat a brilliant red fez. He wore,' she added, 'a tail coat, bottle green with age, black and white check trousers, elastic-sided boots and coffee-coloured spats'.

Actually, when the four students encountered Sickert waiting for them on the platform, his theatrical costume had been transformed into 'a violent orange tweed suit, no collar or tie, only a collar-stud in his shirt -front [flashing] in the sun. His carpet slippers gave him the appearance of a woolly bear'. The lunch – saddle of lamb – was an enormous success:

> Our glasses were filled again and again and more bottles opened. I do not remember the sweet. I remember Mr Sickert waving his spoon and singing more French songs. I remember Mrs Sickert sitting there smiling, still sipping her wine and refusing a second glass. After some excellent gorgonzola, and a glass of port … Mrs Sickert rose from the table and led us to the drawing room.

Then they got down to the business of the visit, first being shown Mrs Sickert's studio, 'quite bare except for an easel, a tidy palette, a neat bundle of brushes on the table, and a grey carpet'. One of her canvases was displayed, a circus scene:

'That's got it', Sickert said as he held her arm. 'The whip is cracking and there's plenty of drawing in that horse. You've got it, my dear, what splendid light … Those rich reds of yours are splendid. You must paint more'.

They then adjourned to Sickert's studio, a complete contrast to his wife's. It was 'a room of hopeless confusion … Paint brushes and palettes were strewn on every table and chair. A pier glass reflected the litter of drawings, engravings, newspapers and the rest that made up the kaleidoscopic effect'. Later, when they had returned to the drawing room:

'Mr Sickert', I said, 'in your studio I noticed you had drawn over a number of photographs'. [He replied] 'Ah yes, people think I paint from photographs. Yes, so I do when I've teased what I want out of them. I draw what I want on top of them. I take a piece of charcoal or a bit of colour and draw, putting in a few tones. There is my secret. I photograph that and work from the new photograph. Sometimes I have it made into a slide for my magic lantern and throw it on to the canvas and draw round … There's my secret, there you are, you go away with something' … We continued to talk in the hall as we put on our hats and coats. 'We will soon be leaving St Peter's. We're going to live in Bath. As soon as we are settled you must come and see us', he said. We thanked them again and looked forward to the day in Bath.

With the threat of another war and the possibility of invasion, it seemed inadvisable for the Sickerts to remain where they were in Kent. He remembered the haven that Bath had been once before, and the inspiration that its fine streets and crescents on the steeply sloping hills had offered for his art. They decided to take a house, St George's Hill, at Bathampton on the outskirts of the city, to which they moved in December 1938. Although many of their friends – including Sir Alec Martin, Sylvia Gosse, and Marjorie Lilly – came to visit them there, it is unrecorded whether Basil Jonzen and his companions managed that 'day in Bath' they had looked forward to. Sickert, however, certainly continued doing what he so much enjoyed: keeping in touch with the young, entertaining and instructing them. Clifford Ellis, the headmaster of the Bath School of Art, recalled how in March 1939

…he wrote to me, and it's a marvellous letter, saying that in due course he will be gathered to his fathers and it would be a pity not to offer to come to my establishment to tell people of the people he'd been fortunate enough to know and then he lists the great French contemporaries and

one thing that I think is very interesting now, that on no account should I think of paying a fee because he was really quite well off. He got £100 or even £150 per painting. In this he was helped by his wife.[29]

Sickert would turn up at the school (then situated on the top floor of the Technical College in Lower Borough Walls), 'regular as clockwork every Friday morning at 11 o'clock'. Kate Fryer, one of the staff at the school, remembers those occasions:

> To get the ball rolling, illustrations were thrown into the epidiascope. At first Clifford selected reproductions found in books – Manet, Degas, etc – but later Sickert brought along his own selection taken from the back numbers of *Punch* or the *Illustrated London News*. Thus we came to know the drawings of the Victorian illustrators, Georgy Bowers, Leech & Keen. Sickert's allusions were sometimes obscene particularly when he was referring to people he had known personally, and he often lapsed into French. But it was all very enlivening and broadening to the minds of a young and unsophisticated audience.[30]

Thérèse was there too, sitting quietly attentive and apparently unremarked. Clifford Ellis, however, describes how on one occasion at least she was brought into the limelight and used to illustrate an important point. While Sickert was discoursing on one of the slides he was irritated

> because out of the tail of his eye he saw something hanging on the wall. This was in fact a lithograph by Duncan Grant in his most Post-Impressionist vein, quite bright bits of colour dancing against one another. Sickert glared at this and he said, 'You know, you don't let off fireworks every day. Life is more sombre and more beautiful'. Then he tried to think of some way of making this statement clearer and he looked around and he saw sitting next to him his wife, long suffering Thérèse and he said,'You know, it isn't done to say that your wife is dowdy but she is, isn't she? She has got that dark almost dirty red ribbon around her hat, and a hat that isn't quite black and that nondescript grey coat and that grey scarf with slightly darker grey flecks in it, but if you go on looking at her and as you look, you realise that this is all relative, and that when you see her there and these marvellous colours she has chosen you begin to see the ribbon burns out bright crimson and that scarf is a tiger skin'. He was a marvellous talker - he'd think of things like this to say.[31]

As well as lecturing to the students Sickert would also give practical instruction to selected groups in a barn which formed part of the outbuildings

Fig.4 (*left*) Walter Sickert opening the exhibition of work by students of the Bath School of Art at the Victoria Art Gallery, Bath, in June 1939.
(*reproduced by courtesy of the Sickert Collection, London Borough of Islington*)

in the grounds of their house. St George's Hill was an extensive property, perched high with spectacular views over the garden and meadow at the rear, taking in the canal, the railway, and the river, and beyond that the city enclosed by further hills. The house itself, built in the early nineteenth century with generously proportioned windows, was spacious enough to allow him and Thérèse to have three studios between them. Sickert had always enjoyed spreading himself over a number of painting rooms: 'My advice to a young painter who wants to get on, is, "Take a large studio! – If you can't afford to take one, take two!"'.[32] The third studio in this case must have been allocated to Thérèse. From the description given by Jonzen of the arrangements at their previous establishment one can imagine the spare and immaculate orderliness she would have preserved in it, contrasting with the chaotic accumulation of objects in Sickert's two workrooms. As well as producing her own work she provided essential help to her husband in taking the photographs that formed the preliminary stage of his compositions. The recipe that he had offered Jonzen for creating a picture reveals that in old age Sickert had become increasingly dependent on photography: the artificial image now needed very little further transformation to turn it into a painting. Thérèse would also assist in preparing the canvas with gesso primings. It is difficult to avoid the conclusion that between them they may then have collaborated in applying the first transparent layer of colour, so similar are their works in tone and texture from this late period of their respective careers.

In his earlier paintings of Bath Sickert had portrayed the stone in rich browns and golds, with touches of deep violet, seen against the blue of predominantly sunny skies. Now, however, he was viewing the scene through different eyes, with the colours dimmed to pale pinks and mauves of an overall chalkiness. His subjects were taken from lower down Lansdown hill than before, including *The Vineyards, The Paragon*, and *Walcot Parade*.[33] Thérèse Lessore, using a range of pastel colours very close to Sickert's, also painted views in the same area:*Walcot from Hedgemead* and *Walcot Church*.[34] She was certainly recognised as an artist of quality in her own right, if not of equal distinction and fame as her husband. It was doubtless at the instigation of Clifford Ellis and his wife Rosemary – both influential members of the Bath Society of Artists – that in May 1940 Sickert and Lessore were honoured by being invited to contribute to the Society's annual exhibition. The works they submitted had no particular Bath connection. Thérèse was represented by *Love in a Mist*, and Sickert by *A Domestic Bully* and *The Miner*. He had always liked to keep a number of canvases going at the same time, some perhaps temporarily laid aside in order to be able to rework the subject later with a slightly different slant. *A Domestic Bully*, for instance, portrays the kitchen of their former house,

Hauteville, at St Peter's-in-Thanet, which had been used as the setting for his painting entitled *The Coffee Mill*. In this version, however, he added a self-portrait on the right (hence the title, possibly ironic) and a female figure (suggesting Thérèse) seated reading a newspaper in the background. *The Miner*, by contrast, is one of the comparatively few subjects he took straight from contemporary life, based on a newspaper photograph of a miner just up from a 'stay down' strike in the pit and embracing his wife. The original title was *Black and White*, emphasising the dramatic clash of their embrace, as the man streaked with coal dust holds his wife close. It had probably been painted about 1935, while they were at St Peter's, and had been noted there by Denton Welch on the occasion of his memorable visit to the Sickerts.[35]

Although this was the last time that Sickert showed his pictures at an exhibition in Bath, Lessore maintained her connection with the Bath Society of Artists, exhibiting as an ordinary member for the next three years. As well as views of Bath including *Pulteney Bridge*, she seems to have returned to her first love of circus scenes. *Swallow's Liberty Horses* now belongs to the collection of the Sickert Trust in Islington Public Libraries; and *Circus in Bath* was presented to Leicestershire Museum and Art Gallery by the Sickert Trust in 1947.

During his final years in Bath Sickert concentrated his attention on subjects that he could paint literally from home, as he looked out of the window at his garden or back from the garden towards the house. He observed the maid scrubbing the doorstep, his wife standing at the window,[36] and the changing aspect of the garden from summer to winter. He painted a poignant self-portrait, titled *The Invalid*, which depicts himself from the back as he gazes over the end wall of the garden at the view beyond. Now in his eighties, he was growing increasingly feeble, and needing the support of a stick. When Cecil Beaton, the most famous photographer of the day, visited the couple in September 1940, he made an unforgettable image of the two of them in the garden (fig.5 overleaf). Sickert dominates the foreground, seeming to act the part of a Biblical patriarch with his flowing white beard ('a magnificent wild and farouche head', Beaton noted), while Thérèse hovers like a self-effacing wraith in the background. She struck Beaton as 'an exquisite objet de vitrine'. The local paper also sent its photographer to record husband and wife together, this time inside the house. She sits upright watching over him, while he lies back reading, with cigar in hand and on his head the favourite nautical peaked cap that he affected when not wearing the fez (shown in another of the Beaton photographs). A makeshift reading stand seems to have been rigged up from a cigar box resting on a plank laid across his armchair. His picture of *Temple Bar* appears in the background. Sickert characteristically saw the potential of this photograph for a painting. The composition that he made from it, entitled

Fig.5 Walter Sickert and his wife Thérèse Lessore in the garden of their home, St George's Hill, Bathampton, September 1940.
(*Cecil Beaton photograph, reproduced by courtesy of Sotheby's, London*)

In the Cabin, gives greater immediacy to the two figures in the foreground, while altering the background to the strong vertical lines of a large bookcase (fig.6).

It was the last time that he painted them together, in the semi-dramatic form that he liked to use for portraiture. It was a splendid way to celebrate their relationship which had developed over the years of their marriage into something so fruitful and fulfilling for them both. Thérèse looked after him tenderly and devotedly during his last year of illness when he suffered a

Fig.6 *In the Cabin*, 1940, by Walter Richard Sickert (1860-1942). Oil on canvas, 43 x 78.5 cm. Based on a photograph taken for the *Bath Chronicle and Herald* in 1940. (*reproduced by courtesy of the Methuen Collection, Corsham Court, Wiltshire. Photograph from the Photographic Survey, Courtauld Institute of Art*)

series of strokes. Marjorie Lilly, his student from the Fitzroy Street days, visited them in the autumn of 1941, by which time Sickert was confined to bed upstairs. She found Thérèse, appearing 'tinier and more frail' than ever, having to cope with a number of evacuees from Balham who had been billeted on them, as well as keeping the peace between Sickert and the nurses who attended him. Lilly offered to take up Sickert's supper, which consisted only of his favourite rice pudding:

> [He] was sitting with his back to the window, dark against the ebbing day. He was so still in his pose of dumb acceptance that he seemed like a figure in one of his own interiors; drifts of light floated over his head and shoulders but the rest was lost in shadow, all depths and blurred contours, losing and finding themselves in the gathering dusk. He was thinner, the concavities of his face more sharply marked, but his hair was thicker than ever, rising from his head in close-piled curls, his eyes blue and clear in their deep orbits. He moved slightly and the shadows fled. I thought what a portrait he would make with his lime green checked coat, the crimson rug wrapped round his knees and the background of trees beyond the window.[37]

Sickert died on 22 January 1942, and was buried in Bathampton churchyard.[38] Thérèse wrote to Marjorie Lilly a month or so later:

… thank you for your kind letter. I know you would have come to help if you could. I had one great difficulty which was solved by the very great kindness of Clifford Ellis. No words can say how kind he has been. He came in every day and sometimes twice, to lift Walter for weeks. When you think of his busy life, it was wonderful. Doing it with such tact and tenderness.

What I shall do now, I just do not know. Find a studio somewhere I suppose – are there any Hendon way? I have no desire to do anything.[39]

In fact what she did was to offer part of the space in St George's Hill as a refuge for the senior students of Clifford Ellis's School of Art. After their premises in Bath had received a direct hit in the bombing raid of 25 April they were invited to work up at the Bathampton house and take their exams there in the summer. It was a gesture appropriately setting the seal on the happy relationship that had existed between Sickert and his students.

Meanwhile Sickert's own work was receiving a great deal of publicity. Even before his death, in the autumn of 1941 a major retrospective exhibition of his paintings and drawings organised by Lillian Browse (and originally intended for the Tate) opened at the National Gallery. Lord Methuen, his former pupil, contributed a perceptive introduction to the catalogue, in which he applied Sickert's own words to what was on show: 'Real quality, like style in literature, is the result of complete knowledge of the subject treated, and of simplicity and directness in the treatment.'

After the exhibition closed at the National Gallery, the various owners of the works generously agreed to an extension of their loans so that it could travel round the country, under the auspices of the Council for the Encouragement of Music and the Arts. It was eventually opened in Bath on 7 January 1943 at the Victoria Art Gallery by Reginald Green. He recalled Sickert as 'a marvellous teacher … [whose] influence has been expressed as much through his writings and through his teaching as through his pictures'.[40] Since then Sickert has been honoured by numerous national and international exhibitions acknowledging the importance of his work both as creative artist and inspirational teacher.

Immediately after his death in 1942 Sickert's dealers at the Leicester Galleries in London had mounted an exhibition in which they displayed his later work, concentrating on the recent street scenes of Bath, as well as his paintings of the house and garden at St George's Hill. His friend, T.W. Earp, wrote an appreciation for the *Daily Telegraph* in which he praised the masterly skill shown in capturing 'the classic beauty of Georgian street and crescent … In splendour of perspective and loving detail [the paintings] reach a flawless truth of record; but with it goes a sense of atmosphere, of spirit of place, that only Sickert could convey'. Sadly, only a month or so later some at least of that classic beauty would be disfigured by the bombing raids in April 1942. Sickert's vision of the peaceful streets would be succeeded by dramatic accounts of the destruction particularly in the areas round Lansdown Crescent, recorded by artists such as John Piper and Clifford Ellis.

Although none of Sickert's later works is yet included in the collection of the Victoria Art Gallery, the small group of his earlier paintings at present belonging to the gallery is a rich and varied one. It begins with the flower piece, *Violets* (c.1883-4), a rare example of him tackling a still-life subject; then the portrait of Lady Noble, which demonstrates the kind of dramatic character study he had perfected following his first stay in Dieppe; while the view of Beechen Cliff from Belvedere – painted in Bath about ten years later – reveals the pleasure he took in recording the urban scene. Another from the same period, of a view from the Assembly Rooms looking up towards Belvedere, is a sparkling account of the effect of sunlight on Bath stone. This little jewel had apparently been left behind in the studio he rented at 10, Bladud Buildings during 1918. It was going to be consigned to the dustbin by his landlady, but was fortunately saved from such a fate in 1925, eventually to find its way to the safe keeping of the gallery. The fact that Sickert was so prolific, and is known to have worked in a number of different studios in the city, leads to the hope that more treasures like this may still lurk somewhere waiting to be unearthed. He himself had found Bath a marvellous source of inspiration. As he put it with such relish: 'Bath is *it* ! There never was such a place for rest and comfort and leisurely work. Such country, and *such* town'.[41]

Notes

1   Osbert Sitwell ed., *A Free House! The Writings of Walter Richard Sickert* (Macmillan, 1941), Introduction p.50.
2   Celia Noble, née James (1871-1962). Lived at 23 Royal Crescent, Bath (1947-50), and at 22 Royal Crescent (1952-62).
3   *L'Américaine* , 1908 (Tate Gallery, no. 5090). The title refers to her hat, which Sickert explained was called 'an American sailor'.
4   Marjorie Lilly, *The Painter and his Circle* (Elek, 1971), p.43.
5   Denys Sutton ed., *Letters of Roger Fry* (Chatto & Windus, 1972), p.417, letter dated 6 October 1917.
6   Sickert's marriage to Ellen Cobden ended in divorce in 1896. In 1911 he married Christine Angus.
7   The Lodge was presumably rented from its current owner, Robert Goldsworthy. For the previous history of the house, see Michael Forsyth, 'Edward Davis: Nineteenth-century Bath Architect and Pupil of Sir John Soane', *Bath History*, Vol. VII (Millstream Books, Bath, 1998), pp.110-111.
8   Undated letter quoted by Denise Hooker, *Nina Hamnett; queen of Bohemia*

(Constable, 1986), pp.116-118. Sickert is referring to the Royal School on Lansdown, where Nina had once been a boarder.

9   Undated letter quoted by Denys Sutton, *Walter Sickert* (Michael Joseph, 1976), p. 190.

10   Undated letter quoted by Denys Sutton, *ibid.*, pp.190-1.

11   BBC Transmissions ,10 February 1961; 19 November 1966.

12   Richard Shone, 'Duncan Grant on a Sickert Lecture', *Burlington Magazine*, November 1981.

13   Wendy Baron, *Sickert* (Phaidon, 1973), p.136. She explains *camaieu* as 'like a grisaille underpainting but composed of two colours'. Sickert's recommendation to Nina Hamnett was white with cobalt for the lights, and white with three strengths of indian red for the shadows. This kept the colours very light in tone, as he wrote: 'practically all white, only just enough coloured to distinguish light from shade'.

14   Quoted by Wendy Baron, *ibid.*, p.136.

15   BBC Transmissions, 10 February 1961; 5 November 1966.

16   Richard Sheepshanks never acknowledged Sickert's mother Eleanor as his daughter, but instead passed himself off as her guardian. It was left to his sister Anne to take an interest in her niece and family, particularly in the upbringing of her godson, the young Walter Richard. In the early 1930s Sickert painted his godmother's portrait, retrospectively, on the basis of an old photograph.

17   Entitled *Beechen Cliff from Belvedere, Lansdown, Bath*, and now in the collection of the Victoria Art Gallery, Bath (no.1942.7). One of the finished versions is in the Tate Gallery, London (no. 5087).

18   This area of Holloway was badly hit in the bombing raids of April 1942. Paradise House (originally No 8 Paradise Row, later No 88 Holloway) fortunately still survives as the Paradise House Hotel, and now incorporates the only other remaining house in the row. All the buildings depicted by Sickert on the opposite side of the road, at the corner of Calton Road, have been demolished.

19   Denys Sutton, *op. cit.*, p.191.

20   *New Age*, 28 May 1914.

21   *Burlington Magazine*, January 1916.

22   See documentation in Victoria Art Gallery archive. The teapot is illustrated in *Wedgwood Ceramics*, by Guy Morrison, fig.364.

23   Friday 21 March 1930.

24   Lent by the Leicester Galleries, London, price £147.

25   Thursday 20 March 1930.

26   Commended by the *Morning Post*, 8 May 1935, as 'a clever portrayal of one of the local beauty spots'.

27   For the first time Lessore also was represented in the 1936 exhibition with her painting of *Newbury Fair* (lent by the Leicester Galleries, and priced at £21.10s.).

28   'A Visit to Mr Sickert at Broadstairs', *Horizon*, September 1943, pp.194-203.

29   Derek Pope ed., *A Celebration of Bath Academy of Art at Corsham* (privately printed, Corsham, 1997), p.99.

30   *Ibid.*, p.11-12.

31   *Ibid.*, p.99.

32   Sitwell ed., *op. cit.*, Introduction p.32.

33   All three were shown in the retrospective exhibition of his work at the Leicester Galleries, London, 1942.

34 These are now in the collection of the Victoria Art Gallery, Bath (no.1946./3 and no.1952.1 respectively).
35 Denton Welch, *A Last Sheaf* (Lehmann, 1951), pp.11-12.
36 Now known as *The Open Window*, in the collection of Leeds City Art Gallery.
37 Lilly, *op. cit.* , p.172.
38 Clifford Ellis carved the tombstone, and added Thérèse's name to it after her death in 1945.
39 Quoted in Lilly, *op. cit.* , p.173, letter dated 1 March 1942.
40 *Bath & Wilts Chronicle and Herald*, 8 January 1943.
41 Quoted by Baron, *op. cit.*, p.156, letter written to Ethel Sands in 1918.

Acknowledgements
I should like to thank the following for their help: Dr Wendy Baron, James Methuen Campbell, David McLaughlin, Jessica Rydill, Dr Susan Sloman, Katharine Wall, and the staff of Bath Central Library.

BATH: UNIVERSITY CITY

R. Angus Buchanan

Let us suppose, for a moment, that Adelard of Bath – that pioneering English schoolman, scientist and academic of the twelfth century – had remained in the town with which he has been identified instead of wandering about Europe in search of Greek and Arabic documents. Had he done so it is possible that he could have attracted one of those seminal groups of scholars who in the twelfth and thirteenth centuries were gathering around outstanding teachers in some European cities and thereby establishing the foundations of the first universities. Or let us suppose that the disgruntled group of scholars who pulled out of Oxford in 1209 had chosen to travel south-west to the busy market town and flourishing abbey of Bath rather than taking off to the north-east into the fenlands around the bridge over the River Cam. In either of these counter-factual situations it is possible that Bath could have become one of the great original university cities of Europe.[1]

Of course, this did not happen, and Bath developed instead as the foremost spa of England, becoming a centre of the incipient leisure and tourist industries. Nevertheless, the point of these speculative 'might-have-beens' is that Bath possessed some distinct advantages as a seat of learning, such as congenial accommodation and convenient access to London, and over half a millennium after the first flowering of European universities in the Middle Ages, it was well placed for consideration in the next phase of university expansion in England. This was in the nineteenth century, when the foundation of University College London in 1826 initiated a prolonged growth in higher education promoted by the increased prosperity of the period and the emergence of wealthy commercial and professional classes. At its foundation the critics of the UCL regarded it as the 'Godless college', because its promoters were utilitarians and rationalists led by Jeremy Bentham, whose mummified body still presides over the institution. So it was quickly followed by the creation of King's College London as a Church of England foundation in 1829, and by the establishment of a traditional Christian university on the collegiate model of Oxford and Cambridge at Durham in 1832.

The same determination to ensure that new universities would be God-fearing institutions animated plans to establish a university in Bath in the 1830s. A prospectus was issued, couched in distinctly pietistic terms, of an evangelical and anti-Catholic flavour, and some design sketches survive for a neo-gothic pile on the lower slopes of Claverton Down (fig.1).

Fig.1 The Project for Queen's College, Bath. This scheme for a substantial 'Saxon' style building on Claverton Down was launched in 1839. It was soon abandoned for lack of funds. (*reproduced by courtesy of the University of Bath*)

But the scheme ran out of funds at an early stage and was abandoned.[2] Another century passed before Bath tried again, and this time more successfully, to become a University City.

Meanwhile, in the neighbouring city of Bristol, other crucial academic developments had occurred in the mid-nineteenth century ferment of new ideas about political liberalism, social reform, and scientific progress. Bristol had long been a thriving port, and had gradually acquired large commercial and industrial activities dominating an extensive hinterland. The rapid expansion of novel industrial processes had generated a national demand for new training establishments, which had been further stimulated by the success of the Great International Exhibition of 1851, and by the enthusiasm of Prince Albert for introducing German standards of technical competence into his adopted home. Technical education thus made an encouraging start at national level in the 1850s, with the Bristol Trade School, set up in 1856, being the local response to this initiative. It was a small step, but it deserves to be recognized as the first formal development in higher education in the West Country, and as the beginning of the institution that became, in the fulness of time, the University of Bath.

The Bristol Trade School itself sprang from a Diocesan Day School, which had been established in 1821 to cope with the missionary problem of the inner-city area. It had not been very successful in recruiting students and had lapsed in 1852, when the trustees had asked Canon Moseley to advise them on the best use of their premises and resources. Henry Moseley (1801-1872), a distinguished Cambridge mathematician, had been Professor of Natural Philosophy at King's College London and an early Inspector of Schools before being appointed a Canon of Bristol Cathedral in 1853. He had already made a reputation for himself as an advocate of technical education, so his advice to the Bristol trustees must have come with no surprise. As the Bristol historian John Latimer observed:

> The Great Exhibition of 1851 having made it clear that, in their knowledge of the scientific principles upon which trades and manufactures are based, English workmen were, for the most part, behind their brethren on the Continent, Canon Moseley conceived the idea of remedying this defect, so far as Bristol was concerned; and after carefully considering the requirements of the city, he submitted to the trustees the scheme of a School of Applied Science, similar to the institutions of the same kind then highly successful in Germany and other countries, but then unknown in England, where youths of limited means could be provided with suitable training for an industrial career.[3]

The trustees accepted this proposal and won the support of Lyon Playfair, another outstanding national campaigner for technical education, so that the opening of the School on 26 March 1856 was accompanied by considerable local and national interest.

The Bristol Trade School took over the premises of the old Diocesan School in Nelson Street, where it grew steadily under the headmastership of Thomas Coomber, and soon became overcrowded. Fortunately for the future of the institution, the Bristol Society of Merchant Venturers (SMV) – a wealthy body of businessmen with a long tradition of charitable and philanthropic benefactions in Bristol – came to take an interest in it. As early as 1863 they had begun to make an annual grant towards the salary for a teacher in navigation, and in 1885 they took over full responsibility for the management of the School, building new premises for it in Unity Street, where it was appropriately re-named the 'Merchant Venturers' School'. When this transformation occurred the School had a teaching staff of twelve, including the Headmaster, and was organized in five departments: Primary, Secondary, Mining and Technical, Chemical and Metallurgical, and an Evening Class. The Evening Class was specifically 'intended principally to carry on the studies of those who have passed through the Day School, but open to all persons whatsoever, without distinction of sex'. This ban on sex discrimination was gradually extended to other departments, and became one of the notable pioneering features of the School. The Prospectus summed up the general objective neatly: 'The School is intended to provide a complete, continuous, and thoroughly sound preparation for an industrial career'.[4]

When Thomas Coomber, the first Headmaster and 'father of technical instruction in Bristol', resigned in 1890 after thirty-three years of service, he was replaced by Julius Wertheimer, BSc, who had previously held a post at the Leeds School of Science. Under Wertheimer, the School was able to take advantage of a new commitment by the state to technical education. From 1870 onwards, successive governments had recognized that the provision of elementary education could no longer be left entirely to private and voluntary organizations, and had undertaken the systematic provision of state schools for all children. This had stimulated the demand for similar provision for secondary education, and especially for technical education, which had resulted in the Technical Instruction Act of 1889, giving local authorities powers to develop technical education. The imposition of a tax on spirits – 'whisky money' – the following year made funds available for such developments. In the case of Bristol, they amounted to the useful sum of £5,700 per annum. Rather than devoting this sum to the establishment of a single great Technical Institute, the Corporation divided it between existing institutions, including the Technical School. This was regarded as a significant lost opportunity by some observers.[5] But the School underwent rapid expansion and in 1894 it assumed a new form when Wertheimer took the title of Professor of Chemistry and Metallurgy and became Principal of the re-styled Merchant Venturers' Technical College (MVTC).

While the MVTC was expanding in this way, a similar growth was occurring in the University College of Bristol, which had been established in 1876 and had shared in the increased liberality of the government towards advanced education. It seemed to several commentators that a merger between the University College and the MVTC was desirable, and negotiations took place intermittently in the 1890s to explore the possibility of a federation between the two institutions. They reached agreement on a title – 'The West of England University and Technical College' – but not much more. Deadlock was reached when both bodies insisted on keeping their own classes in engineering. The problem was resolved in a fashion by the intervention of the Wills family, the tobacco merchants and manufacturers with large factories in Bristol. As prominent members of the Society of Merchant Venturers, the family supported the priority of the MVTC in providing engineering courses. And as princely benefactors of the University College, they were able to insist that when this institution received its Charter and became the University of Bristol in 1909, it should recognize the prior claim of the MVTC in respect of engineering education. Thus, an agreement was made whereby the MVTC provided the Faculty of Engineering in the University, while it relinquished its advanced science teaching to the University, but in all other respects the two institutions preserved their separate identities.

Professor Wertheimer, in addition to being Principal of the MVTC, thus became also Dean of the University Faculty of Engineering. When he died in harness in 1923 he was succeeded in both posts, after a brief interregnum, by Professor Andrew Robertson. Robertson also held the Chair of Mechanical Engineering in the Faculty to his retirement in 1949. The opportunity was then taken to make a major reorganization. In the euphoria after the end of the Second World War, and with the new objectives provided by the Education Act of 1944, the Bristol Local Education Authority (LEA) was anxious to expand the provision of technical education. At the same time the SMV was becoming increasingly apprehensive about the drain on its funds caused by the escalating needs of the College. In 1949, therefore, the SMV relinquished its sixty-four year commitment to the College, which was handed over to the LEA and re-named as the College of Technology, Bristol, with

F.W.Partington as its Principal. The LEA split off the Commercial Department to become a separate College of Commerce, the first Principal of which was W.B.Armstrong. At the same time, the formal links between the Technical College and the University of Bristol were terminated, both institutions acquiring their own departments of science and engineering, with completely separate staffs. Moreover, it was realized that the Unity Street premises, although not themselves seriously damaged in the war, were no longer adequate to accommodate the enlarged role in technical education envisaged for the College of Technology, and a search for larger premises was undertaken.[6]

As it happened, the five substantial buildings that comprised Muller's Orphan Houses on Ashley Down became available around this time. The Orphanage, built in grey pennant sandstone between 1849 and 1870, had been made redundant by the development of alternative facilities within the Welfare State, so the buildings were acquired by the Corporation of Bristol for educational uses. They were put at the disposal of the College of Technology so that, after extensive internal refurbishment between 1953 and 1958, the re-modelled College was fully consolidated at Ashley Down. The Unity Street premises were left to the College of Commerce, and the Department of Art was hived off to become the new College of Art at Ashton Park. George H. Moore had succeeded F.W.Partington as Principal of the College of Technology in 1954. The construction of the new Great Hall and Administration Block at Ashley Down appeared to complete this phase of expansion and prepared the College of Technology for a period of stability under the Bristol LEA. But even more far-reaching changes were ahead.

The first hint of dramatic developments in technical education came in the government White Paper on *Technical Education* in 1956.[7] This emphasized the determination of government to reinvigorate the whole structure of technical education, and as one of the positive actions to achieve this it proposed to designate a few of the larger and more important technical colleges as Colleges of Advanced Technology (CATs), with the intention of concentrating on the development of degree-level courses in technological subjects. Eight of these colleges were soon named, and it was announced that others would be designated when they reached the appropriate standards. It was by no means clear that the Bristol College of Technology, with barely 500 full-time students, could meet these standards. However, the South West of England was specified as one of the desirable areas for the establishment of a CAT, and under the energetic leadership of George Moore the Bristol College began to prepare itself for the role.

As a first step towards fulfilling the requirements of a CAT, it was decided to separate the higher- from the lower-level work in such a way that two distinct colleges could be formed. The higher-level work was then placed largely under the supervision of the National Council for Technological Awards, recently set up by the government to award the new Diploma in Technology for 'sandwich'-type courses of degree level. From the outset, the higher-level college was able to offer courses for the DipTech in Applied Biology, Applied Chemistry, Mechanical Engineering, Aeronautical Engineering, and Electrical Engineering. It also provided courses for the Higher National Diploma in Engineering subjects, advanced level courses in Pharmacy and Architecture, and preparation for various professional qualifications. In accordance with the requirement that for the award of the Diploma in Technology one tenth of the tuition must be of a non-specialized nature, a General Studies Department was created, and there were also strong service Departments in Mathematics and Physics.

Thus equipped, the higher-level work was approved for CAT status, and in September 1960 the College split into a newly designated CAT, now re-named the Bristol College of Science and Technology, and the Bristol Technical College, which took over the lower-level work. Both colleges remained under the auspices of the Bristol LEA, and they both remained on the Ashley Down site. The Technical College was allocated one of the five formidable Orphanage buildings, and the CAT took responsibility for the other four. Many of the amenities, such as the Great Hall and Common Rooms, were shared, but otherwise the two colleges acquired completely distinct administrations, staff and students. George Moore became Principal of the CAT, and E. Poole, who had been Vice-Principal of the College of Technology, became Principal of the Technical College. The existing staff divided between the two new institutions, and both began to appoint new staff of their own. The full significance of this division emerged in subsequent decades, when the CAT became the University of Bath and the Technical College grew to become, first, Bristol Polytechnic College, and then the University of the West of England. Professor R.W.Bolland, who served as the first Head of the School of Chemistry at the University of Bath, moved across to become the first Director of the Bristol Polytechnic, and the sibling institutions have maintained other links.

It was not intended in 1960 that the two colleges should co-habit the Ashley Down site indefinitely. When the split was made, the plan was for the CAT to expand at Ashley Down while a new home would be found for the Technical College. But it quickly became clear that the scale envisaged by the government for the CATs would make the site too small for the higher-level institution, so it was decided that it was the CAT which would have to move. Consequently, it was announced by the LEA in December 1960 that a new site had been found for the CAT at Kings Weston House, an elegant Vanburgh mansion standing in its own grounds on the western edge of Bristol. The mansion was promptly appropriated for the Department of Architecture, and the interior was extensively renovated to equip it for this new function. A distinguished firm of architects, Robert Matthew, Johnson-Marshall and Partners, was commissioned to design new buildings in the grounds of Kings Weston, and all seemed set fair for the development in Bristol of a large institution specializing in high-level technological studies.

Once again, however, things did not work out so simply. By the end of 1962, serious snags had begun to appear in the development plans. The Planning Committee of Bristol City Council had begun to have misgivings about the projected size of the College, and was delaying planning permission for new developments. The problem was accentuated by the fact that in April 1962, together with the other nine CATs, the Bristol College of Science and Technology had been converted into a direct-grant institution, freeing it from LEA control and making it responsible directly to the Minister of Education. The new status was accompanied by a cooling of the relations between the College and the City, culminating in the summer of 1963 when the Planning Committee formally vetoed further development on the Kings Weston site. An alternative site was offered, at Coldharbour Farm on Pur Down, to the east of Filton, but this was not regarded as satisfactory by the Governors of the College, although it subsequently became the home for the Polytechnic. On top of this crisis, the Robbins Report on *Higher Education* was published in October 1963, recommending that the ten CATs should be elevated to university status. The government promptly accepted this recommendation, and planning commenced for the transition from Colleges of Advanced Technology to Universities.[8]

The Bristol College of Science and Technology was thus on the threshold of becoming a university, but had nowhere to call its home, even prospectively. Rumours circulated freely that the Principal had been observed, sometimes wearing gum-boots, inspecting properties in the West Country, in places as far apart as Clevedon and Swindon. But it was in the course of a conversation at a formal dinner that George Moore found the answer to his searches. The dinner was in Bath early in 1964, and speaking there to H.W.Brand, the Director of Education for the City, about his problem he was asked if he had considered Bath as a possible home for the new University. Being himself a Bathonian, Moore responded warmly to the idea, and within a few weeks the scheme whereby Bath City Council generously offered a 150-acre site at

Fig.2 Dr George Moore, the first Vice-Chancellor of the University of Bath, 1966 to 1969. Previously Principal of the Bristol College of Science and Technology. Portrait painted by Dr A.M. Hardie, the first Pro-Vice-Chancellor of the University and an accomplished artist, who also designed the University coat of arms and ceremonial dress.
(*reproduced by courtesy of the Senior Common Room, University of Bath*)

Norwood Playing Fields on Claverton Down had been worked out and accepted by all the parties concerned. Now, at last, the way was clear for Bath to become a University City (fig.2).

While it has been necessary to pursue the emergence of a university in Bath by considering the history of a Bristol institution, it is important to observe that higher education in Bath had made substantial advances in the nineteenth and early twentieth centuries. The city had established a sound educational system with some excellent schools, and had already recognized the growing importance of further and higher education. It had acted as the home base for the Bath and West Agricultural Society from its foundation in 1777, and had enjoyed a flourishing intellectual life through bodies such as the Bath Royal Literary and Scientific Institution, founded in 1825. In 1864 it had hosted a visit from the British Association for the Advancement of Science, and other intellectual organizations had found it a congenial meeting place. A Technical College was set up in 1896 in response to the Technical Instruction Act of 1889, housed first in a wing of the Guildhall and then in the building which had been a Hospital in Beau Street, before moving to the uncompromisingly modern buildings in Avon Street in the 1960s. Bath Technical College did not itself aspire to university status, but it attracted some well-qualified staff such as the distinguished economic historian and historian of Bath, Professor R.S.Neale, who began his teaching career there before going to Australia. A small School of Pharmacy had been set up in Bath in 1907, and when this moved over to Bristol in 1929 it became part of the MVTC and thus became responsible for the strong Pharmacy component in the putative university. And after the Second World War an Emergency Teacher Training College was established at Newton St. Loe, with affiliated departments of arts and domestic science within the city. The Bath Training College, which became Bath College of Education and subsequently Bath Spa University College, undertook degree-level work and came close to merging with the University of Bath in the 1990s. Despite all these developments, Bath faced a novel role in becoming a University City in the 1960s.[9]

The years 1964 to 1966 saw a flurry of activity as the move of the new university from Bristol to Bath began, to the accompaniment of organizational transformation and the construction of a brand new campus. Negotiations for a University Charter were put in hand, to be fulfilled at a ceremony in Bath Abbey on 9th November 1966. Detailed discussion of the composition of the University resulted in the definition of a dozen 'Schools', which were designed to be more inter-disciplinary and flexible than traditional Faculties, and the customary apparatus of university independence – Council, Senate, Court, and Convocation. The architects Robert Matthew, Johnson-Marshall

Fig.3 The University under construction (photographs by R.A.Buchanan)

(*above*) Work began on the 'Preliminary Building', now the 'South Building', soon after the agreement with the City of Bath to build on the Claverton Playing Fields, in the autumn of 1964.

(*right*) After extensive preparations, rapid progress was made on the Chemistry Building, now 4 West, in 1967.

(*below*) The complete Hall, Norwood House, and 2 East Buildings, with early landscaping, 1973.

and Partners, so long frustrated by the Kings Weston debacle, tackled the virgin site with enthusiasm and produced a distinctive design for a linear campus, arranged along a pedestrian deck above a central service road, from which the Schools, the Library, and the Common Room facilities could spring like the vertebrae from a spinal column. The design undoubtedly owed some of its inspiration to an aborted plan for a New Town at Hook in Hampshire, for which the architects had prepared drawings, but it has proved itself to be a very workable pattern for a university campus.

There has been widespread disappointment with the buildings that filled out this excellent design, but the shortcomings were largely the result of financial stringency at the time of construction. The standardized prefabricated buildings adopted from CLASP – the 'Consortium of Local Authority Special Projects' – with their extensive flat roofs and indifferent woodwork, have not weathered well, so that much maintenance and re-building has been required over the past thirty years, and new additions have abandoned the style. However, the landscaping of the site, with a lake, a small amphitheatre, extensive tree-planting and plenty of informal shrubbery, has been a considerable success, toning down some of the harshness of the buildings (fig.3).[10]

The initial building campaign proceeded very promptly, so that by the autumn of 1966, when the University received its Charter, the shape of the future campus was clearly established and several of the Schools were already installed in it. The first or 'Preliminary Building', later styled the 'South Building', was occupied in September 1965, when the School of Biology and the School of Humanities and Social Sciences moved in. The University continued to use premises at Ashley Down, Kings Weston, Rockwells (for the School of Management), and in the centre of Bath at Northgate House (for the School of Education) until the end of the decade, but the consolidation of the campus on Claverton Down was carried forwards with all possible speed, and was complete by the early 1970s. In a remarkably short space of time from the original suggestion, therefore, Bath had acquired a fully-fledged and flourishing University. It was a development that gave a distinctive character to the University, and it also had a profound effect on the city.

Every university is a substantial institution and develops in a sort of symbiosis with the community in which it is set. In the case of Bath, this relationship has been complicated by the long pre-university tradition in a neighbouring city that we have just reviewed. The first area of potential sensitivity between the University and the city in which it has made its home was the question of its title. Senior members of the University were anxious to perpetuate its scientific/technological orientation by keeping the word 'technology' in the title. In its first form this was 'The University of Bath: A

Technological University', but this was such a cumbersome mouthful that it was modified within a few years to 'Bath University of Technology'. Despite the agreeably inquisitorial overtones of the acronym 'BUT', this did not prove popular either, and by the mid-1970s it had been altered once again to its present form, 'The University of Bath'. Only Loughborough, amongst the eight CATs which achieved full university status, has preserved the technological association in its title. For the most part, however, the simple connection between university and city seems to have been accepted happily in Bath by both town and gown.

The question of the title was the tip of a much larger problem, which was that of the academic disciplines composing the University of Bath. With its strong technological emphasis at the outset, many of its original members hoped that this would be retained as a permanent feature of the institution. The powerful argument in favour of this was that it had already established its excellence in engineering and the applied sciences, and that it was desirable to use the limited resources available to strengthen this achievement rather than to experiment in new and unfamiliar fields. On the other hand, it was argued that any fully-formed university needed to offer a wide range of accepted disciplines, which should include the 'humanities' such as History, Literature and Philosophy, in which the new university was manifestly very weak. It was pointed out, moreover, that as an international centre for the arts, music and culture, it was particularly desirable that Bath should have a university which recognized the importance of these as fields of academic study. The debate between these points of view has still not been resolved, partly because of the pressures of financial constraints and new funding structures imposed progressively by governments since the early 1980s, but mainly because of the in-built inertia of the institution which has tended to continue doing those things which it has done well in the past. There is thus something of a conceptual gap enduring between the City of Bath, with its long urban traditions centred on culture, leisure industries and tourism, and the University of Bath, with its dominant commitment to technology and applied science.

This gap has been reinforced by physical separation, because for all the tremendous advantages that the University has enjoyed from being free to develop a virgin site in the middle of open space, the fact that Claverton Down is over a mile from the centre of the city, and that most of this mile is a tough up-hill climb, does place an effective barrier to easy communication between town and gown. Students, once on campus, tend to remain there, and townsfolk do not normally have cause to visit the site, although they are made welcome through a programme of public lectures and theatrical events and, more recently, courses of continuing education. While definitely within the city boundary, therefore, the University has tended to seem in but not of the city. Nevertheless, the city has been proud of, and indulgent towards, its University, from the very first act of outstanding generosity whereby it sacrificed its playing fields in return for a literal 'peppercorn rent', on through the support of countless land-ladies and the whole service substructure of retailing and transport provision. On the part of the University, members of staff have become active in the city societies, and they have supported the theatre and the International Festival of Music, and taken part in local sport and other civic activities. The new sports and swimming facilities have also been made available to citizens. On balance, the symbiosis has successfully overcome the difficulties placed in its way.

One consequence of the transition from a college of technology to a university was that the University of Bath assumed responsibility for awarding its own degrees. This meant that the Diploma in Technology, which had served so well as a degree-level qualification for students at the CATs, was abandoned in favour of degrees designed and taught in the individual Schools of the University. Also abandoned was the exemplary requirement of the DipTech that one tenth of all tuition should be provided in subjects that were outside the specialism of the main course. The implications of this were that all the degree courses became more intensively specialized than they had been before, and that the members of the Department of General Studies who had provided the non-specialist courses for engineers and applied scientists, in economics, history, sociology, and various literary and linguistic studies, were deprived of the service teaching that had been their main function. In anticipation of this deprivation, the Department had begun in 1963 to provide specialist courses of its own, in the form of a Diploma in Sociology, followed almost immediately by a Diploma in Economics and Administration. These courses provided the basis for the School of Humanities and Social Sciences when the University adopted its new constitution.

It was intended that this School would justify its title by acquiring a third degree-level course, which would be in Humanities and would provide specialized academic work for the historians, philosophers, and lecturers in literature. The preliminary discussions for this were well advanced in 1970, and such a development would have made a powerful contribution to the relationship between the University and the city. The fact that it did not happen at that time was due primarily to the loss of impetus through the premature death of the Reader in Humanities, Gerald Walters, in May 1970. Mr Walters was a highly talented and mercurial character who was equally at home in several of the humanities disciplines, and he had already done much to establish the links which could serve the local community and promote the public relations of the University. He had, in particular, supplied the intellectual driving force behind several very successful 'Bath Conferences' on science and society, science and religion, and similar themes. He had also created an enterprizing journal, *The Technologist*, later to become *Technology and Society*, which acted as a mouthpiece for a lively commentary on the problems of a scientific and technological society, and he helped to make Bath University Press a successful venture.

Yet another initiative of Gerald Walters was the establishment, in conjunction with the Holburne Museum, of the 'Holburne Institute' as a vehicle for discussion between Town and Gown on broad areas of social policy. The Museum was and remains a collection of Fine Art with interests in modern craftsmanship and design, and its links with the University were potentially of great value for the development of studies in the Humanities. Walters used the Institute to set up seminar groups on 'Science and Politics' and 'Science and Religion', and both of these acquired a life of their own for several years. But like the Institute itself, as well as the other initiatives inspired by him, they were not able long to survive Gerald Walters' sudden death. The University established a prestigious Memorial Lecture as a tribute to him, but his hopes and expectations for the expansion of a full School of Humanities were not fulfilled, and they have remained unfulfilled to the present day. The University simply lacked staff of sufficient seniority and vision to find the resources necessary for a viable development in the Humanities at that time, and it has proved impossible to restore the situation since.[11]

Early in the 1990s it seemed possible that the University might acquire a School of Humanities as part of a proposed 'merger' with Bath College of Higher Education. The College had developed out of the post-war Emergency Teacher Training College at Newton St. Loe, and had already built up a range of degree courses under external supervision from Bristol and elsewhere, and was ambitious to expand further. It had much to offer the University in addition to a strong Humanities Department, including an attractive campus and several enterprizing vocational courses, but there were also many courses which were not of university standard, involving a considerable number of staff. The plan to fuse the two institutions into a single enlarged University was discussed at length in the summer and autumn of 1991, and went into considerable detail. Teams of staff from different disciplines spent much time devising elaborate schemes for integration at various levels, which generated a great volume of paper-work.

The final proposal was submitted to the University Senate in December of that year and was firmly rejected, overtly because the University feared that the assimilation of too much sub-university standard work would jeopardize the enviable research ratings which were already being achieved. But there were other problems concerning the leading personalities involved, and the tendency of the College to bid for absolute equality of treatment with the University. This was unrealistic and, in the end, made the scheme unacceptable to the academic body of the University. The two institutions went their own way, the College soon achieving an improved status by adopting the title 'Bath Spa University College'. It seems likely that economies of scale will eventually oblige negotiations to be resumed, but meanwhile the University has clearly lost the opportunity of acquiring a well-established group of young scholars in History and Literature who could have provided the critical mass for a genuine School of Humanities. Apart from other considerations, the City of Bath deserves a distinguished academic status in the Humanities, and this can only be provided by the local University. In a sublime city such as this, deeply imbued with history, literature and the arts, it is highly paradoxical that the University has not managed to do more to pay homage to the traditions of the city.[12]

In many other respects, however, the University has undergone continuous growth since its establishment in Bath. When it received its Charter in 1966 it had around a thousand full-time and sandwich-course students, and it is now almost ten times larger. Most of this growth has been accommodated within the original disciplinary parameters and physical design of the campus, but there have been some important changes. Some new Schools were formed, such as the School of Chemical Engineering, which broke away from Chemistry, and the School of Modern Languages added 'International Studies' to its title. But then, in the late 1990s, the School pattern of disciplines was abandoned in favour of a more conventional Faculty structure, with three dominant Faculties in 'Engineering and Design', 'Science' and 'Humanities and Social Sciences' replacing all the old 'Schools' except the School of Management, which preserves its independence. The original Schools have been broken up and made into 'Academic Departments' within the Faculties. An earlier attempt, in the 1970s, to combine the Schools into disciplinary 'Areas' had not been a success, but the recent changes have been more thoroughly instituted.

The University Library, which inevitably lacked many of the advantages of having possessed a longstanding collection of academic works, pioneered new systems of electronic cataloguing and data retrieval under successive Librarians, Maurice Line, John H. Lamble, and Howard Nicholson.

When the University was established in 1966, it was still sufficiently compact for staff to get to know each other across disciplinary divisions, and a strong Senior Common Room was created, with a vigorous social life. It arranged a series of talks and discussions with eminent visitors, and made a substantial contribution to the early negotiations about the constitution of the University.

Fig.4 The University from the air A recent view showing the dominant plan of the campus, with the main buildings arranged like vertebrae off the spine of the service road and the pedestrian deck above it. (*reproduced by courtesy of the University of Bath*)

As far as the physical structure of the campus is concerned, the original linear design has been preserved (fig.4), following the plan to develop at both ends while arranging most of the student accommodation in parallel ranks on the slope of Claverton Down north of the main thoroughfare. The two high-rise accommodation blocks across the Parade have required refacing, and have been partially converted to administration uses. The Library has been extended out over the Parade with a smart new façade in order to provide space for Information Technology Services (fig.5). All the extensions over the last twenty years have departed from the prefabricated CLASP construction and adopted more solid forms and pitched roofs, although grey/cream facing material has been maintained in order to fulfil Bath City planning requirements. An old agricultural building, surviving from the 'Norwood Farm' that occupied the site before it was taken over for playing fields, has been renovated as an 'Arts Barn', supporting a wide range of creative activities. A small theatre has been built next to this. The University has also acquired a high reputation for its sports facilities, including a Sports Hall, Pavilion,

Swimming Pool, Athletics Track and excellent playing fields. Sports are now well integrated into University life, with provision for academic study of its activities in a Sports Institute.

The close links with local and national industry, regarded from the outset as essential to a technological university, were recognized in the choice of the first Chancellor. This was Lord Hinton of Bankside who, as Sir Christopher Hinton, FRS, had played a leading part in the development of the Central Electricity Generating Board and the British Atomic Energy Authority. In accepting this office Lord Hinton let it be known that he would not be happy to regard it as a purely honorific function, and he took an active part in the early discussions about the structure and composition of the University. In particular, he entered with some zest into the

Fig.5 The Library Extension. The original building was extended in the 1990s to provide Information Technology Services in this striking addition cantilevered over the pedestrian deck. (*reproduced by courtesy of the University of Bath*)

task of awarding degrees on Degree Day. For several years, until defects in the restored plaster work made it impossible, degrees were awarded in the Bath Assembly Rooms, which provided a very gracious setting for the occasion. They were, however, too small to admit all the graduands and their families at any one time, so that the function was spread over five or six separate Degree Congregations, and for each of these Lord Hinton diligently prepared a different speech, packed with down-to-earth advice and forthright opinions. These did not endear him to all his listeners, but there can be no doubt that they added a certain liveliness to the proceedings.[13]

Lord Hinton was succeeded as Chancellor by Lord Kearton of Whitchurch, Chairman of Courtaulds, and then by Sir Denys Henderson, Chairman of

ICI, who was followed by the current holder of the office, the economist Lord Tugendhat. The University has been well-served by its Chancellors who, apart from their formal functions, have put their time and professional skills at the disposal of the institution. This has been especially apparent in the attention which they have given to the choice of Vice-Chancellors, the crucial executive office in any British University. Dr. Moore – he had been awarded an Honorary Doctorate on becoming the first Vice-Chancellor of the University in 1966 – retired when he reached the age of 65 three years later. He had guided the University successfully through the difficult years of transition.[14] His place was taken by Dr. Leonard Rotherham, who had served with Lord Hinton in the electricity industry and came to the post with the strong support of the Chancellor. He was also a Fellow of the Royal Society – the first of three Vice-Chancellors in succession with this honour – and an able administrator of large organizations. He was succeeded in 1976 by Professor Paul Matthews, a distinguished physicist; and in 1983 by Professor Rodney Quayle, who came to the post from being Professor of Microbiology at the University of Sheffield. In 1992, the University chose as its fifth Vice-Chancellor an American from Baltimore, David VandeLinde, who had been Professor of Electronics at Johns Hopkins University. The present Vice-Chancellor, social psychologist Professor Glynis Breakwell, took over in 2001.

In the space of thirty-six years the University of Bath has thus made itself thoroughly at home in the city that gave it such a warm welcome in the mid-1960s. It has acquired an enviable reputation for its academic and research work, regularly coming in the top ten of the various ratings which have been contrived to give a competitive edge to British academic life. It has become increasingly popular with students, and has attracted high-quality staff who have contributed directly to its research attainments. It continues to grow, with some good quality buildings and fine sports facilities. But in conclusion it is worth recalling some words of Gerald Walters, written in the book he compiled to celebrate the inauguration of the University in 1966, in which he contemplated the role of the new institution:

It is … with a new university of technology that the real opportunity of finding a coherent relationship between the traditional and the contemporary, between the humanistic and the scientific, lies, since it begins with the fundamental acceptance of the scientific, both in its pure and applied aspects, as the normative activity of contemporary society and with a recognition of the intellectual and social implications of technology. It provides a common frame of reference within which the older traditional activities can find contemporary significance, and science itself recover its role as one of the humanities.[15]

The vision implied in these sentences was essentially forward-looking and catholic rather than traditionalistic, although it was one which fully understood the importance of traditional disciplines and values. It saw the possibility of a new type of university, breaking away from the rigidity of established British institutions to provide 'new types of men who envisage new tasks'. It was and remains a vision pre-eminently appropriate to the University of Bath in the City of Bath. Despite the sound and solid achievements of the University of Bath, however, it is a vision that remains only partially fulfilled.

Notes

1   Little is known about Adelard's personal life, but his achievements have been well reviewed recently by Louise Cochrane, *Adelard of Bath: The First English Scientist* (British Museum Press, 1994). For a more general account of his place in the Twelfth Century Renaissance, see C.H. Haskins, 'Adelard of Bath' in *English Historical Review*, vol.26 (1911), pp.491-98.

2   There is a small file on the project in Bath Reference Library, and a copy of the Prospectus for 'Queen's College, Bath', describing it as 'auxiliary to the Universities of Oxford and Cambridge', in the University of Bath Library. The architect of the winning design was James Wilson of Bath (1816-1900), but neither this nor the alternative scheme proposed by G.P. Manners was ever built: see James Lees-Milne and David Forde, *Images of Bath* (St Helena Press, Richmond, 1982), p.352; and Charles Robertson, *Bath: An Architectural Guide* (Faber & Faber, 1975), p.142. For a brief account of the project, see R.A. Buchanan, 'From Trade School to University: a microcosm of social change' in Gerald Walters ed., *A Technological University: an experiment in Bath* (Bath University Press, Bath, 1966) pp.12-26. I have drawn extensively on this article of thirty-six years ago for the earlier sections of the present essay.

3   John Latimer, *The History of the Society of Merchant Venturers of the City of Bristol* (Bristol, 1903), p.305.

4   *Preliminary Prospectus* of the Merchant Venturers' Technical School, 1885. The emphasis on freedom from sex discrimination is in the original. The *Prospectus* subsequently became the *Year Book*, and a complete series of these from 1885 to 1949 was held in the Library of the College of Advanced Technology at Ashley Down, passing eventually to the Library of the University of the West of England.

5   Latimer, *op.cit.*, pp.323-24, reflected sadly shortly before his death in 1904: 'It is disappointing to observe the lack of public sympathy and support in respect of the proposal to create in Bristol one of those large and complete Technical Institutes which, in the opinion of all experienced authorities, are essential for the future of British manufactures and commerce'.

6   For the later years of the MVTC, see the *Minutes* of the Management Committee of the College in the five volumes of the *Book of Proceedings: Merchant Venturers' Technical College* in the archives of the Bristol Society of Merchant Venturers. I am happy to acknowledge again the kindness of the Society and its Officers in giving me permission to consult these papers many years ago.

180

7   *Technical Education*, HMSO February 1956, Cmnd.9703.
8   The Robbins Report was published as *Higher Education*, HMSO October 1963, Cmnd.2154. Eight of the ten colleges designated as CATs made the transfer to the status of independent universities, while Chelsea College was absorbed into the University of London and Cardiff College of Technology went into the University of Wales.
9   There is no good single account of the development of Further Education in Bath, but see: *The Original Bath Guide* (Bath, 1917), especially pp.75-7 on the RLSI, pp.87-8 on the Bath and West Agricultural Society, and pp.55-7 on the Guildhall and its educational uses. Also W.J. Williams and D.M. Stoddart, *Bath – Some Encounters with Science* (Kingsmead Press, Bath, 1978), pp.76-9; and John Haddon, *Bath* (Batsford, 1973), pp.161-65 and 208-9. See also Helena L.H. Lim, 'Bath & the "Bath and West of England Society", 1777-1851', in *Bath History*, Vol.VI (Millstream Books, Bath, 1966), pp.108-131.
10   Robert Matthew, Johnson-Marshall & Partners, *The Proposed University of Bath, a Technological University: Development Plan, Report Number 1* (Bath University Press, Bath, 1965).
11   In addition to the study edited by Gerald Walters, note 2 above, *A Technological University*, Walters edited several sets of Proceedings of the conferences which he organized and which were published by Bath University Press: see, for example, *Technology and Society* (The First Bath Conference, 1965), edited by G. Walters and K. Hudson (Bath University Press, Bath, 1966). The University preserved a close link with the Holburne Museum: for many years Professor J. Black, Head of the School of Aeronautical and Mechanical Engineering, and an eloquent speaker on engineering design, served as a University representative with the trustees.
12   Details of the merger proposal have not been published, but are recalled here from personal experience on the committee appointed by Senate to conduct the negotiations for the University.
13   Lord Hinton of Bankside, *Some speeches of a Chancellor: addresses ... at his installation ... and at degree congregations* (Bath University Press, Bath, 1982).
14   For his own account, see George H. Moore, *The University of Bath – the formative years 1949-1969* (Bath University Press, Bath, 1982).
15   Gerald Walters, 'A Technological University: the new concept', in the volume he edited, *A Technological University: an experiment in Bath* (Bath University Press, Bath, 1966), p.5.

INDEX TO *BATH HISTORY* VOLUMES I-IX BY AUTHOR

Arnold, Hilary: *Mrs Margaret Graves and her Letters from Bath, 1793-1807*, **VII**, 78

Aston Mick: *The Bath Region from Late Prehistory to the Middle Ages*, **I**, 61

Bell, Robert: *Bath Abbey: Some New Perspectives*, **VI**, 7

Bennet, Robert: *The Last of the Georgian Architects of Bath: The Work and Times of John Pinch*, **IX**, 87

Bettey, J.H.: *Life and Litigation in Bath and its Environs in the Sixteenth Century*, **VI**, 54

Bird, Stephen: *The Earliest Map of Bath*, **I**, 128

Bishop, Philippa: *Beckford in Bath*, **II**, 85

Bishop, Philippa: *The Sentence of Momus: Satirical Verse and Prints in Eighteenth-Century Bath*, **V**, 51

Bishop, Philippa: *Walter Richard Sickert (1860-1942): Painter of the Bath Scene*, **IX**, 138

Blake, Steven: *William Beckford and Fonthill Abbey: A Victorian Showman's Account*, **IX**, 126

Bone, Mike: *The Rise and Fall of Bath's Breweries 1736-1960*, **VIII**, 106

Brown, Malcolm & Samuel, Judith: *The Jews of Bath*, **I**, 150

Buchanan, Brenda J.: *The Avon Navigation and the Inland Port of Bath*, **VI**, 63

Buchanan, Brenda J.: *The Great Bath Road, 1700-1830*, **IV**, 71

Buchanan, Brenda J.: *Sir John (later Lord) Ligonier (1680-1770), Military Commander and Member of Parliament for Bath*, **VIII**, 80

Buchanan, R. Angus: *Bath: University City*, **IX**, 160

Buchanan, R. Angus: *The Bridges of Bath*, **III**, 1

Buchanan, R. Angus: *The Floods of Bath*, **VII**, 167

Cattell, John: *Edward Snell's Diary: A Journeyman Engineer in Bath in the 1840s*, **IX**, 104

Chapman, Mike & Holland, Elizabeth: *The Development of the Saw Close from the Middle Ages*, **VIII**, 56

Clews, Stephen: *Banking in Bath in the Reign of George III*, **V**, 104

Cunliffe, Barry: *Major Davis: Architect and Antiquarian*, **I**, 27

Davenport, Peter: *Aquae Sulis. The Origins and Development of a Roman Town*, **VIII**, 7

Davenport, Peter: *Bath Abbey*, **II**, 1

Davenport, Peter: *Town and Country: Roman Bath and its Hinterland*, **V**, 7

Davis, Graham: *Entertainments in Georgian Bath: Gambling and Vice*, **I**, 1

Davis, Graham: *Social Decline and Slum Conditions: Irish Migrants in Bath's History*, **VIII**, 134

Ede, John & Symons, Roland: *Heraldry in Bath Abbey*, **IX**, 7

Ede, Mary: *Bath and the Great Exhibition of 1851*, **III**, 138

Fawcett, Trevor: *Chair Transport in Bath: The Sedan Era*, **II**, 113

Fawcett, Trevor: *Dance and Teachers of Dance in Eighteenth-Century Bath*, **II**, 27

Fawcett, Trevor: *Eighteenth-Century Shops and the Luxury Trade*, **III**, 49

Fawcett, Trevor: *Science Lecturing at Bath, 1724-1800*, **VII**, 55

Fawcett, Trevor & Inskip, Marta: *The Making of Orange Grove*, **V**, 24

Festing, Sally: *Charles Richter and Bath Cabinet Makers: The Early Years*, **VII**, 146

Forsyth, Michael: *Edward Davis: Nineteenth-century Bath Architect and Pupil of Sir John Soane*, **VII**, 107

Haber, Lutz: *The Emperor Haile Selassie I in Bath, 1936-1940*, **III**, 159
Haber, Lutz: *The First 75 Years of the Holburne Museum*, **V**, 170
Hanna, William: *Bath and the Crimean War, 1854-1856*, **VIII**, 148
Holland, Elizabeth: *The Earliest Bath Guildhall*, **II**, 163
Holland, Elizabeth: see Chapman, Mike
Hopkins-Clarke, Mac: *A Change of Style at the Theatre Royal, 1805-1820*, **IV**, 124
Inskip, Marta: *Two Views of the King's Bath*, **III**, 22
Inskip, Marta: see Fawcett, Trevor
James, Kenneth: *Venanzio Rauzzini and the Search for Musical Perfection*, **III**, 90
Keevil, A.J.: *Barrack(s) Farm, Wellsway, Bath: The Estate and its Holders*, **VIII**, 27
Keevil, A.J.: *The Barton of Bath*, **VI**, **25**
Kinghorn, Jonathan: *A Privvie in Perfection: Sir John Harrington's Water Closet*, **I**, 173
Kite, John: *'A Good Bargain': The Struggle for a Public Library, 1850-1924*, **IV**, 136
Kolaczkowski, Alex: *Jerom Murch and Bath Politics, 1833-1879*, **VI**, 155
Lambert, Robin: *Patrick Abercrombie and Planning in Bath*, **VIII**, 172
Le Faye, Deirdre: *'A Persecuted Relation': Mrs Lillingston's Funeral and Jane Austen's Legacy*, **VII**, 92
Lewcun, Marek J.: *The Clay Tobacco Pipe Making Industry of Bath*, **V**, 125
Lim, Helena L.H.: *Bath and the 'Bath and West of England Society', 1771-1851*, **VI**, 108
McLaughlin, David: *Mowbray Green and the Old Bath Preservers*, **IV**, 155
Manco, Jean: *Bath and 'The Great Rebuilding'*, **IV**, 25
Manco, Jean: *The Cross Bath*, **II**, 49
Manco, Jean: *Saxon Bath: The Legacy of Rome and the Saxon Rebirth*, **VII**, 27
Marks, Stephen Powys: *The Journals of Mrs Philip Libbe Powys (1738-1817): A Half Century of Visits to Bath*, **IX**, 28
Mitchell, Brigitte: *English Spas*, **I**, 189
Mowl, Tim: *A Trial-Run for Regent's Park: Repton and Nash at Bath, 1796*, **III**, 76
Newby, Evelyn: *The Hoares of Bath*, **I**, 90
Noble, Chris: *The New Gaol in Bathwick (1772-1842)*, **IX**, 64
Poole, Steve: *Radicalism, Loyalism and the 'Reign of Terror' in Bath, 1792-1804*, **III**, 114
Rolls, Roger: *Bath Cases: Care and Treatment of Patients at the Bath General Hospital during the mid-Eighteenth Century*, **II**, 139
Root, Jane: *Thomas Baldwin: His Public Career in Bath, 1775-1793*, **V**, 80
Samuel, Judith: see Brown, Malcolm
Sloman, Susan Legouix: *Artists' Picture Rooms in Eighteenth-Century Bath*, **VI**, 132
Symons, Roland: see Ede, John
Tomlin, R.S.O.: *Voices from the Sacred Spring*, **IV**, 7
von Behr, Nicholas: *The Cloth Industry of Twerton from the 1780s to the 1820s*, **VI**, 88
Ward, Owen: *Isaac Pitman and the Fourth Phonetic Institute*, **VII**, 129
Whalley, Robin: *The Royal Victoria Park*, **V**, 147
Wilson, Ellen: *A Shropshire Lady in Bath, 1794-1807*, **IV**, 95
Woodward, Christopher: *'O Lord! Bath is undone; 'tis undone; 'tis undone!': Bath and the Pre-history of Architectural Conservation*, **VII**, 7
Wroughton, John: *Puritanism and Traditionalism: Cultural and Political Division in Bath, 1620-1662*, **IV**, 52

INDEX TO *BATH HISTORY* VOLUMES I-IX BY TITLE

Aquae Sulis. The Origins and Development of a Roman Town, by Peter Davenport, **VIII**, 7

Artists' Picture Rooms in Eighteenth-Century Bath, by Susan Legouix Sloman, **VI**, 132

Avon Navigation and the Inland Port of Bath, The, by Brenda J.Buchanan, **VI**, 63

Banking in Bath in the Reign of George III, by Stephen Clews, **V**, 104

Barrack(s) Farm, Wellsway, Bath: The Estate and its Holders, by A.J.Keevil, **VIII**, 27

The Barton of Bath, by A.J.Keevil, **VI, 25**

Bath Abbey, by Peter Davenport, **II**, 1

Bath Abbey: Some New Perspectives, by Robert Bell, **VI**, 7

Bath and the 'Bath and West of England Society', 1771-1851, by Helena L.H.Lim, **VI**, 108

Bath and the Crimean War, 1854-1856, by William Hanna, **VIII**, 148

Bath and the Great Exhibition of 1851, by Mary Ede, **III**, 138

Bath and 'The Great Rebuilding', by Jean Manco, **IV**, 25

Bath Cases: Care and Treatment of Patients at the Bath General Hospital during the mid-Eighteenth Century, by Roger Rolls, **II**, 139

Bath Region from Late Prehistory to the Middle Ages, The , by Mick Aston, **I**, 61

Bath: University City, by R.Angus Buchanan, **IX**, 160

Beckford in Bath, by Philippa Bishop, **II**, 85

Bridges of Bath, The, by R.Angus Buchanan, **III**, 1

Chair Transport in Bath: The Sedan Era, by Trevor Fawcett, **II**, 113

Change of Style at the Theatre Royal, 1805-1820, A, by Mac Hopkins-Clarke, **IV**, 124

Charles Richter and Bath Cabinet Makers: The Early Years, by Sally Festing, **VII**, 146

Clay Tobacco Pipe Making Industry of Bath The, by Marek J.Lewcun, **V**, 125

Cloth Industry of Twerton from the 1780s to the 1820s, The, by Nicholas von Behr, **VI**, 88

Cross Bath, The, by Jean Manco **II**, 49

Dance and Teachers of Dance in Eighteenth-Century Bath, by Trevor Fawcett, **II**, 27

Development of the Saw Close from the Middle Ages, The, by Mike Chapman & Elizabeth Holland, **VIII**, 56

Earliest Bath Guildhall, The, by Elizabeth Holland, **II**, 163

Earliest Map of Bath, The, by Stephen Bird, **I**, 128

Edward Davis: Nineteenth-century Bath Architect and Pupil of Sir John Soane, by Michael Forsyth, **VII**, 107

Edward Snell's Diary: A Journeyman Engineer in Bath in the 1840s, by John Cattell, **IX**, 104

Eighteenth-Century Shops and the Luxury Trade, by Trevor Fawcett, **III**, 49

Emperor Haile Selassie I in Bath, 1936-1940, The, by Lutz Haber, **III**, 159

English Spas, by Brigitte Mitchell, **I**, 189

Entertainments in Georgian Bath: Gambling and Vice, by Graham Davis, **I**, 1

First 75 Years of the Holburne Museum, The, by Lutz Haber, **V**, 170

Floods of Bath, The, by R.Angus Buchanan, **VII**, 167

'Good Bargain, A': The Struggle for a Public Library, 1850-1924, by John Kite, **IV**, 136

Great Bath Road, 1700-1830, The, by Brenda J.Buchanan, **IV**, 71

Heraldry in Bath Abbey, by John Ede & Roland Symons **IX**, 7

Hoares of Bath The, by Evelyn Newby, **I**, 90

Isaac Pitman and the Fourth Phonetic Institute, by Owen Ward, **VII**, 129

Jerom Murch and Bath Politics, 1833-1879, by Alex Kolaczkowski, **VI**, 155

Jews of Bath, The, by Malcolm Brown & Judith Samuel, **I**, 150

Journals of Mrs Philip Libbe Powys (1738-1817), The: A Half Century of Visits to Bath, by
    Stephen Powys Marks, **IX**, 28

Last of the Georgian Architects of Bath, The: The Work and Times of John Pinch, by Robert
    Bennet, **IX**, 87

Life and Litigation in Bath and its Environs in the Sixteenth Century, by J.H.Bettey, **VI**, 54

Major Davis: Architect and Antiquarian, by Barry Cunliffe, **I**, 27

Making of Orange Grove, The, by Trevor Fawcett & Marta Inskip: **V**, 24

Mowbray Green and the Old Bath Preservers, by David McLaughlin, **IV**, 155

Mrs Margaret Graves and her Letters from Bath, 1793-1807, by Hilary Arnold, **VII**, 78

New Gaol in Bathwick (1772-1842), The, by Chris Noble, **IX**, 64

*'O Lord! Bath is undone; 'tis undone; 'tis undone!': Bath and the Pre-history of Architectural
    Conservation*, by Christopher Woodward, **VII**, 7

Patrick Abercrombie and Planning in Bath, by Robin Lambert, **VIII**, 172

'Persecuted Relation, A': Mrs Lillingston's Funeral and Jane Austen's Legacy, by Deirdre
    Le Faye, **VII**, 92

Privvie in Perfection, A: Sir John Harrington's Water Closet, by Jonathan Kinghorn, **I**,
    173

Puritanism and Traditionalism: Cultural and Political Division in Bath, 1620-1662, by John
    Wroughton, **IV**, 52

Radicalism, Loyalism and the 'Reign of Terror' in Bath, 1792-1804, by Steve Poole, **III**, 114

Rise and Fall of Bath's Breweries: 1736-1960, The, by Mike Bone, **VIII**, 106

Royal Victoria Park, The, by Robin Whalley, **V**, 147

Saxon Bath: The Legacy of Rome and the Saxon Rebirth, by Jean Manco, **VII**, 27

Science Lecturing at Bath, 1724-1800, by Trevor Fawcett, **VII**, 55

Sentence of Momus, The: Satirical Verse and Prints in Eighteenth-Century Bath, by Philippa
    Bishop, **V**, 51

Shropshire Lady in Bath, 1794-1807, A, by Ellen Wilson, **IV**, 95

*Sir John (later Lord) Ligonier (1680-1770), Military Commander and Member of Parliament
    for Bath*, by Brenda J.Buchanan, **VIII**, 80

Social Decline and Slum Conditions: Irish Migrants in Bath's History, by Graham Davis,
    VIII, 134

Thomas Baldwin: His Public Career in Bath, 1775-1793, by Jane Root, **V**, 80

Town and Country: Roman Bath and its Hinterland, by Peter Davenport, **V**, 7

Trial-Run for Regent's Park, A: Repton and Nash at Bath, 1796, by Tim Mowl, **III**, 76

Two Views of the King's Bath, by Marta Inskip, **III**, 22

Venanzio Rauzzini and the Search for Musical Perfection, by Kenneth James, **III**, 90

Voices from the Sacred Spring, by R.S.O.Tomlin, **IV**, 7

Walter Richard Sickert (1860-1942): Painter of the Bath Scene, by Philippa Bishop, **IX**,
    138

William Beckford and Fonthill Abbey: A Victorian Showman's Account, by Steven Blake
    IX, 126